LIONS UNDER THE THRONE

LIONS
Under the Throne

BY CHARLES P. CURTIS, JR.

A STUDY OF THE SUPREME COURT
OF THE UNITED STATES
ADDRESSED PARTICULARLY TO THOSE LAYMEN
WHO KNOW MORE CONSTITUTIONAL LAW
THAN THEY THINK THEY DO,
AND TO THOSE LAWYERS WHO KNOW LESS

HOUGHTON MIFFLIN COMPANY BOSTON

The Riverside Press
1947

The Riverside Press
CAMBRIDGE · MASSACHUSETTS
PRINTED IN THE U.S.A.

Nature itself cannot erre: and as men abound in copi-
ousness of language; so they become more wise, or more
mad than ordinary. For words are wise men's counters,
they do but reckon by them: but they are the money of
fools, that value them by the authority of an Aristotle, a
Cicero, or a Thomas, or any other Doctor whatsoever, if
but a man.

Hobbes, *The Leviathan*.

The student of jurisprudence is at times troubled by the
thought that he is dealing not with things, but with words,
that he is busy with the shape and size of counters in a
game of logomachy, but when he fully realizes how these
words have been passed and are still being passed as money
not only by fools and on fools, but by and on some of the
acutest minds, he feels that there is work worthy of being
done, if only it can be done worthily.

John C. Gray, in the preface
to *The Nature and Sources of Law*.

PREFACE

ISRAELI told someone that Lord Brougham was too good a lawyer ever to be a great statesman. Wilson began at the bar, but he claimed it took him twenty years to get over it. Lincoln practiced law, but fortunately, not so successfully that he did not go into politics. Lawyers, wrote Senator Thomas Hart Benton to Van Buren, 'are no more able to comprehend me than old hack lawyers, according to Burke, are able to comprehend the policy of an empire, and that was no more than a rabbit, which breeds twelve times a year, could comprehend the gestation of an elephant, which carries two years.'

Certainly the law has its own way of assimilating a new notion. Take for the moment a very small example. It may not be a very fair example, but no single example is ever very fair, and there will be more later. What chance has a lawyer got to understand the National Labor Relations Act when he has to look it up in his Digest of Federal Law under the title, Master and Servant?

And contrariwise, look what we do with legal terms. Take a very large example, with which we shall have much more to do. There's a familiar phrase in the Constitution, 'due process of law.' It occurs twice, in the Fifth Amendment and again in the Fourteenth. No one is to be 'deprived of life, liberty, or property, without due process of law.' That is a legal phrase. It was, anyhow, until the

American people succeeded in making it synonymous with
the fundamental principles of political ethics. There was
a period when, indeed, it took in economic theory. And
so it takes more than a lawyer, a man who has outgrown
the law, to understand it.

And yet lawyers play a great part in our system of government. They always have. It surprised de Tocqueville, in 1830. Our judicial organization was the hardest
for him to understand. In every political event he found
that the authority of some judge was invoked. It seemed
to him at first sight as if the judges were participating only
by chance in public affairs, but the same chance, he said,
came up every day. A hundred years or so later when the
Supreme Court was celebrating its one hundred and fiftieth
anniversary Robert H. Jackson, now one of the Justices
himself, told the Court that our system made legal questions of matters that other nations treat as questions of
policy. Every great movement in American history, he
said, has produced a leading case in this Court.

We go to great efforts keeping our judges out of politics.
We put them above politics, and then we lay our great
political issues at their feet and pray a judgment. Because, we say, they involve matters of constitutional law.
Do we bring them to the judges because they are legal, or
do we call them legal so that we may bring them to the
judges?

As a matter of fact, we contrive to have it both ways.
We call our political problems legal and we treat them as
legally as we dare. We require our judges to pretend they
are legal and at the same time we make sure that the
Court has enough political experience not to fumble them.
If you run down the list of Justices from Lincoln's appoint-

ments, and there have been fifty of them, you will find that at least a third had had political experience in high office. Eighteen had been either in the Cabinet or in Congress or both. Four had been in both. One had been President, another a candidate, and a third had suffered severely from presidential ambitions. To put it negatively, nearly half of the fifty had had no judicial experience worth mentioning. None but could talk, as Falstaff pleaded, for God's sake, like men of this world. It makes it easier to treat your political problems as if they were legal when you call in such men to handle them.

Marshall had taken a court of law and made it into an organ of government. We adopted what he did with many misgivings, but with growing pride, and we have been struggling with its difficulties ever since. It is not only difficult. It has one serious drawback. That a statute is legal, that is to say, constitutional, is the least you can say for it, not the best. Much is allowable that is not admirable. We are capable of being wiser than we are legally allowed to be. The more we think of the Constitution, the less we are likely to put our minds on the best we are capable of. We are distracted by the merely tolerable. The Constitution gives us a standard, and that is good, but it is a low standard, and that is bad. Our most precious concerns are better than what can be secured to us by law. The law does what it can for us. We must do the rest ourselves.

THE SCHEME OF THIS BOOK

Chapter   I. The limited usefulness of history,
               and the irrelevance of our fore-
               fathers' intentions   1
               The purpose and function of broad
               words and ambiguities, a legacy of
               responsible choice   3
               An example from the Constitution:
               the admission of new states on equal
               terms   4
               The task of interpretation   7

Chapter   II. The doctrine of judicial supremacy: 9
               The Constitution to be the su-
               preme law   9
               To be interpreted by the Court?   10
               Hamilton's answer   10
               Thayer's exposition   11
               Marshall's answer   13
               The President's quandary   14
               Solutions suggested   15

Chapter   III. The Court's judicial solution: 17
               The theory of it   17
               The length and breadth of words   18
               It is strictly judicial   20
               When is a case not a case?   21

Chapter   IV. A political qualification to the judi-
               cial solution: 24
               Its judicial consequences   26

The Court's quandary 27
The position of Congress 28
The Court's respect for Congress 30
Rational doubt 31
Thayer's explanation 32
Collaboration 33

Chapter V. The power of the Court: 35
Dependent on Congress 35
For its jurisdiction 36
For its terms of court 36
For enforcement of its judgments 37
For the number of its Justices 37
Bryce's comment 37
The Court's temerity in, e.g. 39
The Dred Scott case in 1857 39
The Income Tax case in 1895 41
The real basis of its power 46

Chapter VI. The Court's job: 47
Federalism 47
Natural Rights 50
As absolutes 51
Our idolatry 54
Split decisions 55
Reversals and *stare decisis* 56
The sanctity of decisions and taboos 57

Chapter VII. The advantages of being a law court: 59
Once the Court was only a law court 60
It has still all the advantages: 61

Ancient tradition; and Coke 62
The majesty of the Law 63
The pressure of actuality 64
The pressure of written reasons 65
The fewness of the Justices 68
Their procedure 68
Unanimity and individual opinions 70
Johnson's compromise 73
Dissents 75

Chapter VIII. The Legal Tradition: 79
Personal responsibility 79
But the Court only declares the law 80
An unconstitutional law is void, and always has been 80
Unnecessary, and not true 81
Stare decisis and reversed decisions 83

Chapter IX. Abstractions and the meaning of large words: 84
Bertrand Russell's opinion 84
William Morton Wheeler's 85
Alfred North Whitehead's 87
Lawyers' 88
Conflicting abstractions and drawing the line 89
An example from *Esquire* 91
A useful diagram 92

Chapter X. The impact of the New Deal on the Court 94
The then Justices 95

The first two years of it 99
What the Swedes asked Jackson 100
Five anti-New Deal decisions: 100
Railroad pensions 101
The N.R.A. 112
Hot oil 113
The A.A.A. 121
Coal and Mr. Carter 134
Minimum wages in New York 140
Big Business, Darwin, and
Spencer 141
The Lochner dissent 143
The Adkins decision 145
The Election of 1936 and the Presi-
dent's Court Plan 153
Platforms, Problems, and Propos-
als 154
The Plan 157
After the Election 159
Minimum wages in Washington 160
Lions under the throne: Francis
Bacon 164

Chapter XI. A converted Court 166
Collective bargaining 166
The easy slopes of logic 176
Social security 176
The Tenth Amendment 179
Comment by the Bar Associa-
tion, and others 186

Chapter XII. New Justices: 192
Black, Reed, Frankfurter, and
Douglas 192

A new attitude   194

Federal Common Law   195

Child Labor; and a Holmes dis-
sent   196

The new A.A.A.   198

Fair Labor Standards Act   200

Chapter XIII. The New Court   202

Murphy, Byrnes, Jackson, Rut-
ledge, and Burton   202

A new course or just another tack?   204

Chapter XIV. Federalism and Taxes   205

Can a State tax the Nation?   205

Marshall's view   206

Holmes's protest   207

The New Court follows Holmes   208

Can a State tax interstate commerce?   211

Marshall's view   212

Black's protest   213

The New Court is in doubt   213

Bus lines   216

Air lines   219

Jim Crow cars   220

Can the Nation tax a State?   224

Marshall's view   224

Bradley's protest   224

The salaries of state officers?   226

When a State goes into the
liquor business?   227

Or promotes football games?   229

Or sells soft drinks?   229

The New Court is divided   230

Chapter XV. Delegated judicial legislation   234
            The interpretation of statutes as
            a delegation of legislative power   234
            The intent of Congress   235
              The Sherman Act   236
              The Commodities Clause   238
              Conscientious Objectors   239
            A delegation of responsibility   242
              Discrimination by unions   243
                Racial   244
                Other union men   248
            The rights and responsibilities of
            groups   252

Chapter XVI. Personal liberties   255
            Some assumptions and social dis-
            cipline   255
            Freedom of speech   258
              In the Civil War   258
                Taney and Merryman   259
                Lincoln and Vallandigham   260
                Milligan's court martial   260
              In the First World War   261
                Holmes and Brandeis, and
                the clear and present dan-
                ger rule   261
              In 1925 freedom of speech gets
              into the Fourteenth Amend-
              ment   266
            Madison's rejected proposal   267
            Elihu Root's thought on 'secure'   270
            The insistence of the bar   271
            The Fourteenth Amendment
            and the ingenuity of the bar   273

If property, why not speech? 279
The Court as our conscience 284
The relation between the Bill of Rights and the Fourteenth Amendment 286
Counsel for accused persons 287
Contempt of court and free speech 290
Antiquarianism 292
Jehovah's Witnesses and Religious Liberty 300
Saluting the flag 300
The Court changes its mind 307
A problem for the lower courts 308
A Watch Tower campaign 310
Freedom from taxation in the name of God 313
Transcendental dogma and the latitudinarian alternative 314

Chapter XVII. Conclusions 322
Self-restraint and its relation to wisdom 323
An act of faith 326
Where the democratic process is not working 327
Where it itself is attacked 328
But what of the other cases? 329
The need then for a philosophy 331
Whose? Ours 331

Appendices 335
An abridged version of the Constitution 337

Notes   346
Bibliography   359
Index   363

LIONS UNDER THE THRONE

1

HISTORY IN GENERAL AND OUR FOREFATHERS' INTENTIONS IN PARTICULAR

THIS IS NOT a history of the Supreme Court, nor of the Constitution, and I have no intention of letting it become so. To be sure, we cannot ignore the past. Continuity with the past is a necessity, but, as Holmes said, not a duty. The office of historical research is only that of explaining, and thereby lightening, the pressure that the past must exercise upon the present, and the present, let us not forget, upon the future. We study, Maitland said, the day before yesterday, in order that yesterday may not paralyze today, and today may not paralyze tomorrow.[1] Or better, there is no Past. There is only an eternally new Now that creates itself out of the Past.[2]

We think of ourselves as getting older and wiser. We ought to think of the world in the same way. For the old age of the world is to be accounted the true antiquity, and this is the attribute of our own times, not of that earlier age of the world in which the ancients lived, and which, though in respect of us it was the elder, yet in respect of the world it was the younger. From our age,

1

if it but knew its own strength and chose to essay and exert it, much more might fairly be expected than from the ancient times, in as much as it is a more advanced age of the world. Being a lawyer myself, you must allow me to cite authority. That was the opinion of a Lord Chancellor of England, Bacon.[3]

One element of the past intrudes quite unnecessarily upon the present. We try to make the most of the consequences of what our forefathers did, but there is no reason why we should feel we have to carry out their plans for us. Were they so wise they didn't need to know the facts? The intention of the framers of the Constitution, even assuming we could discover what it was, when it is not adequately expressed in the Constitution, that is to say, what they meant when they did not say it, surely that has no binding force upon us. If we look behind or beyond what they set down in the document, prying into what else they wrote and what they said, anything we may find is only advisory. They may sit in at *our* councils. There is no reason why we should eavesdrop on theirs.

Yet the myth of the intention of the Fathers will probably be the last one to die. The most sophisticated people enjoy a myth, in one way if not in another. In 1935 we find the Supreme Court discussing the constitutionality of the Agricultural Adjustment Act as if it depended on whether it was Madison or Hamilton who was right in their difference over the meaning of the power of Congress to lay taxes to provide for the general welfare. Both were active and prominent members of the Convention, each in an equally excellent position to know, if it could be known, what the Convention meant. They differed. That very fact is enough of itself to show that the Convention had not come to any conclusion. Why then was the Court searching for it in 1936? The Court was indulging either itself or some of the Justices in the myth. For, having expressed its agreement with Hamilton and having officially adopted his view, under which the act might have been sustained, the Court proceeded, wholly apart from that question, to hold the A.A.A. void for other reasons.

The trouble is, not that the Court acts on the myth, but that the talk about it heads the Court in the wrong direction. It backs into the questions it ought to face. It's like going up a one-way street in reverse. This is important. As Holmes warned us, even for practical purposes theory generally turns out the most important thing in the end.[4]

The fact is, when we come upon an ambiguity, we must take it to be deliberate. Of course it may have been negligent, but does it matter to us which it is? And should we not pay the authors the compliment of believing that they meant no more than they said? What they left unsaid, they left open for *us* to decide.

At the same celebration of the Court's one hundred and fiftieth birthday, Jackson spoke of the duties of the Court. It was called upon, he said, by interpretation of the Constitution, to settle doubts which the framers themselves had been unable to resolve. He gave an example. Luther Martin in his great plea in *McCulloch* v. *Maryland* was not only an advocate, he was a witness of what had been and a prophet of things to come, and he told the Court that the whole subject of taxation was full of difficulties which the Convention found it impossible to solve. For, Jackson went on, there were controversies so delicate that the framers would have risked their unity if an answer had been forced, and so they were bequeathed to this Court.

Article IV, Section 3, of the Constitution provides that 'new States may be admitted by Congress into this Union.' That is all. Nothing is said about terms or conditions. Under this section, the number of states has more than tripled. We are no longer a sea-coast, but a continent. Marshall's phrase, the American Empire, has become fact. What could be more vital than the question whether these new states were admitted to the Union as equals? We now take their equality as a matter of course. The Convention of 1787 worried over it. Then they were wise enough to drop it, and put it up to us to decide.

The Committee of Detail reported an addendum to Article 4 in these words, 'If the admission be assented to, the new States shall be admitted on the same terms as the original States.'[5] Gouverneur Morris moved to strike this out. Arguing in favor of his motion, Morris said that he did not wish to bind down the Legislature to admit Western States on the same terms. Not that he meant to discourage the growth of the Western Country. He knew that to be impossible. He did not wish, however, to throw the power into their hands. Colonel Mason even wanted, if it were possible by just means, to prevent emigrations to the Western Country. He thought that might be good policy. But he recognized it could not be done. Madison was wise enough to insist that the Western States neither would nor ought to submit to a Union which degraded them from an equal rank with the other States.[6]

Yet the Convention voted to strike out the provision

that the new states should be admitted on equal terms. Only Virginia and Maryland voted for it.

The question, of course, presented itself from time to time. For Congress was not able to restrain itself from attaching some small conditions to the admission of new states. After all, it was the explicit command of the Constitution that Congress should guarantee them a republican form of government. That duty more than plausibly covered the condition on Nevada when she was admitted in 1864 that the right to vote should never be denied to persons of color, and on Nebraska three years later that neither the vote nor any other right should be denied to anyone, except Indians, and it covered the conditions placed on readmitting the seceding states — or had they never left the Union? — that Negroes should not only vote but never be disqualified for office. Utah raised a nicer question in 1894. Congress admitted her on the understanding of perfect religious toleration, non-sectarian public schools, and — no more polygamy. Is monogamy such a commonplace virtue that it might reasonably be expected of any state? Perhaps Congress's best defense, not arguable by lawyers, is that plural marriages too deeply offend the matriarchal strain that runs through our society and through what we understand to be republicanism.

However, no one insisted on any definite answer until Congress in 1906 made it a condition to the admission of Oklahoma that its state capital and seat of government remain at Guthrie at least until 1913. You may regard that as trivial, or just politics, though as such it becomes matter of sovereignty. You will recall the rival claims of New York and Philadelphia to our national capital, and the same question has not been beneath the notice of the great powers in the United Nations. Any self-respecting state should be able to decide for itself where it wants its seat of government located. And if Congress could require Oklahoma to make her home in Guthrie, by like reasoning could it not make Virginia move out of Richmond?

Oklahoma, by its constitutional convention, accepted the condition. Then Oklahoma changed her mind. By a popular referendum it decided in 1910, three years before the condition ran out, to move to Oklahoma City. There was a great political stir. Could the people of Oklahoma constitutionally do that? If she were on quite equal footing with her sister states, why not? The question was put up to the Court, and the Court proceeded to write into the Constitution the very provision which the Convention had rejected. 'The constitutional equality of the States,' said the Court, 'is essential to the harmonious operation of the scheme upon which the Republic was organized. When that equality disappears we may remain a free people, but the Union will not be the Union of the Constitution.'[7]

That was not part of the Constitution in 1787. Some of the members of the Convention tried to make it a part, those from Virginia and Maryland, but they failed and when the Constitution left the hands of the Convention and was submitted to the people no one could say that the constitutional equality of new states was part of the scheme upon which our republic was organized. What was a part of that scheme was that this question should be left for their elders to make in the true antiquity of the Republic. That part of the canvas was left white, to be painted over later, when the landscape became more visible. The Court undertook to paint it in, in spite of Congress.

What then are the judges looking for, if it is not the intent of those who made the Constitution? They are engaged in doing something, not looking for anything.

When a constitutional provision or a piece of legislation is adopted, and for a little time after, it is only a project, a plan, a design, a mission. Then it slowly turns into an operation. If you ask the Court to seek the intention of the makers, you are asking them to join in its creation, and after the event at that. The Court is not a parent, but the obstetrician. Its function is not legislative, but judicial. When the judges seek the intent of the Fathers, and say they are going to rest their decision on that intent, they are trying to share in the legislative process. They are too late. The judicial process is a part of the operation by which the law is fitted into the rest of law and thus put into effect.

The Court is not dealing with the men who made the Constitution, but what they made. 'A poem,' MacLeish said, 'should not mean, but be'; and this is precisely the case here. The Constitution has become something in its own right. It is an integral part of what men do with it. It has long ceased to be no more than what other men hoped they would do or intended them to do. The Constitution, together with the Court's work, is not so much pushed by the plans of the past as pulled by hopes of the future. It is not stuffed but pregnant with meaning.

The intent of the framers when it is not expressed is only that we, the Congress, the President, and the Court, should be allowed to make good on their best hopes and cash in on their boldest bets. What our forefathers said, they said. What they didn't say, they meant to leave to us, and what they said ambiguously, indefinitely, equivocally, or indistinctly, is in so far not said. If you do not agree, remind yourself that we are doing the same thing for those who in their turn are going to succeed us.

2

THE DOCTRINE OF JUDICIAL SUPREMACY

O NE THING the Constitutional Convention did make quite clear. Their Constitution was to be 'the supreme law of the land.' They had to make certain of that. They were setting up a new government to be endowed by the thirteen states and their people with a number of designated and limited powers, naming them and stating explicitly that all not named were retained by the states and the people. What is more, the first eight amendments added a Bill of Rights which forbade the new government to do certain things. It had a floor, below which the powers retained by the states were not to be disturbed. It had a ceiling, above which the essential and inalienable rights of individuals were not to be infringed. Then, too, but of much less importance, the new government was divided vertically into three departments, Congress, who were to make all the new laws, the President, who was to execute them, and the Court, who were to fit the new laws into the great body of law and apply them by the process of litigation to the hard particular case.

When you set up a compartmental government like that, obviously your Constitution has to be the supreme law of

9

the land. But who is to sustain its supremacy? Who is to prevent the partitions from buckling? The men who make the laws, or the men who execute them, or the Court?

In 1789, when the new government was set up, probably most people expected, at least hoped, that when the meaning of the Constitution was clear and evident it should be the Court. Thus Hamilton declared in *The Federalist* that it must be the duty of the courts 'to declare all acts contrary to the manifest tenor of the Constitution void.' That, of course, was only half an answer, for it covered only the easy cases, when the meaning of the Constitution was clear. In such a case, any one who differed was plainly wrong. But who was to guard the guardians? Could you trust the Court to confine its answers to plain meanings? Its office then would be a sinecure. Some people objected that the Court might decide 'according to the spirit of the Constitution,' in which case its 'errors and usurpations' would be 'uncontrollable and remediless.' Hamilton pointed to the power to impeach the judges. 'There can never be danger that the judges, by a series of deliberate usurpations on the authority of the legislature, would hazard the united resentment of the body intrusted with it, while this body was possessed of the means of punishing their presumption, by degrading them from their stations. While this ought to remove all apprehensions on the subject, it affords, at the same time, a cogent argument for constituting the Senate a court for the trial of impeachments.' [8]

So when Hamilton stood for the doctrine of judicial supremacy, he relied on the Senate to impeach the Justices if they abused their supremacy. That is a reasonable enough solution, though it was not adopted. What would the Senate have done if Roosevelt, in 1937, instead of his Court plan, had sent a message to the Senate asking for the impeachment of the five Justices who were then holding the New Deal unconstitutional? Would the Senate have followed Hamilton?

The solution which we adopted is far more complicated and far less decisive than Hamilton's, and unlike Hamilton's it is not to be found in the Constitution itself. The Convention, perhaps wisely, or discreetly, or in despair of being able to give any other answer itself, did not try to.

James Bradley Thayer, in his life of Marshall, faced and discussed that fact. It is not always noticed, he said, that in making our Federal Constitution, there was an avoidance of any explicit declaration of such a power as touching federal legislation, while it was carefully provided for as regards the States. In the Federal Convention, there was great anxiety to control the States, in certain particulars; and various plans were put forward, such as that Congress should have a negative on state laws, and that governors of the States should be appointed by the federal authority, with power to negative state acts.

But all these, Thayer went on, were at last rejected, and the matter took the shape of a provision that the Constitution and the constitutional laws and treaties of the United States should be the supreme law of the respective States; and the judges of the several States should be bound thereby, anything in the constitution or laws of any State to the contrary notwithstanding. Later, the Committee on Style changed the phrase 'law of the respective States' to 'law of the land.' But the language, as to binding the judges, was still limited to the judges of the several States.

Observe, Thayer says, that the scope of this provision

was to secure the authority of the federal system within the States. As to any method of protecting the national system within its own household, that is to say, as against Congress, it was proposed in the convention, for one thing, that each House of Congress might call upon the judges for opinions; and, again, it was urged, and that repeatedly and with great persistence, that the judges should be joined with the executive in passing on the approval or disapproval of legislative acts — in what we call the veto power. It was explicitly said, in objecting to this, that the judges would have the right to disregard unconstitutional laws anyway — an opinion put forward by some of the weightiest members. Yet some denied it. And we observe that the power was not expressly given. When we find such a power expressly denied, and yet not expressly given; and when we observe, for example, that leading public men, e.g., so conspicuous a member of the convention as Charles Pinckney of South Carolina, afterwards a senator from that state, wholly denied the power ten years later; it being also true that he and others of his way of thinking urged the express restraints on state legislation — we may justly reach the conclusion that this question, while not overlooked, was intentionally left untouched. Like so many other questions, presumably it was so left in order not to stir up enemies to the new instrument; left to be settled by the silent determinations of time, or by later discussion.[9]

So Thayer leaves it like this. The problem was given no answer by the Constitution. A hole was left where the Court might drive in the peg of judicial supremacy, if it could. And that is what John Marshall did. He drove it in, so firmly that no one yet has been able to pull it out.

Marshall saw his chance to establish the doctrine of judicial supremacy right after his appointment as Chief Justice, in the case of *Marbury* v. *Madison*, in 1803. And he seized it cleverly. He held an act of Congress void which would otherwise have required him, so he said, to issue a writ of mandamus against Madison, then Secretary of State. Could Jefferson, the President, object to the establishment of a doctrine which protected his Secretary of State from being told what his duties were by the Court?

Clever? Marshall did more than seize his chance. He made it. For the act which Marshall held void could easily have been construed merely not to apply. The fact is, it was later re-enacted by Congress in almost the very same words, certainly no different so far as Marshall was concerned.[10] The act which Marshall struck down as unconstitutional does not even show a scar. Yet, in the words of one of Marshall's greatest admirers, little short of idolatry, 'Thus, by a coup as bold in design and as daring in execution as that by which the Constitution had been framed, John Marshall set up a landmark in American history so high that all the future could take bearings from it, so enduring that all the shocks the Nation was to endure could not overturn it.'[11]

There is no need of going any further into the history of the doctrine. No more of the past than is necessary to prevent yesterday from paralyzing today, lest today may not paralyze tomorrow. But before taking up the modern doctrine, which is no whit different from Marshall's statement of it, it is important to appreciate that the doctrine might equally well have become Executive supremacy. The Convention left the Court to its own devices, but it made a special provision for the case where the President might find that an act of Congress offended his constitutional conscience. Where it left the Court to work something out as best it could, it gave the President the veto power. There is an analogy.

Suppose Congress passes an act which the President believes to be unconstitutional. He cannot consult and take the advice of the Court, for the Court declines to give advisory opinions. The President has to act first and alone. He vetoes it. It is plainly his duty to veto it if he believes it to be unconstitutional. But then Congress passes this act over his veto by the required two-thirds. What does the President do then? What does he do before his Attorney General can arrange a test case and get the Court to pass on the act, if he can? His constitutional duty is clearly stated, 'he shall take care that the laws be faithfully executed.' [12] But an unconstitutional law strictly is not a law at all.

This is not an academic problem. Taft was in this quandary when he vetoed the Webb-Kenyon Act in 1913 and it was passed over his veto. He thought Congress had no power over interstate commerce to penalize shipping liquor into a prohibition state. The Court got him out of it by holding that it was constitutional. [13] Taft had been threatened with the same problem before, in 1909, when Congress was about to levy an income tax, which the Court had held unconstitutional. Taft got himself out of it that time by persuading Congress of the impropriety of asking the Court to change its mind, and hence the Sixteenth Amendment.

Johnson did not get out of the same quandary so easily. He was impeached when he vetoed the Reconstruction Acts of 1867, though his veto had gone on the express ground that they were unconstitutional. When they were passed over his veto, what should he do? He had sworn to support the Constitution. Should he execute a law which he believed to be contrary to the Constitution? Or should he say what he did say to the Court, through his Attorney General? 'From the moment they were passed over his veto, there was but one duty in his estimation resting upon him, and that was faithfully to carry out and execute these laws.' [14]

The Constitution had given the President the veto to prevent the enactment of unconstitutional laws as well as laws he disapproved of for other reasons. But once he had exhausted that remedy the Constitution gave him no other. That was as far as it expected him to go. After that his conscience became a purely private affair. His situation is politically similar to the Court's, except that the Court has not been provided with any half measure which marks the limits of its authority and its duty. Its veto — for the moment treat it as such, though some lawyers will object — cannot be overridden by any two-thirds vote, even by a unanimous vote, by nothing short of an amendment to the Constitution itself. That is no answer. That is the problem itself.

It has many times been proposed that Congress should be given the power to override the Court's decision that a law is unconstitutional, just as it can override a presidential veto. Theodore Roosevelt proposed it in 1912. Marshall preferred it to the method of impeachment which Hamilton favored. In a letter he wrote to his colleague, Judge Chase, who was then about to be impeached, Marshall said, 'I think the modern doctrine of impeachment should yield to an appellate jurisdiction in the legislature.

A reversal of those legal opinions deemed unsound by the legislature would certainly better comport with the mildness of our character than a removal of the judge who has rendered them unknowing of his fault.' [15]

Shall we impeach them? That was Hamilton's remedy. Should we amend the Constitution to provide for a recall of their bad decisions? That would be better, Marshall thought, and that is what Theodore Roosevelt favored. Franklin Roosevelt proposed another alternative. We shall come to that, but not now and not until we have examined the decisions of the Court which provoked it. What shall we do? Anything?

The Court's answer was the doctrine of judicial supremacy, established by Marshall in 1803. It is what the Court has done with it that counts, but to understand what it has done we must first know in rather precise fashion what the Court says it does.

3

THE DIFFERENCE BETWEEN A POWER
AND A DILEMMA

THEORETICALLY the Court's power to declare laws unconstitutional is not a power at all. It is the consequence of a dilemma. The Court is required to render judgment in the case before it, one way or the other. Someone suggests that the statute says one thing and the Constitution says another. If the Court cannot help but choose, obviously it must prefer the Constitution.

In 1936, when the A.A.A. was held unconstitutional, Roberts, speaking very carefully, explained what he understood the Court was doing. There are other expositions of the doctrine of judicial supremacy, but Roberts's is clear, recent, and authoritative:

'There should be no misunderstanding as to the function of this Court in such a case. It is sometimes said that the Court assumes a power to overrule or control the action of the people's representatives. This is a misconception. The Constitution is the supreme law of the land ordained and established by the people. All legislation must conform to the principles it lays down. When an act of Congress is appropriately challenged in the courts as not conforming

17

to the constitutional mandate, the judicial branch of the Government has only one duty, — to lay the article of the Constitution which is invoked beside the statute which is challenged and to decide whether the latter squares with the former. All the Court does, or can do, is to announce its considered judgment upon the question. The only power it has, if such it may be called, is the power of judgment. This court neither approves or condemns any legislative policy. Its delicate and difficult office is to ascertain and declare whether the legislation is in accordance with, or in contravention of, the provisions of the Constitution; and, having done that, its duty ends.' [16]

Even if the Court can lay them side by side as coolly as a tailor can take your measurements, even then it is not as easy as Roberts makes it seem, this comparing of two meanings.

A good many of us require some visual or mechanical aid to our thinking. Wasn't it Lord Kelvin who said he had to have little models of molecules, though he knew they were not really like that. Kepler drew little demons pulling or pushing the planets along their courses. We think of a cause as somehow pushing things toward its result. Rimbaud ascribed colors to the vowels. This laying the Constitution and a statute side by side and, so to speak, measuring the meaning of both, that, too, is a convenient mechanical aid to thinking about something that is not really measurable at all. So let us pretend we can measure meanings.

Words have size. We can visualize them as blobs of meaning, of different sizes and various shapes, with their margins fading out through a penumbra of chiaroscuro into no-meaning, or overlapping other meanings. We can give them color or even iridescence, if we want to include predilections and prejudices in our metaphor. Or we could simply say, as Roberts implies, that words have only length, like spectra between infra and ultra sense. Or, if you are more auditory than visual, think of scales on a piano.

Make it what you please. The Constitution, or rather some particular provision of it, has a length of meanings, some only a few, some more, depending on the number of specific and particular applications it may be given in practice. So has a statute. Does the particular application of the statute in the case lie within the length of meanings of the relevant provision in the Constitution? Without pulling, without stretching the texture or context? That is the way Roberts visualized constitutional law.

Nor should we stretch a metaphor, good as it is. For the limits of meaning are no more fixed and permanent than they are definite. This is no matter of inches. Words are living things, and *il faut vivre entre les vivants*, as Montaigne well knew. Constitutional law is not much like poetry, but it is far more like poetry than like geometry. Roberts's figure of speech must be left behind.

There have been justices who denied this, but in such a way as really to admit it. Van Devanter, McReynolds, and Butler were three of the Old Guard who stood out against the New Deal in 1935. When the question of constitutionality of zoning laws came up in 1926, they agreed that these were regulations whose wisdom, necessity, and validity, as applied to existing conditions, were so apparent that they should be sustained, though a century ago, or even half a century ago, probably they would have been rejected as arbitrary and excessive. But in this, they said,

there is no inconsistency, for 'while the meaning of constitutional guarantees never varies, the scope of the application must expand or contract to meet the new and different
conditions, which are constantly coming within the field of
their operation. In a changing world, it is impossible that
it should be otherwise. But although a degree of elasticity
is thus implanted, not to the *meaning*, but to the *application* of constitutional principles, statutes and ordinances,
which, after giving due weight to the new conditions, are
found clearly not to conform to the Constitution, of course,
must fall.' [17]

Meaning or application of meaning, it comes to the
same thing. Just as the framers of the Constitution often
chose not to express their own thoughts at all on some
questions, preferring to leave the question unanswered
and open for possibly better men with surely more information, so also they chose their words for size, or length.
Sometimes a big word with many applications, as these
three would put it, sometimes a smaller word when they
wanted to be more specific, nearer the concrete. Now the
difference between a very big word indeed, like the word
'*due*' in due process of law, or the words '*necessary and
proper*' in the provision giving Congress power to carry its
powers into execution, and no word at all comes very near
to the vanishing point. There are words that are all but
the equivalent of silence. What is there then to lay the
act of Congress beside?

The Court is, of course, not faced with the dilemma
at all unless it must render judgment one way or the
other in a law case. The Court is not a lawyer, but a
court, and it made that clear very early in its career.
Washington once asked it for an opinion, and the Court

declined to give it.[18] Frankfurter suggests, in his article on the Supreme Court in the *Encyclopedia of the Social Sciences*, that this was an assertion of the Court's dignity. Maybe. As a law court it would be beneath its dignity to hear anything but law suits. If the President wanted legal advice, let him ask his lawyer, the Attorney General. But it was not only a proper position to take, it was wise.

A statute when it is enacted is only a project. Until it is put into operation, who knows how it will work? Not until then is it itself, an operation which can be observed and appraised. It is only fair to the Court that it should see the statute in actual application. So the Court does well to wait for litigation. Perhaps it ought to be able to wait even longer, until there is enough litigation to make a pattern. And indeed that is precisely what the Court often does. For most of its cases are heard on *certiorari*, where the litigant is required to petition the Court for leave to bring the case before it. One which we shall discuss at some length was heard only after it had refused to hear three other such cases.[19] On the other hand, the Court allowed another case we shall discuss to come up even before the statute by its own terms was to go into effect. Some of the justices felt there was no reason for the Court to be so precipitate.[20] The Court is pretty well able to choose its own time for facing the dilemma. The occasions in which the Court is forced to choose between a statute and the Constitution do not come up to the Court in an inevitable progress on a judicial assembly-line. The fact is, whenever the Court really wants to express its opinion there are several ways it can do it.

One way is to listen to a case which has been made up for the very purpose of obtaining the Court's opinion.

The Court has been very indulgent with the bar about this, not in any particular period, but always, from Marshall down, anyhow until the Court was reconstructed in 1939.

It is of interest that it seems to have happened chiefly in important cases. *Fletcher* v. *Peck*, in 1810, is the stock example. That was the first case in which the Court held a state statute void. It involved a national scandal. The 1795 legislature of Georgia sold its western lands, most of Alabama and Mississippi, to speculators. Perhaps it was the greatest real estate steal in our history. The purchase price was only half a million dollars. The next legislature repealed the statute for fraud, the bribery of legislators, but not before the land companies had completed the deal and unloaded. By that time, and increasingly soon afterwards, more and more people had bought, and their title was in issue. Eleven million of the acres had been bought for eleven cents an acre by leading citizens of Boston. How could they clear their title? Alexander Hamilton gave an opinion, that the repeal of the grant was void under the Constitution as an impairment of the obligation of a contract.

But could they not get a decision from the Supreme Court? Robert Fletcher of Amherst, New Hampshire, had bought fifteen thousand acres from John Peck of Boston. He sued Peck, and he won. Fletcher appealed. Plainly it was a friendly suit.[21] Marshall was nobody's fool. He told Cranch that the Court was reluctant to decide the case 'as it appeared manifestly made up for the purpose of getting the Court's judgment.' John Quincy Adams so reports in his diary.[22] Yet Marshall did decide it, and he held the repeal void, just as Hamilton said it was. 'The fact that Marshall rendered an opinion, under the circumstances,' says Beveridge, 'is one of the finest proofs of his greatness. A weaker man than John Marshall, and one less wise and courageous, would have dismissed the appeal.' [23] That may be, but it was the act of a statesman, not of a judge. The Court has always been able to overcome its judicial diffidence on state occasions.

The modern way is a stockholder's suit. In 1935 the Court permitted Carter, the president and a large stockholder in the Carter Coal Company, to get its opinion that the Coal Control Act was unconstitutional. [24] This was the New Deal's attempt to regulate the coal industry. It is hard to believe that Carter and his company differed as to whether this act violated the Constitution. It is also hard to understand why a stockholder should be able to get an opinion from the Court which would have been refused to the President of the United States.

A test case is different. It is a real controversy. The parties are really at odds over the issue. A test case is only a case that is selected as fairly representative, whose decision will decide the others. It is still justice that the Court is dispensing, though in a sense at wholesale instead of retail.

4

THE DIFFERENCE BETWEEN A RÔLE
AND A FUNCTION

A CERTAIN LACK of candor follows when you are in something of a false position. There are necessary adjustments to be made when a law court finds itself also an organ of government, when the function it finds itself performing differs from the rôle it was expected to play.

Even when the Court has a case, a real case which it must decide and in which it is forced to choose between the Constitution and a statute, even then it does not do it fairly and squarely. You would expect it to give the Constitution the benefit of the doubt, if not the preference. You might suggest that would be only fair to a litigant who is claiming the protection of the Constitution against the statute, a statute which he says Congress, or it may be a state legislature, had no power to pass. But the Court does quite the contrary. It applies the doctrine of judicial review neither logically, nor even fairly to the litigant. It does not even try to make a fair comparison when it lays the statute along the Constitution, as Roberts says it does. It resolves every doubt in favor of the statute. It gives the statute the preference, not the Constitution.

This is the result of an equally classical political qualification to the classical legal doctrine. 'The judicial duty
of passing upon the constitutionality of an act of Congress
is one of great gravity and delicacy. The statute here in
question has successfully borne the scrutiny of the legislative branch of the government, which, by enacting it, has
affirmed its validity; and that determination must be given
great weight. The Court, by an unbroken line of decisions
from Chief Justice Marshall to the present day, has stead-
ily adhered to the rule that every possible presumption is
in favor of the validity of an act of Congress until overcome beyond rational doubt.' That is the Court, speaking
through Sutherland, in the Adkins case, where minimum
wages were held unconstitutional.[25]

Or take it from Holmes, no less sound a lawyer, but of
a different school of thought, when he was dissenting in
the Lochner case, where maximum hours of work were
held unconstitutional. The Constitution was perverted,
Holmes said, when it was held to prevent the natural outcome of a dominant opinion, 'unless it can be said that a
rational and fair man necessarily would admit that the
statute proposed would infringe fundamental principles,
as they have been understood by the traditions of our
people and our law.' These rational doubts, then, are
those of 'a rational and fair man,' or 'a reasonable man,'
as Holmes said, in the next sentence but one.[26]

Plainly a betrayal of the very basis on which the whole
doctrine of judicial review has been based. A betrayal of
the rights of the litigant and the judicial duty owed him by
the Court. If this were strictly a matter of law, he has a
legal right to all the benefits of the Constitution, not wa-
tered down by rational doubts, not stretched and strained

to include what some reasonable man thinks it may mean, but to the Constitution simply, at least to what the Court thinks it is. This has been pointed out.

Chief Justice Gibson of Pennsylvania discussed the doctrine of judicial supremacy when it was still new, not to say novel, in 1825; anyway, before it had been raised to its later exalted position and taken as a matter of course and beyond criticism.

After stating the principle in much the same terms as Sutherland, Gibson said that in such case the party's 'rights would depend not on the greatness of the supposed discrepancy with the constitution, but on the existence of any discrepancy at all; and the judge would therefore be bound to decide this question, like every other in respect to which he may be unable to arrive at a perfectly satisfactory conclusion. But he would evade the question instead of deciding it, were he to refuse to decide in accordance with the inclination of his mind. To say, therefore, that the power is to be exercised but in perfectly clear cases, is to betray a doubt of the propriety of exercising it at all.' [27]

But it is not strictly a matter of justice, any more than the Court is simply a court of law. Only if the Constitution and its meaning were a private affair has he any cause to complain that he is not being treated fairly.

As qualified the doctrine sets aside any comparison of the meanings of the Constitution and the statute. The Court is released from the dilemma and must ask itself quite another question: Can rational doubt, can a reasonable human being, say that this statute falls infra or ultra constitutional sense? The Court's own opinion has become as irrelevant as justice between the parties. That is why it was wise for the Court to set its face against advisory opinions, for they would be called for before Congress had acted, before the President had signed the bill. Then, at that time, if the Court had been asked for its opinion, it could have given only its own opinion, which would in turn be weighed and considered by the Congress and the President. And speaking last they might then have differed. This, I think, is back of Frankfurter's suggestion that the Court's reason for declining to give advisory opinions was a sense of its own dignity. Having to give it first, it might have been overridden. By preferring to give it last, its dignity is secure, but the Court must respect what has already been said.

For by the time the Court has any case before it, Congress has passed the act and the President has signed it. They have both already expressed their opinions. Not only is this a wise move, they have said, it is a constitutional one. Were the judges sitting down with them in council, as indeed it was proposed they should — in the Council of Revision in the plan Virginia proposed to the Convention — they would all have expressed their own opinions to each other and come to some agreement. But they are not. They are acting one after another, and before the Court is called upon both of its colleagues have already said what they thought.

So the Court is always in the same quandary Johnson found he was in. Only it does not mind. He thought the Reconstruction Act unconstitutional and therefore vetoed it. Congress passed it over his veto. Then it came before the Court. Had the Court too approved it, Johnson said he would enforce it. He would have bowed to what they both agreed to. So too President Taft with the Webb-Kenyon Act, passed, vetoed, re-enacted, and approved.

It is all the result of expressing your opinion after and in the light of the opinions of your colleagues when you cannot sit down with them and argue it out into agreement.

Congress acts first and so acts unhampered by doubts raised by or respect owed to others' opinions. Its duties to the Constitution do not include fear of a veto. No more should they include apprehension of the Court's disapproval. Roosevelt was quite right in what he wrote to a member of the House Ways and Means Committee on the Coal Control Act.[28] That was the act which the Court, a majority of them, held invalid in Carter's suit. Roosevelt said, 'I hope your committee will not permit doubt as to constitutionality, however reasonable, to block the suggested legislation.' Some of us will remember the raised Republican eyebrows. Said Snell, the next month, in his keynote speech to the Republican Convention, 'Thank God no Republican President ever violated his constitutional oath by calling upon the members of his party to violate theirs. We bow our heads in shame and sorrow.' What Roosevelt was saying was simply, Do not let your apprehension of what the judges may say swerve you from saying what you think. Things would but run round if each let his opinion hang on what he thought the others' might be. Mutual respect includes self-respect. And Congress, being elected, does not have to think so much of its dignity.

If Congress may not legislate whenever it is beset by constitutional doubts, Congress cannot do its full duty. It would deprive itself by quite uncalled-for self-restraint of a great part of the legislative power which the Court recognizes it possesses by the very fact that it will hold an act of Congress unconstitutional only when it goes bevond 'rational doubt.' Otherwise there would be a legislative no man's land of doubt between Congress and the Court, which would theoretically render the Court's professions quite futile. Were Congress, on Snell's theory, to anticipate the Court's condemnation, it would be a legislative contraception of acts which the Court, as it professes, would hold legitimate.

That is not the only example of the Seventy-fifth Congress feeling it was not to be deterred from its duty of legislating by any apprehension of the Court's disapproval. In May of 1936 the Court held the Municipal Bankruptcy Act invalid in *Ashton* v. *Cameron County*.[29] It was one of the five to four decisions of that time. As we shall see, something came over the Court in the spring of 1937. It had a change of heart, and its recent five to four decisions then began to look more like monuments than precedents. In August of 1937, Congress passed another municipal bankruptcy act, doing its best to save the Court's face, but in at least one respect that was really quite impossible if municipalities were going to get the necessary relief. The chairman of the Judiciary Committee, Mr. Sumners, who had charge of the bill, frankly stated on the floor of the House that the application of the bill to cities and towns, as he proposed, would be unconstitutional under the Ashton case. Yet he felt that it was not only the right, but the duty of Congress to present the question once more to the Court, since that decision, if it were allowed to stand, was a grave threat to the powers of the states to authorize their cities and towns to enter into bankruptcy proceedings, and that he deplored. Congress passed the bill.

The next spring the new act came before the Court and

what Chairman Sumners had said was called to their attention.[30] And the Court held the act valid. Mr. Sumners himself appeared and pointed out that in the case before them it was only an irrigation district, something quite different, he suggested, from a political subdivision of a state. Whether or not this distinction was sturdy enough to save the act, at least it protected the dignity of the Court, which, we may suppose, was Mr. Sumners's chief purpose.[31]

There was really no need of such solicitude. A few years later, in 1943, the Court, commenting on this episode, said, 'Nothing in the history or attitude of this Court should give rise to legislative embarrassment if in the performance of its duty a legislative body feels impelled to enact laws which may require the Court to re-examine its previous judgments or doctrine.'[32] Yet there had been a time when the Court's decisions were more oracular, a golden age when it inspired a feeling more akin to awe than anxiety for its dignity.

The counterpart is the Court's respect for Congress. There must, of course, be a mutual respect of some kind, as between collaborators in a common enterprise. Precisely what should be the Court's demeanor, remembering that Congress acts first and the Court last? An act of Congress must be given 'great weight.' It is constitutional, the Court says, 'until overcome beyond rational doubt,' or in Holmes's words, 'unless it can be said that a rational and fair man necessarily would admit' that the act was invalid. How much weight? What sort and degree of doubt? Who is this man? Plainly the answers go to the very heart of the Court's function and the doctrine of judicial supremacy.

If this rational and fair man, this reasonable man, is a fictitious being, the formula becomes essentially tautological. For, except in such fields as mathematics or logic or other conventional and analytic disciplines, the doubts of that fictitious person are really no more than a reflection of your own. The Court is operating with mirrors. As it approaches the image of this reasonable being, the Justices find that they are approaching themselves, and that the doubts they ascribe or impute to him are really no more than their own. In that case, outside of a purely conventional discipline, the phrase 'beyond rational doubt' comes to mean only a degree of the intolerable, beyond what Holmes once referred to as our Can't Helps,³³ across the no man's land of indifference, and on until they are up against the blind wall of We Can't Stand It. Though this may help us to understand what the Court sometimes does, surely it is of no particular help as a formula for what the Court is going to do. It explains the paradox of how five of the Justices can hold a statute unconstitutional 'beyond rational doubt' when four of their colleagues cherish that very doubt. For each Justice by confusing himself with this fictitious image can come to an honest belief that he is not simply dealing with himself. But we are not running our hare to ground only to dig out a paradox. This formula must be something better than an introspective device. The rational and fair man must be someone else, someone in his own right and on his own feet. Who is he?

To begin with, these are not legal doubts. They are not lawyer's doubts. They are lay doubts. For they are engendered by the 'great weight' which the Court, naturally enough, gives to the fact that Congress has acted as if its act were constitutional, and to the opinion of the President who has not vetoed it, but signed it. These are lay opinions. To be sure, two-thirds of the Senate and half the House may be lawyers, but they are not there professionally. They are representing constituents, not clients.

He cannot be Congress, for in that case the Court, under the formula, could never hold an act of Congress unconstitutional. He cannot be a Justice, for that would be requiring unanimity. The formula would be equally useless if it were merely anyone. Who then is he, or, rather, who are they, whose doubts must guide the Court toward its decision?

James Bradley Thayer found a happy phrase for the people whose opinion the Court is respecting, in an old opinion of the Supreme Court of South Carolina. In 1812, Chancellor Waties said, 'The validity of the law ought not to be questioned unless it is so obviously repugnant to the Constitution that when pointed out by the judges all men of sense and reflection in the community may perceive the repugnancy.' [34]

'When pointed out by the judges.' The perception of such men, *after* the Court has pointed out the issue and explained it, *after* the Court has rendered its opinion. An enlightened popular judgment, then? Why not? There is nothing invidious about that, unless you still insist that judicial review is a purely legal affair, or unless you refuse to accept the democratic process. Those are the men the Court is turning to. It is to them, we may say, that the Court is addressing its opinion, 'all men of sense and reflection in the community.'

We have examined the classic doctrine of judicial supremacy, in the Court's words, and the great qualification, which is equally classic, also in the Court's words. We have tried to analyze it, theoretically; and we have broached a theoretical basis for the qualified doctrine. Obviously we have not got very far. Theory never does get you very far, however necessary it is to start with. The Court defers its own opinion to that of Congress unless it believes it can persuade all men of sense and reflection in the community to take its side and share its view that the statute in question is repugnant to the Constitution. When the Court thinks it can do that, but only then, it is the duty of the Court to declare the statute void and to resist all demands to enforce it. Or, to put the same thing from a different point of view, the Court must restrain itself from the temptation, pardonable enough to a court of law, to judge the case before it according to its own lights, unless it is confident that these men of sense and reflection are going to agree with its decision.

All this may seem a long way round a very low wall. Is there here anything more complicated or more difficult to understand when a statute is held unconstitutional than the spectacle of collaborators who do not agree over their joint work? When the Court calls an act of Congress unconstitutional, is it doing more than trying to ignore some act of nonsense or foolishness or some palpable breach of discipline on the part of its fellow workman? Ignoring it, and as tactfully as possible getting ahead with the work, instead of quarreling over it as Congress is so likely to do with the President? That is true. An unconstitutional act is essentially an unco-operative act, and to be treated accordingly by the Court. And so likewise it would be right for Congress to ignore a decision of the Court equally unco-operative. It is a problem of collaborating between government departments. When they differ, each turns to its own constituents, the Congress to those who have elected them and may or may not re-elect them, the Court to all men of sense and reflection in the community.

5

A TENANT AT SUFFERANCE

So MUCH FOR THE THEORY of judicial supremacy. The first fact to be recognized is that the Court exercises the doctrine at the sufferance of Congress. To begin with, the very jurisdiction of the Court in all important cases is subject to 'such exceptions and under such regulations as the Congress shall make.' That is the language of the Constitution, Article III. To be sure, its original jurisdiction as a court of first instance cannot be taken away from it, but that covers only cases affecting ambassadors, ministers, consuls, and between the States themselves. None of them bring suit very often and when they do it is more important to them than to us. If that were all the business the Court had, the place would be an honorable sinecure for tired lawyers and others, and nobody but themselves would want to write a book about it. It is the Court's appellate jurisdiction that counts, and that is held and exercised at the pleasure of Congress. Congress can even take away the Court's jurisdiction in a case already pending before it. Once Congress did just that, and the Court unanimously agreed that Congress had power to do it.

That was the McCardle case in 1869. McCardle was a Mississippi editor who was arrested and held for trial before a military commission under one of the Reconstruction Acts. After McCardle's case had been argued, Congress apprehended the Court might interfere in a matter of personal liberty. So Congress repealed the section which gave McCardle a right to appeal to the Court. Johnson, stout-hearted fellow, vetoed the repeal right in the middle of his impeachment trial but Congress passed it over his veto. And the Court acquiesced. With dry dignity — the grapes were sour — Chief Justice Chase, for a unanimous court, said, 'Judicial duty is not less fitly performed by declining ungranted jurisdiction than in exercising firmly that which the Constitution and the laws confer.' The Court, he said, was 'not at liberty to inquire into the motives of the Legislature.' [35] B. R. Curtis, the ex-Justice, who had dissented in the Dred Scott case, remarked, 'Congress, with the acquiescence of the country, has subdued the Supreme Court, as well as the President.' Certainly the Fortieth Congress brought the country nearer than it has ever been to a revolution, before or since. We may be grateful that there was no Cromwell among Stevens, Wade, Butler, and the rest of them.

Congress sets the times when the Court is to sit. Once, long ago now, in Marshall's time, the Seventh Congress forced the Court to adjourn for over a year. Senator Bayard asked, 'May it not lead to the virtual abolition of the Court?' Monroe wrote to Jefferson, Suppose the judges were to meet notwithstanding and make a solemn protestation, denouncing the whole proceeding as unconstitutional and the motive as impure. Yet Marshall acquiesced. 'The office still remains,' he said, 'to receive and exercise any new judicial powers which the Legislature may confer.' [36]

Congress has complete power over the enforcement of the Court's judgments. The President might use the Army to prevent their enforcement, just as he can use the Army to enforce the law, which so pleased Sewall Avery that he folded his hands over his complacency and let the soldiers carry him out. If the use of the Army against embattled deputy marshals is too fanciful, the power of Congress to cut off appropriations is not. It could do to the Court what it has done to any other department of the government.

Congress has complete authority under the Constitution to fix the number of justices. It has changed the members more than once. Even the American Bar Association admitted that Roosevelt's proposal to Congress in 1937 to increase the Court to fifteen would be constitutional. They denounced it, and the bar cried out, four to one, that it would be 'constitutionally immoral.' Immoral or not, you will agree, as they did, that it was within the constitutional power of Congress to do it.

Bryce called this 'a joint in the court's armour.' [37] The Fathers of the Constitution, he said, studied nothing more than to secure the complete independence of the judiciary. The President was not permitted to remove the judges, nor Congress to diminish their salaries. One thing only was either forgotten or deemed undesirable, because highly inconvenient, to determine — the number of judges in the Supreme Court. Here, he said, was a weak point, a joint in the court's armor through which a weapon might some day penetrate. And Bryce suggested the weapon. Suppose, he said, a Congress and President bent on doing something which the Supreme Court deems contrary to the Constitution. They pass a statute. A case arises under it. The court on the hearing of the case unanimously declares the statute to be null, as being beyond the powers of Congress. Congress forthwith passes and the President signs another statute more than doubling the number of justices. The President appoints to the new justiceships men who are pledged to hold the former statute constitutional. The Senate confirms his appointments. Another case raising the validity of the disputed statute is brought up to the court. The new justices outvote the old ones: the statute is held valid: the security provided for the protection of the Constitution is gone like a morning mist.

Bryce asks what prevents such immoral assaults on the fundamental law. Not the mechanism of government, he answers himself, for all its checks have been evaded. Not the conscience of the legislature and the President, for heated combatants seldom shrink from justifying the means by the end. Nothing but the fear of the people, whose broad good sense and attachment to the great principles of the Constitution may generally be relied on to condemn such a perversion of its forms. Yet if excitement has risen high over the country, a majority of the people may acquiesce; and then it matters little whether what is really a revolution be accomplished by openly violating or by merely distorting the forms of law. To the people we come sooner or later, said Bryce, and it is upon their wisdom and self-restraint that the stability of the most cunningly devised scheme of government will in the last resort depend.

We have seen that the doctrine of judicial supremacy rests on no express warrant in the Constitution. We have seen, too, how Marshall, a sly genius as well as a statesman, saw his chance and took it. He planted the standard for honest folk and others to repair to. But you know what Franklin told the lady at dinner in Philadelphia after the Constitution Convention, who asked him if we had a republic. Yes, he said, if you can keep it. The Court has kept its supremacy only on sufferance from Congress. In legal terms the Court has been precisely that, a tenant of the doctrine at sufferance. How and why?

The Court did not use Marshall's doctrine for fifty-four years, 1803 to 1857. Then — it sounds incredible, but it seems to be true — the Court tried to use the doctrine to solve what has been, so far, our hardest problem. The only knot which we have not been able to untie, and had to cut. Slavery at that time seemed to hang on the question of whether it could be introduced into the new territories. Kansas had to fight it out. So the Court undertook to solve the problem legally. If we persist in treating our political problems as if they were legal, can you blame our best legal talent for trying their hand? Sometimes the wisest commit the most egregious follies.

The Dred Scott case gave these Justices their opportunity. A couple of weeks or so before Buchanan's inauguration, they became 'convinced that it was practicable for the Court to quiet all agitation on the question of slavery in the Territories by affirming that Congress had no constitutional power to prohibit its introduction.' That is what Wayne said, and Curtis confirms it.[38] Taney agreed and said he would write the opinion. When Grier did not agree, Catron wrote the President-elect, who wrote to Grier, who showed the letter to Taney and Wayne. Grier then wrote Buchanan that he, too, agreed and that the opinion would come down on March 6, two days after he was inaugurated. So Buchanan announced in his inaugural that the question, then pending before the Court, would be 'speedily and finally settled.' 'To their decision, in common with all good citizens, I shall cheerfully submit, whatever this may be.' Which was not hard to do, for he knew.

We, too, know what it was, that a Negro could not be a citizen and that Congress had no power to exclude slavery from the territories. We know also what a better constitutional lawyer even than Taney said about it four years later in his inaugural. 'I do not forget the position, assumed by some, that constitutional questions are to be decided by the Supreme Court, nor do I deny that such decisions must be binding in any case, upon the parties to a suit as to the object of that suit, while they are also entitled to very high respect and consideration in all parallel cases by all other departments of the government. At the same time, the candid citizen must confess that if the policy of the government, upon vital questions affecting the whole people, is to be irrevocably fixed by the Supreme Court the instant they are made, in ordinary litigation between parties in personal actions, the people will have ceased to be their own rulers, having to that extent practically resigned their government into the hands of that eminent tribunal.'

War distracted us from the Court's folly, and the country completely ignored the decision. So much so that when Congress passed an act in 1862 prohibiting slavery in the territories,[39] I cannot find in its debates — they were brief — even a reference to the Court's decision that it had no power at all to do so. The doctrine of judicial supremacy seemed as good as dead.

A candid friend might well have advised the Court to
call it off, give up its fine pretensions to primacy in construing the Constitution, and stick to the law. It would
have been bad advice. For the doctrine was then just
about to begin its career. Charles Fairman has told the
story up to 1890 in his *Mr. Justice Miller and the Supreme
Court, 1862–1890*. I skip to the eighteen-nineties where
we can see the doctrine at the top of its bent. Let us see
how far the Court can stretch it and how the country can
take it.

In 1894 Congress passed an income tax. It was a tax of
2 per cent, flat rate, on all incomes over $4000. Cleveland
had just been elected with a pledge to reduce the tariff,
and Congress, anticipating a reduced revenue, had pru-
dently added this modest tax on incomes.

The legal grounds on which it was contended this income tax was unconstitutional turned on the question
whether an income tax was 'direct' or not. If it was, the
Constitution required that it be apportioned among the
states according to population, which of course it wasn't.
Nobody knows when a tax is direct and when it is not.
In the records of the Convention, it says, 'Mr. King asked
what was the precise meaning of direct taxation. No one
answered.' [40] The idea of a government unable to tax incomes strikes us as silly, and so it did most people in 1894.
An income tax then represented the thin edge of the wedge
which a great hammer — the same hammer we now see in
the device of the U.S.S.R. — was driving into our capital-
istic economy. The result was the same hysteria we saw
in the nineteen-twenties. Listen to a paragraph out of
Joseph H. Choate's argument, and you will recognize the
same raised voice.

'The act of Congress which we are impugning before you is communistic in its purposes and tendencies, and is defended here upon principles as communistic, socialistic — what shall I call them — populistic as ever have been addressed to any political assembly in the world. I do not believe that any member of this court ever has sat or ever will sit to hear and decide a case the consequences of which will be so far-reaching as this — not even the venerable member who survives from the early days of the Civil War, and has sat upon every question of reconstruction, of national destiny, of state destiny that has come up during the last thirty years. No member of this court will live long enough to hear a case which will involve a question of more importance than this, the preservation of the fundamental rights of private property and equality before the law, and the ability of the people of these United States to rely upon the guaranties of the Constitution. With the deepest earnestness and confidence we submit that all patriotic Americans must pray that our views shall prevail.' [41]

And they did. The Court agreed with him. Five to four. It was really even closer than that, for someone shifted his vote at the last minute. Contemporary rumor thought it was Shiras. Corwin thinks it was Gray. Others suggest Brewer. No matter. It was as close as could be, if not closer. Four to four with the fifth man, whoever he was, himself divided by doubt. Not a very solid foundation for a decision? Well, it took an amendment to the Constitution to undo it.

Tariff revenue worked out better than Congress expected. McKinley, not Bryan, was elected. The country had other things to think about. It was not until 1909 that the country again felt the need for an income tax. Then Bailey of Texas, Borah of Idaho, and Cummins of Iowa proposed a 3 per cent flat rate tax on incomes over $5000 as a rider to the Payne-Aldrich tariff. Aldrich did not want that, of course. So he and Lodge went to see Taft about it. They found him most sympathetic.

None of them wanted an income tax and they discussed the best way to prevent one. What was the strongest argument they could find to defeat this income tax in the Congress? Taft gave it to them: 'I think it exposes the Court to very severe criticism whatever it does.' [42] So they agreed to propose a constitutional amendment.

The best argument against an income tax was disrespect for the Court, and so, when Senator Root made the speech in the Senate, its theme was not the tax but the Court. I ask you to compare what Lincoln said in his inaugural. Root said, 'If they yield, what then? Where then would be the confidence of our people in the justice of their judgment? If they refuse to yield, what then? A breach between the two parts of our government, with popular acclaim behind the popular branch, and setting against the independence, the dignity, the respect, the sacredness of that great tribunal, whose part in our government is the greatest contribution that America has made in political science.' [43]

Root did not argue that an income tax was unconstitutional. Indeed, he said he thought the dissent in the Pollock case 'had the weight of the argument.' But that was now irrelevant. He argued that the Court had held it was unconstitutional, and that was that. That was enough. He preferred, all things considered, that the Court should stay in error to its being forced to admit error. Or even given the opportunity to correct itself.

Possibly his real reason was nothing more than the fear the Court would confess its error. Root said he had 'more than doubts' that the Court would reverse itself. But the fact is, the Court seemed quite ready to do just that, given the opportunity. Of the old majority of five, only Fuller, the Chief Justice, and Brewer remained. Moreover, Brewer died the next March,[44] and the case could scarcely have reached the Court sooner. Of the four dissenters, there were two left, Harlan and White. They could be counted on to sustain the tax. And the intervening years had brought Holmes, McKenna, Day and Moody. It is hard to see them holding an income tax void. That makes six and that's enough. No doubt the senators had all this in mind. They were trying to defeat the tax, or at any rate postpone it.

But the point is the argument Root chose as the most persuasive. It was not only Root's own opinion. It was what he thought would move other senators, and it did. 'If they yield ——.' This is a curious way of putting it, as if they would be yielding to Congress against their better judgment, and not to that judgment. '—— where then would be the confidence of the people in the justice of their judgment?' A curious justice and a curious attitude, startlingly different from what the Court said in 1943 about reversing the Ashton case.

As we all know, Congress ditched an income tax for the time being and submitted the Sixteenth Amendment to the country. 'The Congress shall have power to lay and collect taxes on incomes, from whatever source derived ——.' Perhaps a broader grant of power than even a reversal of the Pollock case would have given. However, the country preferred to do without a tax on incomes until it had gone through the ritual of amending the Constitution, sooner than even seem to offend the sensibilities of its Court. 'Tis mad idolatry to make the service greater than the god.

This was the heyday of the Court's power and prestige in Congress and at the bar. Between 1865, the end of the Civil War, and 1935, when the Court attached the New Deal, it held some thirty-six acts of Congress unconstitutional.[45] During the same period, the Court invalidated some two or three hundred state statutes, over two hundred under the Fourteenth Amendment.[46] It is useless to be precise, for statutes are not of comparable importance. There is no unit of value. If we try to appraise each act and statute by hindsight, we run into might-have-been's, would-I-might's instead of may's.[47] For the question always is, as it was with the income tax, Is the statute worth either a constitutional amendment or pressure on the Court? Neither is easy. The one takes time and organization. The other subjects you to a charge of sacrilege. The New Deal had to face the horrid question after the 1936 elections. To put it rudely, the Court has a high nuisance value.

One thing, though, these figures do prove, and that is the deference Congress and many of us paid the Court during this era, these seventy years. Time after time, dozens of times, Congress bowed its belief that a measure was constitutional before the Court's belief that it was not, and forsook what it wanted to do out of respect for the Court's opinion that it should not do it. The income tax is but one example. The prevention of child labor is another. Twice Congress proposed to stop it. Twice the Court said no, once in 1918, again in 1922. Congress was willing to wait until the National Labor Relations Act was held valid in 1937. Deference to the Court during this era of our history gave it such power that Stone was led to say, in 1936, that the only check upon its exercise of power was its own sense of self-restraint.[48] Needless to say, Stone was dissenting.

What is the basis of this power so great that Stone could think of no limit save self-restraint? Why did the country let the Court — let it? — insist that it should have this power? What is the magic? There is no magic. It is the most commonplace of situations. When a great people finds that there are certain things they want done, and no one specially appointed to the work, a job to be done and no one named to do it, they look around. When an applicant appears, shovel on his shoulder, they take him. He proves quiet, industrious, and discreet. What if he does go on a drunk now and then? He sobers off and goes to work again. Before you know it, John is a fixture. He likes his job. He is a good worker. He's a member of the family. No one else seems to know how to do the work so well.

The clue to the Court's power lies partly in the need that the job be done, and partly in the way the Court has done the job.

6

THE COURT'S JOB

Federalism

THE HOLE shapes the peg just as the peg shapes the hole. The Court is fashioned by the need which it fills, the function it performs. What it does determines what it is. Almost, it is what it does. This is true of an individual. It is peculiarly true of groups and organizations. For theirs is at best a synthetic personality, compounded out of its function, unless, of course, they are dominated by one man, as the Court was once dominated by Marshall. So an understanding of the job to be done is a way to understand the Court. The job and the workman are two sides of the same thing.

What then is the job to be done? This is a *federal* state where *natural rights* are secured. That calls for two quite separate jobs for someone. And there is also some need for an alignment and discrimination of function in any state that is set up with a separation of its power between the legislative, executive, and judicial. They are not naturally and inevitably distinct. A strong centripetal force pulls them together.

But take now only the first two: the preservation of a federal system, lest the national government either dissolve in a centrifugal chaotic swirl or stagnate into unity; the protection of the inherent, inalienable, and natural rights of the individual against any government at all.

Federalism is simply a tribute paid, or owed, to space. We have not conquered space. We are on the way to conquering time, but that's another matter. The weeks we used to take in getting from one place to another have become days, and the days are by way of becoming hours, but miles are no shorter than they were. Communities have spread themselves out because we have shortened the time it takes to get to work or away from work and home, but there is still a vast difference between commuting and traveling. The state capital is still a long way from your town, and for a man in Montana the distance to Washington is still measured in miles. The Bell System makes it easier to arrange an appointment, but it's no substitute for the conference when you get there. So the aeroplane and the telephone can annihilate time as fast as they choose, but space will remain. Nothing is going to make personal intercourse obsolete.

The democratic process in government calls for the personal participation of the citizen in that government, not simply control over his government, nor only representation in the process of government. Remote control is not enough. Nor is it enough for the citizen to feel he is participating vicariously, through statesmen that are one of them, like Lincoln. That is no more than watching the game. It's not playing it. This is not only my government. I must also be some part of it, and that requires personal intercourse. We can't all of us move up into official position. So the government must also move down to you and me, nearer us, as near as it can get to us.

This is not hard to do in a small community. It has been done several times with spectacular success. But personal intercourse is a matter of space, not time. We are undertaking to do it over two or three thousand miles. It is not enough to say the problems are national, and it is not true to say that the railroads, the telephone, the aeroplane, and the radio have made our continent a small community. We think if we kill time we kill space, too. No. We think that we Americans are all much alike and need uniform treatment. To a degree that is true. But uniformity of treatment is only a simplification of the problem, to make it seem easier of solution. It is no reply at all to a failure to bring government down to the individual citizen. Not if we propose to govern ourselves by the democratic process.

At the same time, the democratic process and the personal participation of the citizen in his government is not all we want. It is a way of government, not its goal. There are things we want that only the whole nation acting together can give us. The most recent example is success in this last war, but that is a brutally big example. Again and again we have come up against things that local community effort cannot give us. Local ambition and local zeal indeed stand in our way. Child labor could not, cannot be got rid of state by state. The plight of agriculture is not, and cannot be, the business of the agrarian states alone. A national market must be opened from above, not bit by bit from below. There are other things, short of national, which yet must transcend state lines. The TVA is one. It is a matter of a whole river valley, and nothing short of that.

Our industry was showing us that this was so, and

taught our unions it was so, before our government learned it. The government only saw that it had to keep up with them. For local government cannot keep pace with a national business. If government did not nationalize itself, too, it would be turning us over to be ruled by one or the other. For as life got more complicated, it became more apparent that there is not more or less government. There is always just about so much and the real question is, Who is doing it? If the government does not, or cannot, some-one else will. For example, there are three ways of handling labor relations. There is individual bargaining, each employee with his company. Economic dominance then makes the employer practically a dictator. There is compulsory arbitration. Then the government may make itself the dictator. And there is collective bargaining, which rests on the hope that it will work by itself, *laissez-faire* them both.

The reconciliation of national government with local participation and then the further reconciliation of the political result with the economic power of business and labor, that is the federal problem.[49]

Natural Rights and Some Absolutes

Federalism is one of the Court's jobs, and plainly it calls for statesmanship. The other is different and harder and it calls for something more than statesmanship, almost priestcraft. There is certainly something about it that is either religious in a large sense or akin to religion. We have not only a government that we want to keep federal. We have a government to which some things have been wholly denied. We recognize certain natural inherent rights in man as an individual which we believe no government, municipal, state, or national, may abridge or infringe. Who is going to see to it? This is the other job we expect the Court to do.

In the bright fragrance of our revolutionary dawn, Jefferson, with editorial advice from Franklin and Adams, wrote the Declaration of Independence. In it he said, 'All men are created equal and endowed by their Creator with certain inalienable rights, among which are *life, liberty, and the pursuit of happiness.*' 'Among which' leaves room for four more. But let that pass. The point is, Jefferson had no doubt that his rights were absolutes. In his *Notes on Virginia* he wrote, 'Can the liberties of a nation be thought secure when we have removed their only firm basis, a conviction in the minds of the people that these liberties are the gift of God?'

That was in 1776, in the flush of revolt. By 1791 it was daylight and when Congress wrote into the Constitution the Bill of Rights, Jefferson's phrase had become the right of every person not to be deprived of 'life, liberty, and *property,*' and, they added, 'without due process of law.' Yet over these words, 'life, liberty, and property without due process of law,' in spite of the revision and notwithstanding the qualification, there still shone, and there still shines now, the flush of the revolutionary zeal that speaks only in absolutes.

Perhaps no one understands what absolutes are who does not believe in them. *Man lernt nichts kennen als was man liebt.* The best Holmes could make of them was to say, 'It is not enough for the knight of romance that you agree that his lady is a very nice girl — if you do not admit that she is the best that God ever made or will make, you must fight. There is in all men a demand for the superlative, so much so that the poor devil who has no other way of reaching it attains it by getting drunk. It seems to me that this demand is at the bottom of the philosopher's effort to prove that truth is absolute and of the jurist's search for criteria of universal validity which he collects under the head of natural law.' [50]

There seem to be two sorts of us, the all-or-noners and the more-or-lessers. The all-or-noners are perfectionists. If they can't get everything just right, they're not having any. And if they do get it right, or think they have, they may be a little arrogant about it. Naturally, therefore, they prefer a world where perfection is possible, and that is a world of ideals. They seek ideological security, as others do economic security. In the world of the more-or-lesser, things are never like that.

He admires an absolute and ultimate right, but always as one admires something that does not belong to him. The fact is, he tries to understand it and he can't. Probably he turns in his mind to something very much like what William James said. 'Take any demand, however slight, which any creature, however weak, may make. Ought it not, for its own sole sake, to be satisfied? If not, prove why not. The only possible kind of proof you could adduce would be the exhibition of another creature who should make a demand that ran the other way. The only possible reason there can be why any phenomenon ought to exist is that such a phenomenon actually is desired. Any desire is imperative to the extent of its amount; it makes itself valid by the fact that it exists at all. Some desires, truly enough, are small desires; they are put forward by insignificant persons, and we customarily make light of the obligations which they bring. But the fact that such personal demands as these impose small obligations does not keep the largest obligations from being personal demands.' [51]

Who drives fat oxen must themselves be fat. It is the truth of that proposition that concerns us. Don't we feel that somehow the Justices must be like the oxen they drive, that somehow they must believe what we look to them to expound? Dealing with ultimates and absolutes, as they do, we impute something ultimate and absolute to their opinion. This was Holmes's fear for judges. He wanted them to learn that they are not God. There are some few, I know one, so do you, who seem to be able to do without abstractions and reach and touch facts directly. The rest of us have to use them, either for our own satisfaction or for the satisfaction and persuasion of others. If it is for our own, we fall into faith in them. If we use them on others, our own lack of faith enhances our belief in the credulity of others. Either way they are dangerous, either as playthings or as weapons.

This is a country that has most emphatically rejected the divine origin of government. For us the power of government wells up from the people. It does not descend from heaven. We have no king, no peerage. To tell the truth, this leaves a void, which we seek somehow to fill, disguising what we are doing under new and different names. Honorary degrees take the place of titles. A photogenic face or a voice that can be electrically modulated takes the place of Norman blood and noble faith. The distinction of being a lawyer, though only honorary, is quite as great as wearing the Garter or sporting a Golden Fleece. We believe the chance that good looks are associated with talent quite as great as that it should be inherited. One is as irrational as the other.

Likewise the Court's power seems to be more than can rationally be ascribed to its competence in its work. There seems to be some undisclosed factor in the equation, and its presence is indicated by excessive admiration.

The most influential treatise on political science in the decades just after the Civil War, when, and not really until then, the doctrine of judicial supremacy was taking hold, turning from theory into practice, was by Theodore Dwight Woolsey, ex-president of Yale and then professor of political science. He not only reflected the prevalent attitude from which the practical application of the doctrine sprang. We must credit him with being something of an influence, too. 'Judges,' he taught, 'are in no sense representatives of the people or the king, or of any will whatever, except so far as they take a place which the people or the king filled before. In a higher sense, they are not representatives of the community nor of its chief magistrates, but of justice and of God.' They must have, Woolsey taught, the spirit of the old prophet, who, when a king's messenger was sent to ask him to speak well of the king, replied, 'As the Lord liveth, what the Lord saith unto me, that will I speak.' And Woolsey meant just that, for he went on to say, 'They are in fact more immediately servants of God than any other men who manage the affairs of a country.' [52]

Some day, not now, you will run across, perhaps read, more in the same strain. This is enough for now. In 1898, about the time Senator Root was pleading with the Senate, at the very height of the Court's heyday, Mr. Justice Brewer made an address. He said, 'It is a mistake to sup-

pose that the Supreme Court is either honored or helped
by being spoken of as beyond criticism. On the contrary,
the life and character of its justices should be the objects
of constant watchfulness by all, and its judgments subject
to the freest criticism. The time is past in the history of
the world when any living man or body of men can be set
on a pedestal and decorated with a halo. True, many citizens may be, like their authors, devoid of good taste, but
better all sorts of criticism than no criticism at all.' [53] Time
and again the most candid criticism has come in the dissenting opinions of its own Justices. When what they say is
repeated, as Thurman Arnold pointed out at the time of
Roosevelt's Court plan, they are denounced as untrue and
mischievous, but only in the mouths of those who have the
bad taste to repeat the language of these dissenting opinions in public.[54] Once more, 'Tis mad idolatry to make
the service greater than the god.

This idolatry is reflected in the way people are puzzled,
and even more in the way we are vexed, at split decisions,
six to three, four to five. We expect unanimity. The
Court's authority is hurt, we say, when the justices differ
among themselves. We take for granted that the validity
of a law can be derived by reason from premises that are
given and certain. Usually it is the dissenters we are
vexed with, unless we have an opinion of our own. For
we have also an irrational belief that a majority must
somehow be in the right in matters that depend on logic
and reasoning as well as in other things. What we are
doing is concealing a fear that the vision of the major
premise is denied to those we disagree with.

You can see how the Court has encouraged us into this
attitude by constantly telling us how it never holds a

statute unconstitutional unless it was so far so, so much so, as to be beyond any rational doubt. Go back and re-read what Sutherland said in the Adkins case. Beyond rational doubt. If you don't agree, you are irrational. You are no more than a fool.

We are even more puzzled when the Court reverses an earlier decision. We are vexed when it was an old decision to which we have become accustomed and to which we have adapted ourselves and our business. It was this puzzlement that Senator Root was so anxious to avoid. Not, that he was naïve enough to lose respect himself for the Court if it reversed the Pollock case. He was thinking of the effect on our opinion of the Court, for on that he knew the power of the Court rested. Perhaps he was underestimating our perspicacity, but his anxiety shows how much he relied on our idolatry.

There is a good deal to be said about the doctrine of *stare decisis* in constitutional law, the doctrine that a court should stand by its former decisions. In ordinary law, *stare decisis* is one thing. You and I, and especially our lawyers, have a right to know, think we know, what the law is and what the court is going to say in our case. But in constitutional law, which isn't law at all, we have no right to any such expectation. There the doctrine is either something quite different or entirely out of place. There you can defend the doctrine only if you assert that the Constitution meant, means, and will mean the same thing today, yesterday, and forever. And in the Bill of Rights you have to assert that they are absolute, unchanged, unchanging, and unchangeable. You cannot do it.

Lawyers, and others who insist on the sanctity of the Court's decisions, are always insisting, as Root did in

1909, and as so many did in 1937, that the only proper way for the Court's decisions to be changed is by an amendment to the Constitution. That is, of course, the logical consequence of the application of *stare decisis* to constitutional law. They justify it popularly and on the merits by saying that the Court is a brake on democratic temerity, a curb on mass recklessness and passion. Let us not argue with them. The demand for an amendment instead of simply giving the Court a chance to reverse itself is but another tribute to the irrationality, the idolatry of our attitude toward the Court. For what would we do? We would sooner change the Constitution than let the Court change its mind. The Constitution becomes something less holy and less sanctified than the Court's mind. God does not change His mind. No, but this, too, may be said, He cannot have been wrong. It is also true that He can afford to confess His mistakes, even make them.

At times, I think, you will detect a curious feeling, half conscious, never explicit, that the government cannot abridge these rights, not that it ought not, but cannot. In other words that there is something compulsive as well as obligatory about the Bill of Rights, so far as the Court is concerned. You need not go mystic to detect it. It is the remnant of what once dominated men's minds almost to the exclusion of everything else. When the Court holds a statute unconstitutional, it is laying a taboo on the state. Let me quote from Frazer's *The Golden Bough*.[55]

Frazer is speaking of kings and royal taboos. 'A king of this sort lives hedged in by a ceremonious etiquette, a network of prohibitions and observances, of which the intention is not to contribute to his dignity, much less to his comfort, but to restrain him from conduct which, by disturbing the harmony of nature, might involve himself, his people, and the universe in one common catastrophe. Far from adding to his comfort, these observances, by trammelling his every act, annihilate his freedom and often render the very life, which it is their object to preserve, a burden and a sorrow to him. Of the supernaturally endowed kings of Loango it is said that the more powerful a king is, the more taboos he is bound to observe. In the crater of an extinct volcano, enclosed on all sides by grassy slopes, lie the scattered huts and yam fields of Riabba, the capitol of the native king of Fernando Po. This mysterious being lives in the lowest depths of the crater, surrounded by a harem of forty women, and covered, it is said, with old silver coins. He exercises far more influence on the island than the Spanish governor at Santa Isobel. In him the conservative spirit of the Boobies or aboriginal inhabitants of the island is, as it were, incorporate. He has never seen a white man and, according to the firm conviction of all the Boobies, the sight of a pale face would cause his instant death.'

I do not say, you would not have me say, that this is at all a fair picture of the Court. No, take it as an allegory of what these people would make of it. Their attitude springs from deep inherited sources and it is nothing we can ever hope to understand. All we can do is recognize its existence. And we must recognize, too, that it is a source of great power for the Court.

7

A COURT OF LAW AND ITS ADVANTAGES

THE MOST IMPORTANT HISTORICAL FACT about the Court is that it started its career as a law court for the decision and disposition of law cases. That was what it was set up to do by the Constitution, and that is what it did do. Here history is of the first importance. The Constitution expected its Supreme Court to be a law court, and the debates on the Convention show that if the Court was going to nullify legislation it would be expected to do it strictly in line of its judicial duties. What was first proposed, in the Virginia Plan, was a Council of Revision which was to have the veto power instead of the President. This was opposed on the ground that it would give the Justices a double chance to veto an act of Congress, once on grounds of policy in the Council, and again on the grounds of unconstitutionality when the act came before them in a law suit. Gerry added that it was quite foreign to the nature of the office to make them judges of the policy of public measures. Whatever the reason, the Convention rejected the proposed Council and gave the veto power to the President alone.

So the Court started as an ordinary law court and it continued to be an ordinary law court for a long time.

The Justices sat on the bench, they heard the arguments of counsel, they gave written opinions, just like any court in the ancient tradition of the Common Law. The procedure was, and, of course, still is, the same, writs, declarations, bills in equity, pleadings, judgments, and decrees. Aside from the few cases in which the Constitution gave them original jurisdiction, their appellate jurisdiction was fixed by Congress in the First Judiciary Act of 1789, but it was broadly fixed and there was more to it than cases arising under the Constitution and the laws of the United States. There were 'controversies between citizens of different States,' as the Third Article of the Constitution permitted, and they covered every kind of question of law.[56]

In the early days about 60 per cent of its business was made up of ordinary law suits between individuals which depended on the ordinary principles of law, either the common law or the special rules that obtain in the three chief fields that have been taken away from the state courts and given to the federal courts, admiralty, bankruptcy, and patents. Anyhow, almost two-thirds of its business was ordinary law suits between individual litigants. And this continued until after the Civil War. In 1875, the proportion was a little less, but not much, 56 per cent. But fifty years later, in 1925, we find a great change. It was only about 15 per cent. Now, in 1945, it would be pretty safe to say that this kind of business had almost entirely gone. Thumb your way through one of the recent volumes of the Court's reports, and you will find what Frankfurter and Landis, whose figures I have used, call 'a different world of ideas.' You find the Court passing on the meaning or the validity of legislation, on the use and abuse of the powers of this or that board or commission, on the

right of a state to tax or regulate this or that corporation
or union, on the constitutional propriety of this and the
other court's handling of some criminal prosecution, on
tax matters, on suits against the government. This is a
great shift into matters of public concern and public interest. Disappointed litigants often say they will carry their
appeal right up to the Supreme Court of the United States,
if necessary. They do not get there. For the Court has
all but ceased to handle ordinary private litigation.

And yet the Court has never ceased to conduct its business under the guise and with all the tools and procedures
of an ordinary law court. We think of it as a law court.
In its tradition and procedure it is a law court. Only its
business has changed to far transcend ordinary litigation.
It would not be true — but a good half truth won't do us
any harm — to go back and wonder if the Council of Revision, thrown out of the window by the Convention, has
not come back down the chimney, and without the President being a member, only the Justices. That is not quite
true, but sometimes some of the Justices have acted as if
it were true. If the Council of Revision had been included
in the Constitution, would it have survived? Democracy
elbowed aside the equally undemocratic Electoral College.
A Council on which the judges sat and openly and candidly passed on the wisdom of legislation, would that have
stood?

Anyhow, it was as a court of law that the Court undertook after the Civil War to exercise its great power over
legislation. Not, of course, only because it sat on a bench
and wore robes. It had also all the many and great advantages that a court of law possesses in dealing with
political and economic questions; and at the same time its
disadvantages. The Justices are quite well aware of both.

The Tradition of the Law

In a very real sense the Court is older than the Constitution, much older. The tradition of the law goes back into history almost far enough to satisfy lawyers. That tradition belongs to the Court. McIlwain wrote an essay on the Fundamental Law Behind the Constitution. He said, 'For the growth of constitutionalism specifically, the tracing of modern tendencies can hardly begin much later than the second or third centuries B.C.' [57] We will let nineteen centuries slip by unnoticed and begin, as late as we dare, with one particular episode.

On Sunday, November 10, 1612, which was the fifth year of the reign of James I — that is the way the lawyers used to keep the calendar — James called Chief Justice Coke and the other judges before him. There had been differences between them over James's authority to try cases himself. The converse, you will note, of the Court taking part in legislating. This was not long after the settlement of Virginia, not long before the Pilgrims landed on Cape Cod. What was said is reported in Coke's *Reports*, volume 12, on pages 64 and 65. While you read his brief account, remember that Coke's words have reverberated down between courtroom walls from that day to this. The last four are engraved in stone over the Harvard Law School. That is of interest, because Bracton, from whom Coke quotes these four words, was the author of a textbook on law which he wrote as long before Coke as Coke is before us. Coke made it as living in his time as we have kept Coke alive into ours. We are dealing with a very ancient notion.

Here is what Coke said he said to James. 'A controversy of land between parties was heard by the King, and sentence given, which was repealed for this, that it did belong to the common law: then the King said, that he thought the law was founded upon reason, and that he and others had reason, as well as the Judges: to which it was answered by me, that true it was, that God had endowed His Majesty with excellent science, and great endowments of nature; but His Majesty was not learned in the laws of his realm of England, and causes which concern the life, or inheritance, or goods, or fortunes of his subjects, are not to be decided by natural reason but by the artificial reason and judgment of law, which law is an act which requires long study and experience, before that a man can attain to the cognizance of it: and that the law was the golden met-wand and measure to try the causes of the subjects; and which protected His Majesty in safety and peace: with which the King was greatly offended, and said, that then he should be under the law, which was treason to affirm, as he said; to which I said, that Bracton saith, *quod Rex non debet esse sub homine, sed sub Deo et lege.*'

That is a brave statement and there are accounts other than Coke's own, in which he did not behave as bravely as he spoke. One is to the effect that James lost his temper, offered to strike the Chief Justice, who promptly fell on all fours before his king.[58]   But what actually happened has had no effect whatever on legal or political thought, and what Coke said has had enormous consequences.

A Law, higher than all of us, higher even than the Constitution. The Justices are its exponents and this accounts for that faint air of superiority toward the Constitution which they sometimes reveal in their opinions. That, however, is not the immediate point. You may embrace the notion of this higher law or you may reject it. You cannot deny that it does for the law much what ancient tradition does for the Court. As the law derives a semblance of eternal stability from this idea that the law is over all government, so tradition lends a feeling of ancient stability to the Court. As the laws we enact are felt to be only a part of Law itself, so the Court feels that it belongs in a judicial lineage that is far older than the Constitution which it is interpreting and expounding. The Court, in fact, was already sitting and had been sitting for centuries before the Constitution was entrusted to its keeping, and Marshall's announcement of the doctrine of judicial review was, in one sense, the most natural thing in the world. The legal tradition gives the Court that subtle pride which springs from the humility of knowing you are only a part of something vaster than yourself. What's more, it is not only vast. It is exclusive. For though this legal tradition is a large heritage, it is not shared by all of us, only by lawyers and judges. 'We few, we happy few, we band of brothers,' to apply Henry the Fifth's proud exclamation to the last thing he had in mind.

Practically, what does this tradition do for the Court? For one thing, it is a mighty barrier against personal preferences and predilections. Not only selfish preferences, but special causes. Not only personal ambitions, but what has sometimes even more vicious consequences on the exercise of wisdom, altruistic devotion to some smaller cause. A Negrophile is as unjudicial as an anti-Semitic. And the tradition likewise keeps the Court reasonably non-representative, of class as well as of locality. With exceptions, the Justices have become, if they were not already, much less representative than we generally suppose. He's a tool of the banks, just as it used to be a slave-holding Southerner, or he's labor-minded. We owe much to the competition of the loyalty to the judicial tradition. It is a relief to be released by a better duty from the burden of reflecting vicariously the views, interests, hopes, fears, and hysterias of people whose qualification to possess them is measured by their ability to express them. Of course the Court follows the election returns, but it is the national elections. Why not? They are a national court. They are appointed for life. This is a democratic government. It is theirs as well as ours. Their decisions may be fashioned for permanence, but they are made at the present moment. It is hard to overestimate the value of the judicial tradition in this respect. It is more than worth the expense of much sentimental, even tawdry talk, delusion and idolatry. It is well to be candid, but candor can be very destructive.

The Pressure of Decisions and Written Opinions

The judicial tradition makes two quite direct and specific demands upon a court, both so usual that we take them for granted and miss perhaps their efficacy. One is that the case be decided one way or another and as soon as possible. The other is that the judges give written opinions, reasoned statements of what the case is, what they decide and why. Other government officials may have to act, and sometimes quickly under the pressure of events. A court is always under the pressure of the tradition, and no other government official is required always to give his reasons. He may or he may not, as he deems best and when it is expected of him, but it is always expected of the

Court. A strange inconsistency bids some people deplore criticism of the one governmental body that is required always to offer itself for criticism. The Justices know better, as Justice Brewer said.

But the requirement of an immediate decision, not contingent on events, is the more important and the more valuable. Not that justice delayed, as the saying is, is justice denied. That is so in private litigation, but in public matters, as in every decision, the advantage of an immediate decision is not so much the disadvantage of delay as the peculiar virtue of being right up against the problem. Psychologically there is a chasm between a question you some day will have to answer and a problem that now confronts you. While it is remote, you had better prepare for it. That is all to the good. But do not try to anticipate your answer. Wait until it is an actuality. Wait until you are charged with the electrical emanations of its immediate presence. When it becomes concrete and actual, then you will discern all the variables that you ignored because it had been safe to ignore them, while your decision was only an abstract possibility, and ascertain many of those for which you had to assume only an approximate value. The pressure of events brings political problems near enough to other departments of the government, meanwhile keeping those that do not call for decision remote enough not to interfere. For the Court it is the traditional duty of deciding the instant case that serves this purpose. Not until a problem is immediate and unavoidable is a man at his best to solve it. This is the reality-principle of Freud taking the place of the pleasure-principle. The anticipated decision of a problem, when it is not preparation in general, has a kinship with fantasy-making and day-dreaming. It is conducted by what Freud calls the pleasure-ego. As the problem comes closer, the reality-ego takes over. The best individual does best under pressure and in a pinch.

If we compare the very unjudicial advisory opinion, which the Court wisely and true to the judicial tradition rejected, we shall see the difference. Frankfurter referred to the dignity of a law court, but he also truly and wisely said that the whole milieu of advisory opinions on proposed bills is inevitably different from that of the litigated case over contested legislation. However much provision may be made on paper for adequate arguments, advisory opinions are bound to move in an unreal atmosphere. The impact of actuality and the intensity of immediacy are wanting, he said.[59] And if the Court calls for argument the same is true of the bar. Instead of the instant case, counsel must suppose instances. They have no client who has in fact felt the actual bite of the law. They are debating, not arguing.

These two demands of the judicial tradition work happily together. The Court is faced with a problem it knows it must now decide, and in its deliberations it knows, too, that it is going to have to give its reasons. A body of men that must explain itself to a public that is going to criticize. The function of the bar on these public questions is sometimes not fully understood. The bar not only aids the Court by arguing the issue before it. The bar is a special set of experts retained by the public at large to read the Court's opinions and expound them to the people. The people not only have a right to criticize the Court. They have professionals to help them do it. It is a double pity when the bar is so eager to defend the Court's prestige that it goes back on its public clients.

The Fewness of the Justices and their Procedure

But the great advantage the Court has over Congress but not over the President, is the fewness of the Justices. They are few enough to make it possible for them to work together. The judicial tradition has tended to keep their numbers down, but the credit must equally well be given to Congress which has, as we know, complete authority to fix the number. The vice in President Roosevelt's Court Plan was the risk that the older Justices would not resign and so bring the number up to fifteen. That is too many. The Court is now nine. It is a pity that they have been doing their several bests to make that as many as possible.

Every body of men devoted to a purpose has an optimum number, which depends less on what they are up to than how they are trying to do it. We must, therefore, go into the Court's procedure. Perhaps it will bring into relief several things we have already discussed and others that we have yet to mention.

Take the physical architecture of the Court House first, because it is the least important, particularly for that Court. They could sit in the back of a barroom with equal dignity. So we need not linger over where they now sit. Imagine what you think the Parthenon could never have looked like. That is the exterior. Inside there are more great columns and heavy red curtains. At the further end of the chamber there is the bench, and on it nine high-backed and plainly comfortable chairs. In front of them is a small lectern, such as a sermon requires. But you can not preach to people four feet above you. In these comfortable chairs sit nine informal, not to say chatty, individuals. To them the attorney who is arguing the case addresses his argument. Behind him sit the public, visitors to Washington, connoisseurs, lawyers, cranks, and more visitors. They sit in silence. The Justices do not. They whisper to each other, they ask questions of the arguing attorney, they pass notes, which are borne by small boys who lurk in the folds of those red curtains behind the Justices.

I may have given you an impression of a certain lack of dignity. Then I am very wrong. The Justices have had submitted to them elaborately printed records of what has occurred in the case and long printed briefs of the argument of counsel. They are more than aware of what goes on and the attorney is equally aware of that very pertinent fact. His respect for the Court permeates the courtroom, and when he is asked a question he replies with deliberation. He had better. All in all it confirms the ancient observation, the higher the tribunal, the less formality, and the less necessary to its dignity. The columns and the red curtains are singularly out of place, and when you leave, do not look back at the façade of the building.

In the old days the arguments were interminable. The Court had fewer cases and more time. Webster went on for days, not hours. The Court had time for a contemplative life. In 1849 the Justices set a two-hour time limit. It is now an hour per lawyer, in all ordinary cases. Arguments start at noon on weekdays except Monday and Saturday. Why noon? That is an ancient tradition, too, from Marshall's time. They enjoyed each other's company the night before in those spacious days more than we do.

On Saturdays, the Court confers. Deliberates. From

noon to four-thirty. The Chief Justice states each case and the Justices 'recite' — that was Holmes's word — and then they vote, juniors first, an ancient tradition in all courts. That evening the Chief Justice, who has heard them recite, sends round to each Justice the case in which he is to write the opinion. If there are dissents, the senior dissenting Justice takes charge of them.

The opinion, written by the Justice assigned, is printed and circulated. There are in the Harvard Law School bound volumes of Holmes's opinions in proof, with the comments in the margin by the other Justices. You will not be allowed to see them because they are the comments of individual Justices before they had a chance to pool their minds. They are contributing to a joint product which is not yet complete. The comments and suggestions are then discussed, and the opinion of the Court, that is, the conclusion of the majority of the nine, is then put into final form.

On Mondays the opinions are announced. Each Justice reads the opinion given him, then come the dissents. To say he reads is too precise. Citations of precedents are skipped or slurred over. Sometimes there is some ad libbing. McReynolds had a way of saying more than he wrote and industrious persons would take it down and you may find it in *Time* and elsewhere. Some Justices lend feeling to what often needs it. Each has his own way. Roberts startled people by reciting his opinions verbatim without even a glance at the print. Black is eloquent. The spectators try to hear more in an opinion than can be read out of it.

But such effort is somewhat futile. The Court's opinions are written to be read, and they are read, and they are

read carefully, painstakingly. Juniors in law offices read
them and abstract them. Seniors read and discuss them.
They are read on trains and in bed at night. Newspapers
take the more spectacular and make hideous abridgments.
Law professors select what they think are more significant
and write articles on them, then they reprint them in case
books for their students. The common fold finally get the
gist of them, which is all too much like condensed novels
and abbreviated books. All in all, first, second, third, and
further hand, the opinions of the Court do get round.

The Court's procedure is an exploitation of the fewness
of its members to the end of joint co-operative action. A
pooling of minds is what Lawrence Lowell called it, here a
pooling of powerful and diverse minds, which have not
brought themselves together. The Justices do not fill
their own vacancies with minds of their own choosing.
Each one of them has been separately selected for separate
reasons. In an ideal world, nevertheless, these diverse
minds would melt into a clear surface of decision. They
do not. It is the most difficult and delicate of all the processes of co-operation. Man at his rare best can do it. If
you have never done it, shared in it, or even seen it done,
you have missed a spectacular satisfaction. We find fault
with the Justices when they do not succeed. That is either
our high expectations, the best of compliments, or it shows
an utter and rather deplorable failure to understand how
hard it is for powerful minds to do, or we do not know
what we are talking about. This is not a matter of light-
minded agreement on the dead level of the least common
denominator. Nor at its best of compromise, a splitting of
differences. The judicial tradition sets its face against
that. It is a give and take of persuasion, toward a com-

mon end and under a common major premise. And all this goes on through a procedure which is alternately public and secret: public argument — secret deliberation — public reasons.

Dissents, Occasional, and Persistent

Yet the single opinion for the Court, ideally unanimous, is not in the ancient tradition. It never obtained in the higher courts in England. There each judge speaks his own opinion. Of course, one turned out to be the chief opinion, and often judges would simply add their complete concurrence with what so-and-so had said. That was the way our own Court started under Chief Justice Jay. But only for a dozen or so years. Marshall took over in 1803 and for a time delivered all the opinions himself. All of them. Even on occasion a dissenting opinion.

Marshall was a strong judge and he left his mark on almost everything he touched. His strength was devoted to the Court, not to himself, and this is the basis for his strong feeling for unanimity. So much so that he would sink his own personal view in order to get unanimity. The opinion in *Little* v. *Bareme* has been pointed out as an example of this. 'I confess' — Marshall is delivering the opinion — 'the first bias of my mind was very strong. But I have been convinced that I was mistaken, and I have receded from this first opinion. I acquiesce in that of my brethren.'[60] Acquiesce, that is the word; precisely.

Convinced, and yet he but acquiesces. Unanimity sometimes is little more than conventionality, but in political life it is power. When a committee's deliberations end in a decision, there is a plea for serried ranks and a united front. Dissent becomes dissension, vexatious and unmannerly, disturbing. The dissenter is regarded as a deserter. The man who deplores dissenting opinions, unless his emotions are involved in them, is usually thinking solely of the Court's prestige. Engaged in making a court of law into a department of government, Marshall of all things most needed power. He required of his court the same unanimity which the British Cabinet requires of itself, and which you can see pursued by any commission which the United Kingdom sends on a foreign mission. They reach their decision by the time-honored method of internal dissension, but it is a purely domestic operation. They deliberate severally, they act jointly. Our cabinet ministers are personal administrators and advisors, who find unity only in the personal command of the President. Their several executive duties go their own ways for their own reasons. Their loyalties run only to him, not to each other. His term of office is fixed, theirs depend on his pleasure. None depends on Congress. Now that the Court is established in power and the doctrine of judicial supremacy is secure, the Court is dependent on no one, and the Justices' loyalties run less to the Court than to their several selves. Unanimity is not worth its cost in conscience and personal pride.

If Marshall is the father of unanimity, William Johnson, the youngest man ever to be appointed to the Court, is the father of our present practice. He was appointed by Jefferson at the age of thirty-two, not so young then as it is now, in 1805. For four years Marshall had been in command. Johnson found him delivering all the opinions, even some in which he did not agree. They were the opinions of the Court and he was its Chief. Johnson had been appointed from the state bench in South Carolina, where the usual English practice prevailed of each judge delivering his own opinion. Jefferson favored that practice and Johnson wrote him expressing his surprise at finding Marshall giving all the opinions and saying that he had remonstrated in vain. 'The Answer was he is willing to take the trouble, and it is a Mark of Respect to him. I soon however found out the real Cause. Cushing was incompetent. Chase could not be got to think or write. Paterson was a slow man and willingly declined the Trouble, and the other two are commonly estimated as one Judge.' These other two were Marshall and Bushrod Washington.

Johnson went on to say that he delivered his own opinion as 'a thing of Course,' and during the rest of the session 'heard nothing but Lectures on the indecency of Judges cutting at each other, and the Loss of Reputation which the Virginia Appellate Court had sustained by pursuing such a Course. I therefore bent to the Current, and persevered until I got them to adopt the Course they now pursue, which is to appoint some one to deliver the Opinion of the Majority, but to leave it to the rest of the Judges to record their Opinions or not ad Libitum.' [61]

Johnson's compromise between the two extremes has become the general practice in all courts of appeal in this country. It is more than a compromise. It is a third way. The object of a dissent is not merely, as Johnson described one of his own, 'to avoid having an ambiguous decision hereafter imputed to me, or an opinion which I would not wish to be understood to have given.' [62] Dissents serve a larger purpose than either to cover scruples of conscience or to save your judicial reputation as a good lawyer. Dissents are competing opinions in their own right. They are what the dissenter would have said if he had persuaded enough of his colleagues to agree with him. We have had, we still have, we should always have powerful dissents, four to five, three to six. They are two pools of mind. There has been a fission and now there are two cells, almost two Supreme Courts of the United States, or, if one, schizophrenic. The majority exercise all the powers of the Court, but the minority have a curious concurrent jurisdiction over the future. For a dissent is a formal appeal for a rehearing by the Court sometime in the future, if not on the next occasion.

This has proved so even if the dissenting Justices do not intend it to be so. Among the great dissents were those of Taft, Sanford, and Holmes in the Adkins case,[63] where a minimum wage was held unconstitutional. A few years later, in 1925, the same question came up and the same majority again held a minimum wage void. And all three dissenters acquiesced. 'Mr. Justice Holmes,' the report says, 'requests that it be stated that his concurrence is solely upon the ground that he regards himself bound by the decision in the *Adkins* v. *Children's Hospital*.'[64] Yet it was their dissent which persisted, not their acquiescence, and was the base on which the Adkins case was later overruled. Hughes in the opinion overruling it expressly cites and quotes from Taft. His 'challenge persists and is without any satisfactory answer.'[65] As views and major premises shift in that periodicity which general opinions seem to possess in common with most of nature, dissents have a way of becoming the most persuasive of precedents. Perhaps some majority opinions will again come into their own in the same cyclic fashion.

There are some who feel uneasy, and some who even

resent the present Court's practice of many, almost an individuality of opinions. They long for a single authoritative opinion, and they regard any dissent as smelling of heresy or disloyalty. They must not let their feelings run too far ahead of them. By pressing toward the perfection of unanimity they are undermining the very basis of the judicial process. Just as those others are doing, who from the other side strike toward the same center with proposals that more than a majority of the Court be required to hold a statute unconstitutional on the theory that if four of the Justices believe a statute within rational doubt five others cannot logically hold it irrational. For if you require unanimity, you make compromise inevitable, in the Court as everywhere else. Compromise is as alien to the feelings of the judicial process as what Solomon offered to do with the baby was to the feelings of the mother. At the same time, it is typical and essential in the political process. Byrnes, who was one of the Justices and who is now Secretary of State can speak with authority here. In his report on the session of the Council of Foreign Ministers which was held in London in the fall of 1945, he said, 'The first session of the Council of Foreign Ministers closed in a stalemate. But that need not, and should not, deprive us of a second and better chance to get on with the peace. In the past I have been both criticized and commended for being a compromiser. I confess that I do believe that peace and political progress in international affairs as in domestic affairs depend upon intelligent compromise. The United States delegation acted in that spirit at Berlin. We acted in that spirit at London. And we shall continue to act in that spirit at future conferences. That spirit is essential in international conferences where action can be taken only by unanimous agreement. When any one member can prevent agreement, compromise is a necessity. Men and women who have served on a jury can appreciate that.'

The persistent dissent, which amounts to schism, is something quite different. Two popes cannot both be right, and it is not good for the prestige of either, or for the power of the Court, which rests on prestige. Like the old adage, the silly ass thought two could pass where one had gone before. But this is true only when there is something qualitative about their difference between the majority and the minority. If they are only on different sides of the line that has to be drawn in any quantitative affair, no great harm is done. It is just a close case. It only shows that the line runs between them and not on either side of both of them. And yet how near they are is beside the point. They may be near enough to grasp hands and yet if they come from different directions, they are facing each other and not marching side by side.

Here we have something really qualitative, an instance where the qualitative is not swallowed up in the quantitative. There are mixtures, colloids, in chemistry, which are composed of the same elements in the same proportions and yet which are quite different. The chemists call them isomeric. They are different, with different properties, only because they have not been put together in the same way. The order in which you follow a recipe from a cookbook is as important as the amounts you stir together. So judges may reach what seems to be the same conclusion, or differ by what seems to be the merest trifle, and yet be worlds apart, because what seems to be the same opinion or all but, has been put together differently. A converted sinner or an enlightened conservative is not the same as a retrograde saint or a retarded progressive, though they may even stand and speak from the same platform. Men can be isomerous, and so also can their opinions.

8

THE LEGAL TRADITION AND *STARE DECISIS*

W E ARE SECURED to the past by a cable of many
strands, by habit, by nostalgia, by what the
psychoanalysts call regression, by a sense of
comfort and security. It may even at times be wise to do
again what wisdom dictated before, or again just what
seemed just before, for men may conform their behavior to
what they expect to be done again. 'The prophecies of
what the courts will do in fact, and nothing more preten-
tious, is what I mean by the law,' said Holmes.[66] The
Legal Tradition, by the doctrine of *Stare Decisis*, is insistent that 'our friend the bad man,' of whom Holmes is
speaking, should have as secure a basis as possible for his
prophecies.

But we are talking about judges, not about criminals.
The strongest strand that ties a judge to previous decisions
is the desire to avoid the intolerable burden of personal
responsibility. He no more wants to be free than we want
him to be. This is not peculiar to the lawyer. Lloyd
Garrison, who has had abundant experience with administrative tribunals on which laymen as well as lawyers sit,
says, 'I have received the distinct impression that laymen

in a judicial position are quite as eager as lawyers in pursuing, and quite as contentious in dissecting the available
precedents; and that precedents are thus magnified not
because of any notion of the social desirability of certainty,
but because they are a godsend to men harassed by the
necessity of making up their minds in close cases and of
justifying their decision when made.' [67]

So a court of law declares only what the law is. Not a
court in Anglo-Saxon Christendom but says that this is all
that it does and denies that it makes law. I do not mean
only by that slow process that Holmes somewhere com-
pares to the growth of a coral isle, bit by bit, by the accre-
tion of each case that is by just a little bit different from
any of the myriad of cases that preceded it. No court can
help making law as well as declaring it in that way so long
as it goes on deciding cases, until every case gets to be the
same as every other case. But judges do legislate whenever they deviate from the logically inevitable pattern of
the precedents. Obviously so when a precedent is overruled. That is a fresh start on the old process and it is the
making of new law. Except in the literal sense that legislation is only what is enacted by a legislature, courts make
law.

But they are supposed not to and so naturally they deny
that they do. The judges put it this way. They say that
all they do is declare what the legislators meant, or in the
interpretation of the Constitution, as we have seen, what
the Convention meant, or what Congress meant in the case
of an amendment. It follows that whatever meaning they
ascribe to the Constitution must have been its meaning
from the beginning. If a statute is unconstitutional, it
must always have been unconstitutional. Void, as they

say, *ab initio*. The classic statement is Field's, 'An unconstitutional act is not a law; it confers no rights; it imposes no duties; it affords no protection; it creates no office; it is, in legal contemplation, as inoperative as though it had never been passed.' [68]

This shining simplicity is the theory, and as theory it is hard to impeach it, so hard that sometimes courts even act on it, but it won't work of course, and the present Court knows it. This is an actual, not merely a theoretical world we live in. Even the Legal Tradition, though its branches may move freely in the upper air, has its roots in fact.

When recently a lower court acted on the theory, in 1940, Hughes said, 'The courts below have proceeded on the theory that the Act of Congress, having been found to be unconstitutional was not a law; that it was inoperative, conferring no rights and imposing no duties. It is quite clear, however, that such broad statements as to the effect of a determination of unconstitutionality must be taken with qualifications. The actual existence of a statute, prior to such determination, is an operative fact and may have consequences which cannot justly be ignored. The past cannot always be erased by a new judicial declaration.' [69]

Can it ever? If ever, must it not be done by a fiction, not a mere theory? Fictions are useful if they are recognized for what they are. There is no objection to the Legal Tradition having this fiction up its capacious sleeve for use on occasion. It is a fiction. The medieval doctors used to say that there was one thing that even an omnipotent God could not do, undo what had been done.

You can do what you please with fictions. Why should

not judges date the unconstitutionality of a statute from any time it pleases? If they can make it retroactive, why cannot they make it prospective?

They can. Some few lawyers live so high up in the branches of the Tradition that they would doubt this, doubt even that it would be constitutional. At least one brought the question up on appeal. But the Court ruled that a state supreme court could do this, and what a state court can do, the Court can. In the Sunburst case,[70] Cardozo, in 1932, denied that the Constitution had anything to say upon the subject. 'A state may say that decisions of its highest court, though later overruled, are law none the less for intermediate transactions. On the other hand, it may hold to the ancient dogma that the law declared by its courts had a Platonic or ideal existence before the act of declaration, in which event the discredited declaration will be viewed as if it had never been, and the reconsidered declaration as law from the beginning.'[71]

Cardozo refers to the prior Platonic existence of the subsequent ruling of the court when it declares what the law is. In *Phaedo* Socrates' first argument for the immortality of the soul is that as our souls existed before birth, hence they must continue to exist hereafter. That is just what the Legal Tradition has tried to do with the Law. In many branches of the law there is no gainsaying that it is the very stuff and being of law. But here perhaps more clearly than anywhere else ordinary law and constitutional law fork.

The Court's opinion upon the construction of the Constitution, Taney said, is always open to discussion where it is supposed to be founded on error.[72] And Field, 'It is more imperative that the Court should be right on later and more elaborate considerations of the cases than consistent with previous declarations. Those doctrines only will eventually stand which bear the strictest examination and the test of experience.' [73] The Constitution speaks with the voice of experience. Hughes, as we shall have occasion to see, justified the reversal of a precedent by an intervening change in economic considerations.[74] Frankfurter, more poetically, refers to the erosion of time.[75]

The Court overrules its own prior decisions, or, if you prefer, the decisions of prior Courts, fairly often. It corrects errors. It sometimes recants. At other times it just does something quite different from what a prior Court very clearly would have done, but, out of courtesy to their predecessors, without saying so. Leaving these silent deviations out of account, the Court overruled about one precedent every three years from the Civil War down to 1932, twenty-one cases during those sixty-five years.[76] If we listen to the voice of experience, this was not enough to keep up with time. For the reconstructed New Court, in the eight years between 1936 and 1944, overruled sixteen cases, two a year, six times as many. Time's chariot had forged ahead of the old judicial bus.

9

FACT AND FANCY

LEGAL AND CONSTITUTIONAL DOCTRINES are played on a mental keyboard where the scales run down from high abstractions to the most particular pattern of concrete fact. Strike the key of abstract doctrine and you will get a high clear note. Touch on a matter of fact and you get a low reverberation. Or better, drop the simile of a piano and compare matter of fact with all sorts of noises, from screeches to rumbles, and contrast them with the clear modulations of the abstract. Or even compare abstractions to the frozen words that fell on the deck and Pantagruel picked up and gave to Panurge. They looked like sugarplums of many colors, red, green, blue, black, gold, and in his hand they melted into the sounds of battle.[77]

That is enough of the metaphorical. Bertrand Russell put it this way. The world of universals, he said, is unchangeable, rigid, exact, delightful to the mathematician, the logician, the builder of metaphysical systems, and all who love perfection more than life. The world of existence is floating, vague, without sharp boundaries, without any clear plan or arrangement, but it contains all thoughts and feelings, all the data of sense, and all physical objects, everything that can do either good or harm, everything that makes any difference to the value of life and the world. According to our temperaments, we shall prefer the contemplation of the one or of the other.[78]

William Morton Wheeler perceived the same difference in his students. He saw that he was dealing with a difference in mental type. On reviewing his students and the mature investigators he had known during the past half century, he found that most of them belonged to two extreme types, while the remainder were intermediate or ambiguous composites. These extremes corresponded, he thought, with the romanticist and classicist types respectively, which Ostwald distinguished among physicists and chemists, and also agreed very closely with the two general psychological types which Jung called extraverts and introverts. The more numerous romanticists or extraverts are the naturalists; the classicists or introverts are the biologists in the strict sense.

The naturalist is mentally oriented toward and controlled by objective, concrete reality, and probably because his senses, especially those of sight and touch, are highly developed, is powerfully affected by the esthetic appeal of natural objects. He is little interested in and may even be quite blind to abstract or theoretical considerations, and therefore inclined to say with Goethe:

> Grau, Freund, ist alle Theorie,
> Und grün des Lebens ewig goldener Baum.

He is primarily an observer and fond of outdoor life, a collector, a classifier, a describer, deeply impressed by the overwhelming intricacy of natural phenomena and revelling in their very complexity. He is, therefore, more or less irrational, intuitive, receptive, and passive in his attitude toward natural objects, synthesizing rather than analyzing, a poor mathematician, an amateur in the proper sense of the word. When philosophically inclined he is apt to be a tough-minded Aristotelian. In his output he is clearly of the romanticist type, publishing copiously and easily, but often without much sense of literary form or proportion.

The biologist, on the other hand, Wheeler goes on, is oriented toward and dominated by ideas, and rather terrified or oppressed by the intricate hurly-burly of concrete, sensuous reality and its multiform and multicolored individual manifestations. He often belongs to the motor rather than to the visual type and obtains his esthetic satisfaction from all kinds of analytical procedures and the cold desiccated beauty of logical and mathematical demonstration. His will to power takes the form of experimentation and the controlling of phenomena by capturing them in a net of abstract formulas and laws. He is a denizen of the laboratory. His besetting sin is oversimplification and the tendency to undue isolation of the organisms he studies from their natural environment. As a philosopher he is apt to be a tender-minded Platonist. In his output he is a true classicist. The total volume of his writing is apt to be small, but of high quality.[79]

Russell was describing two extreme forms of thought, Wheeler two equally extreme corresponding types of men. It is certain that in this world we live in we need both. For we stand in the center of our world, holding an abstract conception in one hand and a concrete fact in the other, trying to tie them together. But as soon as we get them secure, we find that for some reason or other we have

knotted the wrong strands or the knot is pulling out. So
we have to free the end of the notion and fasten it to the
loose end of another fact, or *vice versa*. And they are hard
to tie and hard to untie, for the demons of life are pulling
at the facts and twitching them out of our hands.

Let Whitehead, who is a philosopher, state the respective advantages and disadvantages of these two view-
points. What follows is taken from the first part of the
fourth chapter of his *Science and the Modern World*.

The advantage, Whitehead says, of confining attention
to a definite group of abstractions, is that you confine
your thoughts to clear-cut definite things, with clear-cut
definite relations. Accordingly, if you have a logical head,
you can deduce a variety of conclusions respecting the
relationships between these abstract entities. Further-
more, if the abstractions are well-founded, that is to say,
if they do not abstract from everything that is important
in experience, the scientific thought which confines itself
to these abstractions will arrive at a variety of important
truths relating to our experience of nature. We all know
those clear-cut trenchant intellects, immovably encased in
a hard shell of abstractions. They hold you to their abstractions by the sheer grip of personality.

The disadvantage, says Whitehead, of exclusive attention to a group of abstractions, however well-founded, is
that, by the nature of the case, you have abstracted from
the remainder of things. In so far as the excluded things
are important in your experience, your modes of thought
are not fitted to deal with them. You cannot think without abstractions; accordingly, it is of the utmost importance to be vigilant in critically revising your modes of
abstraction. It is here that philosophy finds its niche as

essential to the healthy progress of society. It is the critic of abstractions. A civilization which cannot burst through its current abstractions is doomed to sterility after a very limited period of progress. An active school of philosophy is quite as important for the locomotion of ideas as is an active school of railway engineers for the locomotion of fuel.

Now abstractions are specially tempting to judges. Not only are reasons expected of them, but also, as Learned Hand said, 'It always gives an appearance of greater authority to a conclusion to deduce it dialectically from conceded premises than to confess that it involves the appraisal of conflicting interests.'[80] But as lawyers, too, they are specially liable. Lawyers are likely to think and live at their happiest, easiest, and best in the world of abstractions, unlike those who cannot keep themselves away from the heat and grime and excitement of facts. Lawyers like to deal with abstractions, good clean things they can make as neat and polished as they please. Few of them, in other words, have green fingers. Few of them enjoy messing into the loam of fact. Do not find fault with them. Facts are not strictly their peculiar business. Perhaps they do well to recognize where their legal function comes to an end, as indeed they do — by their respect for experts, the medical expert, the engineer, and that expert on the common facts of ordinary life, the jury. And yet, though a lawyer's disinclination from facts may make him more lawyerlike, it will not help his practice. He will be all the more successful for a love of facts. By the same token a distaste for them disqualifies him for dealing with the Constitution. To do that well, he must be wise enough to recognize his abstractions for what they are. He must know they are instruments with which to find his way about this variegated world. He must know too that they are devices which give him prestige and claim the assent and approval of others to what he chooses to say. And he must know that they are no more than this. There are lawyers who have not been able to shake off the Legal Tradition. They may neither agree with this, nor perhaps even understand it.

Most of the Court's decisions call for drawing a line somewhere between opposing and conflicting abstract principles. Thus Black in one case, 'We have two declared congressional policies which it is our responsibility to reconcile. The one seeks to preserve a competitive business economy; the other to preserve the rights of labor to organize to better its conditions through the agency of collective bargaining.'[81] He was speaking of the Sherman Act as against the Clayton Act which required that nothing in the anti-trust laws be construed to forbid the existence and operation of labor organizations. It is even plainer in constitutional questions, as, for example, where the sovereignty of a state must be reconciled with the power of the national government to tax.[82] It may not be so plain, but it is still true in the conflict between the right to freedom of religious belief and the principle of the plurality of principles underlying toleration, which, as Frankfurter recognized, had to be reconciled in the flag-salute case.[83]

This business of drawing a line comes hard with minds which work in the conceptual world. The qualitative mind curiously shuns the spectrum where the colors run into each other and are scarcely distinguishable where they meet and merge. To the quantitative, that is only natural, no more than what it expects and approves. Conflicting principles, though quite distinguishable when they do not approach each other, may yet, like the intervening colors between white and black, approach so nearly as to perplex the understanding, as colors perplex the vision in marking the distinction between them. Yet the distinction exists, and must be marked as the cases arise.[84]

The last two sentences were said by Marshall, and it was the same man, but not the same Marshall, who had held in *McCulloch* v. *Maryland* a few years before,[85] that the states had no power to tax United States banknotes, because the power to tax involved the power to destroy.[86]

Holmes fixed that, with his nominalist eye, 'In those days it was not recognized as it is today that most of the distinctions of the law are questions of degree. If the states had any power it was apparent that they had all power and that the necessary alternative was to deny it altogether. But this court which so often has defeated the attempt to tax in certain ways can defeat an attempt to discriminate or otherwise go too far without wholly abolishing the power to tax. The power to tax is not the power to destroy while this Court sits.'[87]

Not while this Court sits. When the time comes, yes — to follow Holmes's thought through, when the exercise of the power will in fact encroach on what the Constitution is there to preserve, then the Court will act. But not prematurely, not by anticipation, not running to meet the evil consequences, as your abstractionist will do. *Obsta principiis*, he says. It is his favorite argument, the entering wedge.

Of course his abstraction may be ill-founded, distorting the facts or leaving some relevant portion of them out of account. In that case, instead of the approximately actual results which will follow from the decision, the logical consequences of accepting and acting on his ill-founded principle will bring up against something quite unexpectedly. But suppose his abstraction to be well-founded, as true a version of the facts as we have any right to expect, now he must draw the line between it and its conflicting competitor, and it must run through the area where they overlap and conflict. For if there were no overlapping and no such area, there would be no problem. His immediate duty to decide the immediate case requires him to draw the line of decision through that area which is common to both principles, but his devotion and loyalty to his own principle or his fear or even abhorrence for the other, or both his predilections and his prejudices, will lead him to draw the line safely within the confines of his own abstraction. He is so repelled by what conflicts with it that he is reluctant even to recognize its existence. And so he is basing his decision, not on the exigencies of the instant case at all, but on a reluctance to recognize the validity or the relevance of the competing abstraction. He fears that his successors, abusing or abused by the doctrine of *stare decisis*, which he devoutly believes in, in subsequent cases will take his recognition as a precedent and move the line farther and farther away from what he believes in. For *stare decisis* controls only the validity of the conflicting principles. It has nothing to say about where the line should run through the area they both cover. He is treating the case before him not as a case at all, only as a precedent.

The only difficulty in picking an example is their multitude. The Court was recently unanimous in its decision that *Esquire* had a right to the privilege of second-class mail, and Douglas wrote an admirable opinion. But in the course of it he gave as one reason for the decision that 'to withdraw the second-class rate from this publication today because its contents seemed to one official not good for the public would sanction withdrawal of the second-class rate tomorrow from another periodical whose social or economic views seemed harmful to another official.'[88] And a very good reason, but consider the following comment by Frankfurter in his concurring opinion. 'It seems to me important strictly to confine discussion in this case because its radiations touch, on the one hand, the very basis of a free society, that of the right of expression beyond the conventions of the day, and, on the other hand, the freedom from constitutional compulsion to subsidize enterprise, whether in the world of matter or of mind.' And he referred to the questions which the Court must confront when it considers 'the basis on which government may grant or withhold subsidies through low postal rates, and huge subsidies, if one is to judge by the glimpse afforded by the present case.' It meant a matter of five hundred thousand dollars a year to *Esquire* to keep or lose its second-class rates. Frankfurter concluded, 'It will be time enough to consider such questions when the Court cannot escape decision upon them.'

I visualize the two abstract principles as the overlapping arcs of two circles making a lanceolate common area, down through which must somewhere run the line of decision. If you push the line so far away from your favored abstraction that it does not cut through its arc at all, unless, of course, the other competing and conflicting abstraction is irrelevant to the question, in which case that is no common area at all, you have made your abstraction into an absolute, for you have insisted that no line of decision can cut through it. You have isolated it from fact. You have cut it off from the living world and there is nothing but logic left to protect it.

A diagram proves nothing. Every man must make his own. Let us turn to the cases.

10

OLD COURT AND NEW DEAL

D ID THE COURT in the late autumn of 1932 have any clear idea of what had happened? Of course, some of them did. Brandeis, and Stone, and Cardozo did. Hughes, the Chief Justice, certainly did. Roberts must have known, but the others, Van Devanter, McReynolds, Sutherland, and Butler seem to have been taken by surprise. At least they thought it would blow over. Anyhow, all of them, particularly the Chief Justice, had a difficult job of statesmanship before them, a more difficult job than any of their predecessors. Marshall? *Marbury* v. *Madison* was academic. Taney? The Dred Scott case was hopeless.

There is one person who can really tell the story and that is Hughes. He is retired now and perhaps some day we shall hear it. In 1928, four years before, he had given a series of lectures on the Supreme Court, and he said, 'Much that I should like to say must be omitted.' How much more he has that he must want to tell us now!

There was schism in the Court, four and four, Van Devanter, McReynolds, Sutherland, and Butler against Hughes, Brandeis, Stone, and Cardozo; and, defying classification, there was Roberts.

94

Van Devanter was the oldest of the five. He was seventy-seven. Born in Indiana, he had moved to Wyoming at twenty-five, where he served in the Territorial Legislature and became Chief Justice of the State Supreme Court at thirty. After a year or so he resigned to practice law, with lumbermen, cattlemen, and the Union Pacific for clients. Back into politics again as Republican National Committeeman in 1896, when he helped McKinley and Gold beat Bryan and Silver. In 1903 Roosevelt appointed him to the Federal Circuit Court, and seven years later, in 1910, Taft raised him to the Supreme Court. A courteous, kind, skilled counselor-at-law, with a deep political experience as a Republican. 'My mainstay in the Court,' Taft wrote to his daughter Helen, and in conference 'far and away the most valuable man in court.'[89]

McReynolds was seventy-four. From Tennessee, where he ran unsuccessfully for Congress as a Gold Democrat in 1896. Then he became a professor in Vanderbilt University. After that he practiced law in New York City. As assistant attorney general, he prosecuted the Tobacco Trust. Wilson made him his Attorney General (instead of Brandeis) in 1913, and appointed him to the Court in 1914. 'He has a continual grouch,' wrote Taft, he 'seems to delight in making others uncomfortable ... always offended because the court is doing something that he regards as undignified.'[90]

Sutherland was also seventy-four. He was brought to Utah when he was a baby by his English father, and there he grew up into law, but also into politics. After a few years in the State Legislature he went to Washington, first as Congressman, then as Senator, as the colleague of Smoot. A Taft man in 1912, President of the American

Bar Association in 1918, close to Harding in 1920. Harding appointed him to the Court in 1922, when he failed of re-election to the Senate. A conscientious learned jurist and a politician with all kinds of Republican experience.

Butler was seventy. An Irishman and a Catholic. Born on Saint Patrick's Day on a farm in Minnesota, whence he had made himself into a highly successful lawyer. A lawyer, not a politician. He was appointed to the Court by Harding, in 1922, over the bitter opposition of Senator Norris.

In 1929, Chief Justice Taft wrote to Justice Butler: 'The most that could be hoped for is continued life of enough of the present membership to prevent disastrous reversals of our present attitude. With Van and Mac and Sutherland and you and Sanford, there will be five to steady the boat. We must not give up at once.' [91]

The next year, 1930, Taft retired and Hughes took his place as Chief Justice. Sanford died in March, 1930, and Roberts succeeded him. But Van and Mac and Sutherland and Butler kept on 'steadying the boat.'

Roberts was the youngest of them all, but sixty-one at that. A Philadelphian. Professor of law in the University of Pennsylvania from the time he graduated from its law school in 1898 until 1919. Then assistant district attorney in Philadelphia. When Coolidge decided to prosecute the oil cases, he appointed Roberts to do it. After that, in 1930, Coolidge appointed him to the Court, when the nomination of Judge Parker had been rejected by the Senate. A spectacularly competent lawyer, and very much a lawyer.

The other four were Hughes, Brandeis, Stone, and Cardozo.

Chief Justice Hughes was seventy-four. He had been governor of New York in 1906, after conducting a great and successful investigation of fraudulent insurance companies. He was first appointed to the Court in 1910 by President Taft. In 1916, he resigned to run against Wilson, nearly but not quite successfully. He was Harding's and then Coolidge's Secretary of State. He was President of the American Bar Association in 1924–25. Hoover appointed him Chief Justice in 1930.

Brandeis was the oldest. Eighty. An active and successful practicing lawyer in Boston until he was appointed to the Court by Wilson in 1916, and confirmed over the bitter opposition of most of the bar, including Root, Taft, and five other past presidents of the American Bar Association. His service on the bench is only half of a distinguished career. The father of savings bank insurance. The author of the factual brief. The People's Advocate. And, as Holmes said, 'Whenever he left my house, I was likely to say to my wife, There goes a really good man.' [92]

Stone was sixty-four. Born in New Hampshire, but by experience a New Yorker. Dean of Columbia Law School for some thirteen years. Then, for a while, a member of the big firm of Sullivan and Cromwell in New York City. Attorney General for President Coolidge in 1924, who appointed him to the Court in 1925. Taft had something to say about him, too, 'a learned lawyer in many ways, but his judgments I do not altogether consider safe. He definitely has ranged himself with Brandeis and with Holmes in a good many of our constitutional differences.' He was to succeed Hughes as Chief Justice, head a troublesome Court, and die with his shoes on in 1946.

Cardozo was sixty-six. A New Yorker. A judge, first

in the lower courts of New York, then from 1914 a judge of its highest court. Originally by appointment of a Republican governor, and later by election. He was its Chief Judge from 1927 until 1932, when he was appointed to the Court by Hoover, on the insistence of Norris and Borah, as our most distinguished judge and jurist.

It would have taken a shrewd appraiser of background, character, and record to have foretold the line-up. Age versus youth is arguable, but the average age of each group was just about the same, about seventy-one; and the youngest, Roberts, parted company with the oldest, Brandeis. Nor was it political, if their appointments are the test. There was a Wilson appointee and a Coolidge appointee on each side. Harding appointed Sutherland and Butler, but it was Hoover who appointed Cardozo, and he made Hughes Chief Justice. Politics had little to do with it. Hoover told the Republican Convention in 1936, 'You might contemplate what would have happened if Mr. Roosevelt could have appointed enough Supreme Court Justices in the first year of his administration.' Within a few months, it did happen anyhow before Roosevelt appointed anyone.

Where then was the common denominator in each group that pulled them so far apart? Van Devanter, McReynolds, Sutherland, and Butler had all grown up and made great careers for themselves out of the pioneer life of Turner's frontier. That was their America and they loved it. When a man starts from nothing in a pioneer community and emerges with a great career or a fortune or both, it is impossible for him to believe there is anything really wrong with the society in which he did it. In the best and soundest sense he is conservative. Francis Biddle put it well in his memorial as Attorney General to Butler,[93] 'He was brought up in a school of thought which had not learned to doubt the implications of its perhaps over-simplified assumptions — *laissez-faire*, individualism, free competition. These things meant the American way. By this way he had come to the top and the failure of others to arrive seemed to indicate personal fault rather than economic disadvantage. The frontiers were open. Success was at the end of a straight road.' Elizabeth Cobb said, 'It always seems to me a strange thing that so often the self-made man becomes the great reactionary, frightened that the world he knew, and in which he was able to make his mark, should ever change. Perhaps all successful men are egotists, must be egotists, are required to be egotists — and so they cannot abide the idea of a world which they cannot dominate, and as they are no longer young enough to learn how to dominate this new one they both hate and fear it.'[94]

The other five too made their own careers, but not in the same society, Brandeis in Boston, Roberts in Philadelphia, Hughes, Stone, and Cardozo all in New York.

As a whole it was a typical Court. All lawyers, but one national committeeman, two Attorney Generals, one Senator, one Governor and presidential candidate and Secretary of State, one straight judge, and three straight lawyers. But none of them inexperienced in politics. Much as the Court has been from the beginning.

Through 1933 and 1934, the first two years of the New Deal, the Court seemed to regard the New Deal quite placidly. In January of 1934, indeed, there was a decision that sustained the Minnesota Moratorium on mortgage foreclosures.[95] Later in the year the Court even smiled on price-fixing legislation. In the Nebbia case[96] the Court sustained New York's Milk Control Law, in an opinion which not only encouraged liberals and made them think that at last the Holmes-Brandeis-Cardozo line of dissent had become settled law, it put them quite off their guard. In the Nebbia opinion, which Roberts wrote, the Court said, 'So far as the requirement of due process is concerned, and in the absence of other constitutional restriction, a state is free to adopt whatever economic policy may reasonably be deemed to promote public welfare.' But Van and Mac and Sutherland and Butler were steadying the boat. They had to dissent. Roberts was not yet with them.

We are going to postpone one and skip another of the first two anti-New Deal decisions. The one to be postponed is the Hot Oil case, which came in January of 1935.[97] We skip the Gold Clause cases,[98] where bad constitutional vinegar was mixed with good legal olive oil, and it takes a very good lawyer to relish the result, to say nothing of understanding the recipe. The Court declared that Congress could not constitutionally reduce the amount of gold in the dollar, only to add that under the legal rules of damages bondholders could not prove any actual loss when they were paid in the new dollars.

When Jackson went abroad that summer, Swedish lawyers and bankers asked him some questions, which he reports in his book, *The Struggle for Judicial Supremacy*. 'How could you Americans let your national monetary and economic policy be dependent on the outcome of a law suit between private parties over a difference of $15.60? How could American business intelligently function over a year and a half while such basic questions were pending in the Court? Why could you not learn the answer earlier? Why should within one of a majority of your Court hold that a private contract between two citizens should deprive the nation of power to change its monetary policy? And why, anyway, should lawyer-judges be supreme over the national parliament, the President, the Treasury, and the whole government in a matter so vital to economic life?' Jackson told them they did not understand our legal tradition and left them, he said, unsatisfied.

We will begin with the Railroad Pensions decision, which came down in May, 1935. Roberts joined the Four and wrote the opinion. What he said, or rather what they said, makes a good introduction. For it reflects their attitude toward social legislation in general.

Railroad Pensions

Railroad pension systems were half a century old in 1934. By 1910 half the railroad employees were covered; by 1927, four-fifths. All of them, of course, had been set up by the roads themselves. Each road had its own system, set up as each thought best, each under its own control, and each was terminable when the railroad chose.

In 1934 Congress established a uniform and compulsory system for all interstate lines. Since there were over a million people working for the railroads, it was a large order. It was done as an exercise of Congress's power to regulate interstate commerce, and it was done because the separate voluntary systems of each road were not satisfactory. Mr. Eastman was the Co-ordinator of Transportation and he can testify. The experience with voluntary systems has been unsatisfactory, he said; the depression brought clearly to light their many weaknesses and uncertainties.[99]

Congress's scheme was this. All the interstate roads were treated as one big employer. Each road was to pay into one fund, deposited in the United States Treasury and administered by a Board appointed by the President, two per cent out of every man's pay and double that amount out of its own pocket. Out of that fund the annuities would be paid.

One hundred and thirty-four railroads, two express companies, and the Pullman Company at once brought suit in the District of Columbia asserting that the Act was unconstitutional and asking for an injunction against its enforcement. In view of 'the importance of an early and final decision,' the Supreme Court took the question up. They heard arguments in March, 1935, and two months later they announced their decision, that the Act was not constitutional. Five to four. Roberts wrote the majority opinion for the Court, Hughes the dissent.[100]

The railroads called the Act bad for two separate reasons. One went to the validity of any such act, that this really was not a regulation of commerce at all, but simply social legislation. The other attacked this particular act. It was that many of its provisions were in violation of due process of law, particularly the provision for a single fund, because that would result indirectly in one railroad paying the pensions of another's employees.

Roberts discussed due process first, and found the Act invalid on that ground. Then he went on to the other and said it was not really a regulation of commerce at all.

You will see that there was no need of going on to say that. If the plan was invalid because Congress had done it badly, it was unnecessary for the Court to say anything more. It was more than unnecessary to do what they did, go on and say that Congress could never set up any pension system at all for the railroads. It was an advisory opinion that no one, barring railroad counsel, had asked them to give.

That was, to Hughes and the minority, the gravest aspect of the decision. 'It does not rest simply upon a condemnation of particular features of the Railroad Retirement Act, but denies to Congress the power to pass any compulsory pension act for railroad employees. If the opinion were limited to the particular provisions of the Act which the majority find to be objectionable and not severable, the Congress would be free to overcome the objections by a new statute. But after discussing these matters, the majority finally reach a barrier that the subject matter itself lies beyond the reach of the congressional authority to regulate interstate commerce. In that view, no matter how suitably limited a pension act for railroad employees might be with respect to the persons benefited, or how appropriate the measure of retirement allowances, or how sound actuarially the plan, or how well adjusted the burden, still under this decision Congress would not be at liberty to enact such a measure. That is a conclusion of such serious and far reaching importance that it overshadows all other questions raised by the Act. Indeed, it makes their discussion superfluous.'

It was superfluous to the decision, and superfluous to Hughes, but not to us.

The commerce clause in the Constitution reads, 'to regulate Commerce . . . among the several states.' Now railroads are plainly engaged in 'commerce' and interstate lines are plainly run 'among the several states.' What Roberts denied was that pensions are regulations.

Safety appliances had been required. Restrictions on the hours of continuous work had been prescribed. A standard day's work had been established. The road's liability for injuries to employees had been regulated. Provisions had been enacted for the settlement of disputes with employees. Employees had been protected in their freedom to organize. All those regulations had been held constitutional. But a compulsory pension system is not a regulation?

The Government's first suggestion, through the Solicitor General, why pensions were a regulation of interstate commerce, was that they made the railroads run better. It helped the roads retire superannuated employees. Mr. Eastman, the Co-ordinator of Transportation, had testified that there was excessive superannuation among railroad employees: 'Men who have grown old in the service decline in efficiency. The carrier pays in wages an amount out of proportion to the service rendered. There is now a large body of superannuated employees in railroad service who, for the good of the service, ought to be retired.' [101]

Roberts simply denied that this was so. The facts did not indicate, he said, that the older men were inefficient or incompetent, but quite the contrary. Train accidents had decreased over the last ten years. Casualties among employees per man hours had decreased. As for efficiency, the average speed of freight trains had increased in the last five years from eleven to over fifteen miles an hour. Roberts said that incontrovertible statistics showed a steady increase in both safety and efficiency.[102]

'But that gratifying fact,' replied Hughes for the minority, 'does not establish that further improvement is not needed or obtainable, or that a sound pension plan would not be of considerable benefit to the carriers' operations. At best, the question as to the extent of superannuation, and its effect, is a debatable one, and hence one upon which Congress was entitled to form a legislative judgment.' [103]

Roberts went on, 'If the promotion of efficiency, economy, or safety demand the elimination of aged employees, their retirement from the service would suffice to accomplish the object. For these purposes the prescription of a pension for those dropped from service is wholly irrelevant. The Government, conscious of the truth of this statement, endeavors to avoid its force by the argument that social and humanitarian considerations demand the support of the retired employee.'

In other words, since it would be constitutional for Congress to require the railroads to discharge all their employees as soon as they reached sixty-five, it is constitutional to require them to pension them.

Hughes picked that up, 'Congress may, indeed, it seems to be assumed, compel the elimination of aged employees. A retirement act for that purpose might be passed. But not a pension plan. The government's power is conceived to be limited to a requirement that the railroads dismiss their superannuated employees, throwing them out helpless, without any reasonable provision for their protection.' [104]

In respect to the 'social and humanitarian considerations' which Roberts referred to, they were talking at cross-purposes. Roberts, I think, was referring to such considerations on the part of Congress. Of course they were not a proper basis for an exercise of its power. But I don't think the Government was saying that. It was urging social and humanitarian reasons on the part of the railroads, not of Congress. It comes hard to say that they are irrelevant. When a road is making up its mind whether or not to fire an old employee, surely it is easier to retire him if you know he is going to be pensioned.

If Congress had the power to insist on the retirement of superannuated railroad men, and Roberts as much as says so, Congress certainly has the right to recognize that it was going to be done by human beings and make it decently easy for human beings to do it. Roberts was confusing the recognition of humanitarian feelings in others with humanitarianism in yourself, two very different things.

The Government's next argument was that pensions improved morale. Almost all the carriers had voluntarily adopted pension plans of their own, and for two principal reasons, the Government said. One was the creation of loyalty. The other was the encouragement of continuity of service. These were business reasons. Congress was requiring pensions for the same business reasons that had impelled the roads themselves to give pensions voluntarily.

Well, said Roberts, if the purpose of these voluntary pension plans was to create loyalty to the employer who establishes them, and continuity in his service, then 'to us it seems axiomatic that the removal of the voluntary character of the pension and the imposition of it in such form as Congress may determine, upon all employees, and irrespective of length of service, or of service for the same employer, will eliminate all sense of loyalty or gratitude to the employer, and remove every incentive to continuance in the service of a single carrier.' [105]

'The surest way,' said Roberts, 'to destroy loyalty in any privately owned business is to substitute legislative largess for private bounty and thus transfer the drive for pensions to the halls of Congress and transmute loyalty to employer into gratitude to the legislature.' [106]

The railroads which had already adopted pensions had not done it as charity, but as good business. If that is so, why cannot Congress make all of them adopt the same system? If it is good business for them, why is it not good regulation for Congress? What is the difference?

Because the 'loyalty or gratitude' which the railroads obtained from their voluntary pensions springs only from the very fact that they are voluntary. If the employees knew their employers had to do it, loyalty to the employer becomes gratitude to Congress. Manhood is melted into curtsies, valor into compliment. You will agree that there is something wrong here.

The Solicitor General turned to the sense of security which pensions give, and which, he said, was a good thing for the railroads. Surely, he said, that sense of security does not depend on who gives the pensions or whether they are given voluntarily or by compulsion. Why is not that a proper basis for regulation? he asked. To which Roberts replied:

'We think it cannot be denied, and, indeed, is in effect admitted, that the sole reliance of the Government is upon the theory that contentment and assurance of security are the major purposes of the Act. We cannot agree that these ends if dictated by statute, and not voluntarily extended by the employer, encourage loyalty and continuity of service. We feel bound to hold that a pension plan thus imposed is in no proper sense a regulation of the activity of interstate transportation. It is an attempt for social ends to impose by sheer fiat non-contractual incidents upon the relation of employer and employee, not as a rule or regulation of commerce and transportation between the States, but as a means of assuring a particular class of employees against old age dependency.' [107]

Hughes said simply that 'the fundamental consideration which supports this type of legislation is that industry should take care of its human wastage, whether that is due to accident or age. That view cannot be dismissed as arbitrary or capricious. It is a reasoned conviction based upon abundant experience. The expression of that conviction in law is regulation.' The flash of accident and the slow rub of age. To Roberts and the Four, maintenance, repair, and obsolescence were only for accountants. Were they living in the industrial revolution in England and echoing the hymns of Isaac Watts or in the pioneer days of American business? In either case, it is the nineteenth century, and there we must leave them.

There are two wrong ways of arguing about constitutional law. One of them is to say, It's Constitutional, therefore it's Right. That is not the same as saying, It's Constitutional, and therefore it's not Wrong. Not being wrong may be very different from being really right. For you can be right in so many degrees of rightness. Good, better, or best. Not being wrong is only the bare minimum. The Constitution doesn't prescribe the best way of doing things. It leaves that to Congress. All the Constitution says is, If it's Unconstitutional, it's Wrong.

The other wrong way is what the majority were saying here. They were arguing, or at any rate they were coming fearfully close to arguing, It's Wrong, therefore it's Unconstitutional.

Take it that they started with the thought that this act was Wrong. And the thought took hold and before they knew it, it had become a Major Premise. It's wrong, the majority said to themselves, for the railroads to be compelled to do what they can do and are doing very well by themselves. If it's Wrong, then it must be Unconstitutional. Perhaps they were not aware that their thought had taken such a hold on them, but it had. Then it was up to them to give some reason for it, and the best they found was this distinction between voluntary and compulsory pensions. It is really not a bad argument, granted their Major Premise.

Needless to say, Congress was not persuaded. The Court's opinion was announced in May, 1935. In August Congress passed two acts on the same day, the twenty-ninth. They were announced as 'companion bills.' One was substantially a re-enactment of the pensions, but neither the carriers nor their employees were expected to pay them. They were all made payable out of the United States Treasury. All that was expected of the carriers, and the word in the act was 'expected,' was not to reduce their pension payments beyond the amounts appropriated by the act. How could the carriers object to that?

The companion bill was entitled the Carriers Taxing Act of 1935. It imposed an 'income tax' on the railroad employees which was equal to the percentages which the old statute, now defunct, had deducted from their pay. At the same time it laid an 'excise tax' in the same amount on the carriers. Both were made payable into the United States Treasury, as 'internal revenue collections.' How could you find anything wrong about that? Congress has the power to tax. Too smart? Too obvious? Certainly not a very candid nor a very dignified way of legislating. Nor had the Court's opinion been in its best manner.

What the Court would have done with this companionate device, we may guess when we see the way it dealt with the A.A.A., but no one ever gave it an opportunity. The validity of these companion acts was never presented to any court until 1942, and then they came up (as they were re-enacted in 1937) before the Circuit Court of Appeals in California. That court, through Judge William Denman, had a keen sense of the ridiculous.[108]

'It is true,' Judge Denman said, 'that in *Railroad Retirement Board* v. *Alton Railroad Company* the majority of the court takes judicial notice that Congress in 1934 could not rationally conceive that the minds of railway workmen were so constituted that absence of fear of the loss of a railway job by lessened commerce or injury or old age could in any way add to the efficiency of their service. Morale, the court apparently thought, could be improved only if a pension were granted by the "largess" of the employer. Sufficient had then been generally disclosed of the railway workmen's motivations for the four dissenting Justices to disagree with the facts as found on judicial notice, by the majority.

'Probably there never has been a period in modern legislative history when the concepts and motives of the minds of working men were more fully explored in the course of enacting or amending labor laws or in the discussion of unpassed labor bills, than in the three year period between the enactment of the first and third Railroad Retirement bills. Congress certainly could have a rational concept of the effect of a legislatively enforced railroad pension different in 1937 from that in 1934. To

hold that it rationally could have had the concept we have
stated above in 1937 concerning the later law, does not
overrule the Alton case and does not violate *stare decisis*.
Each decision rests on different facts — nonetheless facts
whether judicially noticed or proved.

'We take judicial notice, based upon our present knowledge of the minds of workmen, that the following is a
rational concept concerning interstate railway employees
sufficient to sustain the Railroad Retirement Act of 1937
against the charge that it is unconstitutional because it
would not effectually aid interstate commerce: That experience has shown that men's participancy in railroading
produces a strong loyalty to the organization of which
they are creative parts. That it is a loyalty of men of
character devoted primarily to the service to which their
minds and bodies are given; and that their loyalty to their
employer *as employer* is subordinated to the loyalty to the
organization as an all-embracing entity. That loyalty to
the employer disappears once railroad men feel that he is
not of them. That employee loyalty to the distant cor-
porate president or banker-controlled board of directors is
practically non-existent. That one of the primary induce-
ments to *draw men* of the required high character *into* such
an organization and *keep them there* is the certainty that it,
the living entity to which they belong, will afford them and
their dependents a secure old age. That to a man of such
required character, a pension giving such security has a
stronger appeal to his loyalty to his service if it is a certain
internal function of the organization, than if it rests in the
uncertain and insecure largess of the employer.'

The N.R.A.

You will remember that when Roosevelt took office, in his first inaugural, in March, 1933, he asked Congress for 'broad executive power to wage war against the emergency, as great as the power that would be given to me if we were invaded by a foreign power.' If you do remember, you will not have forgotten the emergency. Nearly a third of labor could not get work. Our national income off a half. No purchases, no sales, no profits — national bankruptcy, and, as Stuart Chase has said, the Federal Government became our receiver.[109]

Two months later Roosevelt asked Congress 'for the machinery necessary for a great co-operative movement throughout all industry to obtain wide re-employment.' The National Industrial Recovery Act was promptly passed, on June 16, 1933. Roosevelt said, when he signed it, 'History probably will record it as the most important and far-reaching legislation ever enacted by the American Congress.' What the N.R.A. proposed to do to the country's industry can be compared only to what has been done twice, once before, in 1917, and once since, in 1941, when we were at war. It was too big an ark to float in time of peace. Only in time of war do you get a great enough wave of 'co-operative movement' to submerge Mount Ararat.

Each industry was given a code. Trade associations, labor unions, leaders of all kinds, and a lot of others were got together, and by a process of collaboration and cajolery they worked out a code. If they couldn't or wouldn't do it for themselves in a way the President would approve, then the act provided that he could make one up for them. So there was a certain amount of legal insistence behind the cajolery. They were called Codes of Fair Competition, and there were certain provisions that every code had to contain. Collective bargaining, maximum hours, minimum wages, no child labor, and miscellaneous appropriate business practices. Including these provisions, each code became a fairly detailed manual of law for its industry.

There would not have been a great deal left for Congress to do about industry and business once they had all got codes, except to revise and amend them. And pretty nearly every industry and every business did get a code. Not only the key industries, not only those that were depressed and in particular trouble. Nearly all of American industry was covered. Congress had loaned to the Executive a great deal of its power. But there is this to be said, Congress could at any time have repealed or amended the N.R.A. In fact, at the very time the Court declared it unconstitutional, its two years of life were about to expire. The President had recently asked for another two years, but the Senate Committee on Finance had just reported out an extension of only ten months. Ways and Means in the House were prepared to report. But they never did, because on the eve of their action the Supreme Court held the whole N.R.A. experiment hopelessly unconstitutional.[110] But that was in June, the June of 1935, and in January the Court had already cut out one section and held it unconstitutional. Let me go back and begin there. It was the first piece of New Deal legislation to be hit. This was the Hot Oil case.[111]

The condition of the oil industry was as acute as the rest of industry. The wholesale market was below the cost of manufacture. The market was flooded with cheap gasoline. It was being dumped at what price it would bring. Consequently the oil-producing states were trying to restrict production, but enforcement was difficult, more than difficult. Oil was being unlawfully produced, hot oil and hot gasoline, and it was sold, of course, for even less than legal oil. It was worse for the independent producers who did not dare shut down for fear of losing their regular customers.[112]

The New Deal Congress offered to help. Section 9(c) of the N.R.A. authorized the President to forbid the interstate shipment of oil that was produced, or withdrawn from storage, in violation of any state law. A month later, in July, Roosevelt made an Executive Order forbidding such shipments. This section, and with it this order, was what the Court held unconstitutional as an undue delegation of legislative power.

The Constitution says this, 'All legislative powers herein granted shall be vested in a Congress of the United States.' Obviously you can't lay too much stress on that word 'all.' Congress cannot go into details. Congress must tell someone, including the President, what it wants done and leave it to him to see that it is done. In brief, Congress must delegate its powers. This does not mean it can abdicate them. In the inevitable descent from the general to the particular, from the abstract to the concrete, which is required by force of circumstances of all legislators, more or less in ratio to their numbers, why shouldn't Congress go so far as it chooses? It can always take the power back. It can always call a halt and recall the delegated authority. This is not the Weimar Republic.

If you do not agree, consider what the wisest of our

elder statesmen, Hughes, has said, 'The Constitution has
never been regarded as denying to the Congress the necessary resources of flexibility and practicality, which will
enable it to perform its function in laying down policies
and establishing standards, while leaving to selected in-
strumentalities the making of subordinate rules within
prescribed limits and the determination of facts to which
the policy as declared by the legislature is to apply. Without capacity to give authorizations of that sort we should
have the anomaly of a legislative power which in many
circumstances calling for its exertion would be but a
futility.'

Lawyers like to think of the Constitution as an enactment of *law*, pointing to the phrase in the Preamble, 'We,
the People — *do ordain and establish* this Constitution,'
which are apt words for the enactment of a law. Every
now and then they need to be reminded of what Marshall
told them, that this is a constitution which they are expounding. Which makes Hughes's words almost apolo-
getic. And in truth they were, for he said them in this
very opinion in the Hot Oil case,[113] where the Court held,
on January 7, 1935, that Congress had offended the Constitution when it gave President Roosevelt authority to
penalize interstate shipments of the hot oil produced in
violation of state law.

The decision is hard to understand, and not worth trying to explain. Cardozo's dissent did not even argue with
the majority. He simply denied that this was too much
delegation. 'There is no fear,' he said, 'that the nation
will drift from its ancient moorings as the result of the
narrow delegation of power permitted by this section.
What can be done under cover of that permission is closely

and clearly circumscribed both as to subject matter and occasion. The statute was framed in the shadow of a national disaster. A host of unforeseen contingencies would have to be faced from day to day, and faced with a fulness of understanding unattainable by anyone except the man upon the scene. The President was chosen to meet the instant need.' [114]

Perhaps the way Congress detoured the decision is explanation and argument enough. The decision had come down on January 7, 1935. Within weeks, Congress passed the Connally Act, which simply turned the discretion delegated to the President inside out or upside down. Congress began at the other end by flatly prohibiting all interstate shipment of hot oil and then authorizing the President, by proclamation, after stating the facts, to lift the prohibition when and where he deemed expedient. And it has never even been questioned in the courts, high or low, as an unconstitutional delegation of power. In other words, in the N.R.A. Congress simply went about it hind-end to. But that depends at which end you are standing.

This Panama Hot Oil case is really the only case, not just the first, in which an act of Congress has been held void under this doctrine that Congress cannot delegate its power. In the two others the doctrine was used as an additional reason for invalidity, only as a *coup de grâce*. They came a few months later. One was in coal control. The other was the Schechter case, where the whole N.R.A. was held void.

When the Justices filed into the courtroom on May 27, 1935, they were looking cheerful. Particularly, it was pointed out, Chief Justice Hughes, McReynolds, and

Stone. The Chief Justice had every right to be pleased. The Court was going to deliver a unanimous opinion. McReynolds may well have been pleased, because it was going to be unanimous against the New Deal. Why did Stone look pleased? Perhaps it was the cherry blossoms outside.

For one thing, the whole act delegated so much more to the President that now even Cardozo agreed it was void.[115] We may leave it at that, and turn to the Court's other reason. It was void, too, because it transcended Congress's power over interstate commerce. Congress had passed it as an exercise of that power. As to that, Cardozo concurred, but he and Stone took a different slant from the others on the way that question should be approached. At the time, their different approach was scarcely a cloud in the clear unanimous sky, but it was different and, as it proved, pregnant with thunder.

Donald Richberg, the general counsel of the N.R.A., had picked out the Live Poultry Code to test N.R.A.'s constitutionality, and under that code the misbehavior of a small poultry slaughterhouse in Brooklyn. Joseph Schechter and his brothers, Martin, Alex, and Aaron, ran a wholesale poultry slaughterhouse in Brooklyn. They bought their chickens alive in coops in the Manhattan Terminal and the West Washington Market, both in New York. From there they were trucked over to the slaughterhouse in Brooklyn, where the Schechters killed and dressed and sold them to the retailers.

The Schechters were convicted in the Federal District Court in New York, for paying their men less than the minimum wage of fifty cents an hour, for working them more than forty hours a week, for 'selective killing,' for selling an unfit chicken, for selling some chickens before they had been inspected, for not reporting their daily prices and sales, and for trading with unlicensed dealers, all in violation of the Code.

They had bought their chickens in Manhattan, killed them in Brooklyn, and sold them all within the State of New York. How could you say that this was interstate commerce? It is true that most of the chickens, maybe all of them, came from out of state. This was certainly a regulation of the Schechters' business, but was that business interstate commerce?

The Court has in many cases spoken of a 'stream' of commerce and allowed Congress to regulate the activities of those whose business dealt with the 'flow' of the 'current' of the stream, even if their activities were all carried on within the state. The Court had said this about Federal regulation of the stockyards in Chicago, for example. But here the 'stream' of poultry stopped in New York. It did not flow through. Hughes said there was no warrant for the argument that the poultry handled by defendants at their slaughterhouse markets was in a 'current or flow' of interstate commerce and was thus subject to Congressional regulation. 'The mere fact that there may be a constant flow of commodities into a State does not mean that the flow continues after the property has arrived and has been commingled with the mass of property within the State and is there held solely for local disposition and use. So far as the poultry here in question is concerned, the flow in interstate commerce had ceased. The poultry had come to a permanent rest within the State.'[116] Hughes meant that the chickens were eaten in New York.

Yet the chickens were shipped into New York only be-

cause the Schechters, among others, were going to buy
them, and then only to sell them to people who would eat
them in New York. The poultry would not have come at
all, there would have been no such commerce, if the
Schechters and their like were not buying them.

Could you not, therefore, say that the Schechters' poultry business *affected* interstate commerce? If it did, then
regulating it was indirectly regulating that commerce,
even if the business itself was not *in* it or a part of it.

No, said Hughes. 'Where the effect of intrastate transactions upon interstate commerce is merely indirect, such
transactions remain within the domain of state power. If
the commerce clause were construed to reach all enterprises and transactions which could be said to have an
indirect effect upon interstate commerce, the federal authority would embrace practically all the activities of the
people and the authority of the State over its domestic
concern would exist only by the sufferance of the Federal
government. The distinction between direct and indirect
effects of intrastate transactions upon interstate commerce must be recognized as a fundamental one, essential
to the maintenance of our constitutional system. Otherwise, as we have said, there would be virtually no limit to
the federal power and for all practical purposes we should
have a centralized government.' [117]

Hughes was applying the metaphors and the metaphysics which the Court had been using in interstate commerce cases. He tried the 'stream' or 'flow' of commerce
theory, and found no stream or flow here. He tried the
distinction between 'direct' and 'indirect,' and found that
the code had at most an indirect effect on interstate commerce. By none of the accepted tests was this interstate
commerce. Congress had exceeded its power.

Cardozo and Stone concurred in the result, but they reached it in an entirely different way, and what they said was important because the whole future of the Commerce Power hinged on the difference. They rejected these tests. They knew they were dealing with one of those questions of degree *in fact* with which the law has to deal, and to which it always resigns itself in the end.

'The law,' they said, 'is not indifferent to considerations of degree. Activities local in their immediacy do not become interstate and national because of distant repercussions. What is near and what is distant may at times be uncertain. There is no penumbra of uncertainty obscuring judgment here. To find immediacy or directness here is to find it almost everywhere. If centripetal forces are to be isolated to the exclusion of forces that oppose or counteract them, there will be an end to our federal system.' 'Motion at the outer rim,' they said, 'is communicated perceptibly, though minutely, to recording instruments at the center. A society such as ours is an elastic medium which transmits all tremors throughout its territory; the only question is of their size.' [118]

They were quoting from the opinion of Judge Learned Hand in the Circuit Court of Appeals below, whose decision the Court was reviewing. Hand had been less respectful of the general principles which Hughes applied. He regarded it as disingenuous to pretend that the *ratio decidendi* of such decisions is susceptible of statement in general principles. 'That no doubt might give a show of necessity to the conclusion, but it would be insincere and illusory, and appears formidable only in case the conclusion is surreptitiously introduced during the reasoning. The truth really is that where the border shall be fixed is a question of degree, dependent upon the consequences in each case.'

Again, what did Congress do? The Court's objection to the delegation of power was easy. All Congress had to do, and what it did do, was to turn the codes it had asked the President to draw up into its own acts of Congress. This is what it did for the soft coal industry in the Guffey Act, and for the provisions on labor in the National Labor Relations Act. The Court would have to deal with both of these later on different grounds, as we shall see.

But the abstract distinction between the direct and indirect effect on interstate commerce was not easy. There was no legislative detour around that obstacle. That would have to wait for a change in the whole approach of the Court toward the question. Nothing could be done about that until the Court dropped its metaphors and metaphysics and accepted the factual quantitative approach of Cardozo and Stone.

The A.A.A.

Miller once referred to 'the old argument often heard, often repeated, and in this court never assented to, that when a question of the power of Congress arises the advocate of the power must be able to place his finger on the words which expressly grant it.' [119] Miller was saying, in terms of constitutional law, the same thing Lincoln had said at Gettysburg twenty years before. It is important to recognize the identity. A new nation had been brought forth on this continent. That was a fact for the Court to reckon with, particularly because it was part of that nation. It was a fact the Court could not ignore when it was dealing with the Constitution. Put out your hand to place your finger upon a particular word, and you find your palm against the body of a nation.

The 1914–1918 War took some fifty million acres of crops in Europe temporarily out of cultivation. We in America responded and put more of our lands under cultivation. So did other countries — the Argentine, Australia, etc. The result was, after the war we had some thirty, forty millions of acres producing crops which could not be sold, not at any price that would keep the farmer alive. And his farm was mortgaged. He couldn't even pay his taxes.

The problem was only too obvious. What was the answer? Reduce this excess of production? Control this excess acreage? Take these millions of acres out of production?

It would be a great mistake to think this answer was a party issue. The Republican platform of 1932 said, 'The fundamental problem of American agriculture is in the control of production to such volume as will balance supply with demand. In the solution of this problem the co-operative organization of farmers to plan production and the tariff to hold the home market for American farmers, are vital elements. A third element, equally vital, is the control of acreage of land under cultivation, as an aid to the efforts of the farmer to balance production.' And that is just what the Democrats did. As soon as Roosevelt became President, a great meeting was called, and the Agricultural Adjustment Act was agreed on. It was passed on May 12, 1933.

The A.A.A. attempted to reduce our acreage of crop production to our domestic consumption plus as much as we could export with profit. Wallace, then Secretary of Agriculture, called it 'an orderly retreat from surplus acreage.' If that could be done, farmers would be providing just about what people needed, not more. Let's see how this was to be done, and just who was to pay for it. This calls for a few details.

The Act required the Secretary of Agriculture to determine what had been the farm price for cotton during the five years 1909–1914, the years just before we had expanded our acreage. I take cotton as an example because it was cotton that figured in the case we are coming to. It had been 12.40 cents a pound.

Then the Act required the Secretary to figure the price index of the commodities which farmers buy. He figured it had gone up a little since those years 1909–1914. Not much, only 3 per cent. So, to bring the 12.40 cents up to date, he had to make it 12.40 plus 3 per cent. That was 12.77 cents.

The current 1933 price of cotton was only 8.7 cents. There was, therefore, a difference of some four cents between the market and the price which would give the cotton farmer enough to buy as many commodities as he used to be able to buy before the war.

What the Act did was authorize the Secretary to offer this four cents a pound to growers who agreed to plant less cotton. It was money offered by the United States to each farmer to make it worth his while to grow less, and so sell less, and thus make the orderly retreat from the surplus excessive acreage. Do not forget that there was no law against each individual grower's holding out and making more by selling all he could produce at the higher price which the reduction of the rest had established.

Where was the Government to find the vast sum which this four cents a pound would come to? Out of general taxes? No. Why not from the cotton mills? Why not the ultimate consumer, the people for whom the farmers grow the cotton? Are not they the ones who ought to support the farmer? On the other hand, a tax directly on the consumer is too hard to collect. A tax on the mills which made the goods could be passed on to the consumer by raising the price per yard by whatever corresponds to four cents a pound. So the ultimate consumer would, as he should, ultimately pay. That was the idea.

So the Act imposed a 'processing tax' on the mills. The amount of the tax was to be fixed by the Secretary at what he judged was just enough to pay the four cents. It was to be paid into the Treasury. At the same time it was appropriated out of the Treasury to pay the cotton farmers who had agreed to reduce the acreage they otherwise would have planted.

The theory was this. The United States was to take money from the people who turn cotton into cloth, leaving it to them to take it out of the people who buy that cloth, then turn the money over to farmers who would agree to produce less cotton the next year, all in the hope that that much less cotton would raise the price of cotton by the amount of the tax, which would then stop. In theory, the tax would gradually dwindle to nothing. Is that good economics? The lawyer who argued the case for the cotton mills, said the United States 'had robbed Processor Peter in order to pay Producer Paul.'

This was the experiment which came before the Supreme Court for argument on December 9 and 10, 1935. It came up to the Court this way. The Hoosac Mills in New Eng-

land had gone into bankruptcy. Its receivers had refused
to pay the processing tax. The District Court had directed them to pay it. They had appealed to the Circuit
Court of Appeals in Massachusetts, which had told them
not to pay it, because it was unconstitutional. The Government had taken it up to the Supreme Court.

Stanley Reed, now Mr. Justice Reed, was the Solicitor
General who defended the Act. The lawyer chosen to attack constitutionality was George Wharton Pepper. He
was well chosen, for he believed sincerely and deeply that
the A.A.A. was not constitutional, as strongly as Mr.
Choate felt about the income tax.

Mr. Pepper told the Court, 'I have tried very hard to
argue this case calmly and dispassionately, because it
seems to me that this is the best way in which an advocate
can discharge his duty to this Court. But I do not want
your Honors to think that my feelings are not involved
and that my emotions are not deeply stirred. Indeed, may
it please your Honors, I believe I am standing here today
to plead the cause of the America I have loved; and I pray
Almighty God that not in my time may "the land of the
regimented" be accepted as a worthy substitute for "the
land of the free."' [120]

Within a month, on January 6, 1936, the Court announced its decision.[121] The Act was unconstitutional.
In slow, precise tones, seldom consulting the written
opinion that lay before him, it was again Roberts who
spoke the decision of the majority.

This time that majority included Hughes. Six to three.
The Four, plus Roberts, plus Hughes, against Brandeis,
Stone, and Cardozo. Why did Hughes join the Four?
Perhaps some day he will tell us. It made no difference in

the result, but it avoided another five-to-four split, which had become notorious. Too much so. Six to three was better for the morale of the country. However, we do not know. Let us examine the opinion.

This was the occasion when the Court indulged itself in the history of Hamilton's versus Madison's views of what their Constitution meant.

The Constitution gave Congress the power 'to lay and collect Taxes, Duties, Imports and Excises, to pay the Debts and provide for the common Defence and general Welfare of the United States.' Madison took the view that the words 'general welfare' must refer to the specifically granted powers of Congress to regulate commerce, to coin money, etc. So, he said, the power to tax must be confined to these specifically granted powers otherwise committed to Congress. The difficulty with Madison's view is that taxation is a necessary incident anyway to the exercise of any power. Why, then, don't the words mean as much as they seem so clearly and concisely to say? Hamilton stated very clearly that he thought they did. He regarded it as an independent power which was limited only by the three purposes stated, to pay debts, to provide for the common defense, and to provide for the general welfare.[122]

The Court discussed these two opposing views, and plumped for Hamilton. Congress, it said, does have power to tax and spend for the general welfare generally, not only in aid of its other powers.

And so — No, that was only the beginning. That did not decide the case. That, you might almost say, was only to give the A.A.A. a fighting chance for its life. It did not follow, Roberts said, that this tax was valid. For this is not really a tax at all. It is part of a plan. So not the tax alone, but the plan was what they had to consider.

Stop for a moment, and let us consider. If Congress has power to lay taxes and spend money for the general welfare beyond its specifically granted powers, as Hamilton asserted, and as the Court had just agreed, why can it not require that the money be in fact spent for the purpose it was appropriated for? Congress has often made the payment of the money it has appropriated conditional upon the recipient doing what he was expected to do with it. For one example, it makes grants to state universities to teach agriculture.

Is there a difference here? So it seems. The A.A.A. did not offer simply a conditional grant to a farmer. It required him to sign a contract to reduce his acreage before he got the money.

There is an obvious difference, Roberts said. 'We are not here concerned with a conditional appropriation of money, nor with a provision that if certain conditions are not complied with the appropriation shall no longer be available. By the A.A.A. the amount of the tax is appropriated to be expended only in payment under contracts whereby the parties bind themselves to regulation by the Federal Government. There is an obvious difference between a statute stating the conditions upon which moneys shall be expended and one effective only upon assumption of a contractual obligation to submit to a regulation which otherwise could not be enforced.' [123]

So if Congress had preferred to hold up payments until the farmer had actually reduced his acreage, done it instead of only agreed to do it, the Act would have been constitutional? Hardly. Yet that is what Roberts implies.

Take another and entirely different tack. May Congress purchase a compliance which it is powerless to command? No, said Roberts. 'That is coercion by economic pressure. The asserted power of choice is illusory.' [124]

Suppose it was not illusory. Suppose you could convince Roberts that an individual cotton grower could in fact hold out. Would the A.A.A. then be constitutional? No, it would not. 'If the plan were one for purely voluntary co-operation,' Roberts went on, 'it would stand no better so far as federal power is concerned. At best it is a scheme for purchasing with federal funds submission to federal regulation of a subject reserved to the states. The Congress cannot invade state jurisdiction to compel individual action; no more can it purchase such action. Congress has no power to enforce its commands on the farmer to the ends sought by the Agricultural Adjustment Act. It must follow that it may not indirectly accomplish those ends by taxing and spending to purchase compliance.'

Why 'must' it follow? Because, said Roberts, the Constitution and the entire plan of our government negative any such use of the power to tax and to spend as the act undertakes to authorize.

There we are. What are Roberts' reasons?

The first is the argument *ad horrendum*. This clause of Section 8 of Article I would become the instrument for total subversion of the governmental powers reserved to the individual states. 'If the act before us,' he said, 'is a proper exercise of the federal taxing power, evidently the regulation of all industry throughout the United States may be accomplished by similar exercises of the same power. We have held in the Schechter Case that Congress has no power to regulate wages and hours of labor in a local business. If the government is right, this very end may be accomplished by appropriating money to be paid to employers from the federal treasury under contracts whereby they agree to comply with certain standards fixed by federal law or by contract.'

Why not? Because, said he, 'a possible result would be that every business group which thought itself under-privileged might demand that a tax be laid on its vendors or vendees, the proceeds to be appropriated to the redress of its deficiency of income.'

Roberts said he gave this illustration, not to suggest that any of the purposes of the A.A.A. were unworthy, but to demonstrate the scope of the principle for which it stood, and to test the principle by its applications, and 'to point out that, by the exercise of the asserted power, Congress would, in effect, under the pretext of exercising the taxing power, in reality accomplish prohibited ends.' And, he added, 'The supposed cases are no more improbable than would the present act have been deemed a few years ago.'

This brought Roberts to his second reason, the novelty of it. 'Until recently no suggestion of the existence of any such power in the Federal Government has been advanced. The expressions of the framers of the Constitution, the decisions of this court interpreting that instrument, and the writings of great commentators will be searched in vain for any suggestion that there exists in the clause under discussion or elsewhere in the Constitution, the author-ity whereby every provision and every fair implication from that instrument may be subverted, the independence of the individual states obliterated, and the United States converted into a central government exercising uncontrolled police power in every state of the Union, superseding all local control or regulation of the affairs or concerns of the states.'

The fact is, Roberts's reasons come down, simply enough, to one thing. This just Can't Be. It Must be Wrong. 'Hamilton himself, the leading advocate of broad interpretation of the power to tax and to appropriate for the general welfare, never suggested that any power granted by the Constitution could be used for the destruction of local self-government in the states. But to this fatal conclusion the doctrine contended for would inevitably lead. And its sole premise is that the makers of the Constitution, by a single clause, gave power to Congress to tear down the barriers, to invade the states' jurisdiction, and to become a parliament of the whole people, subject to no restrictions save such as are self imposed. The argument when seen in its true character and in the light of its inevitable results must be rejected.' [125] And it was. And for that reason.

Brandeis, Stone, and Cardozo dissented. Stone expressed their opinion. 'The power of courts to declare a statute unconstitutional is subject to two guiding principles of decision which ought never to be absent from judicial consciousness. One is that courts are concerned only with the power to enact statutes, not with their wisdom. The other is that while unconstitutional exercise of power by the executive and legislative branches of the government is subject to judicial restraint, the only check upon our own exercise of power is our own sense of self-restraint. For the removal of unwise laws from the statute books appeal not to the courts but to the ballot and to the processes of democratic government.'

Pause for one comment on this sentence, 'The only check upon *our own* exercise of power is *our own* sense of self restraint.' I have emphasized these words, for they are a direct retort to what Roberts had said about Congress, that it would 'become a parliament of the whole people, subject to no restrictions save such as are self-imposed.' [126] Roberts had got it from Pepper's argument, 'that Congress, originating as a federal legislature with limited powers, has somehow been transformed into a national parliament *subject to no restraint except self restraint.*' [127]

This is the kernel of the case. Here is a great power, a very great power indeed, exercised over agriculture. No one can point to any particular words in the Constitution which give Congress power to regulate agriculture. No one can point to any particular words which forbid Congress from doing what it did in the A.A.A. Pepper and Roberts do not trust Congress, and they are appalled at the strength of a nation, at Leviathan stirring and restrained by nothing but a sense of duty. To which Stone says, Brother, consider the restraint in your own bosom.

What is the answer when neither trusts the other, when the Court lacks faith in Congress and Congress does not trust the Court? That is matter for reflection. But I want now to go on with what Stone is saying, for it is one of our great dissents.

Stone went on, 'That the governmental power of the purse is a great one is not now for the first time announced. Every student of the history of government and economics is aware of its magnitude and of its existence in every civilized government. Both were well understood by the framers of the Constitution when they sanctioned the grant of the spending power to the federal government, and both were recognized by Hamilton and Story, whose views of the spending power as standing on a parity with the other powers specifically granted, have hitherto been generally accepted.

'The suggestion that it must now be curtailed by judicial fiat because it may be abused by unwise use hardly rises to the dignity of argument. So may judicial power be abused. "The power to tax is the power to destroy," but we do not, for that reason, doubt its existence, or hold that its efficacy is to be restricted by its incidental or collateral effects upon the states. The power to tax and spend is not without constitutional restraints. One restriction is that the purpose must be truly national. Another is that it may not be used to coerce action left to state control. Another is the conscience and patriotism of Congress and the Executive.'

'A tortured construction of the Constitution is not to be justified by recourse to extreme examples of reckless congressional spending which might occur if courts could not prevent — expenditures which, even if they could be thought to effect any national purpose, would be possible only by action of a legislature lost to all sense of public responsibility. Such suppositions are addressed to the mind accustomed to believe that it is the business of courts to sit in judgment on the wisdom of legislative action. Courts are not the only agency of government that must be assumed to have capacity to govern. Congress and the courts both unhappily may falter or be mistaken in the performance of their constitutional duty. But interpretation of our great charter of government which proceeds on any assumption that the responsibility for the preservation of our institutions is the exclusive concern of any one of the three branches of government, or that it alone can save them from destruction is far more likely, in the long run, "to obliterate the constituent members" of "an indestructible union of indestructible states" than the frank recognition that language, even of a constitution, may mean what it says: that the power to tax and spend includes the power to relieve a nation-wide economic maladjustment by conditional gifts of money.'

Is this a Court constrained in deciding a case to follow the Constitution rather than an act of Congress? No, these are men frightened by the power of the purse. And so, logically enough, they had to rest their decision, as they did, on the consequences, the 'fatal conclusion' to which the power of the purse must, they thought, lead. 'In its true character and in the light of its inevitable results' the power must be rejected. Appalled, too, by the novelty of it, they denied that Congress could use that power for ends which seemed to them fatal to the America they, and Mr. Pepper, loved.

If Congress were subject only to self-imposed restrictions, they, these Justices, were subject only to their own self-restraint, and when the America they loved was in peril, it was no time for self-restraint. They sprang to its defense and threw all the weight of the power and prestige of their Court into the breach. Like good soldiers they sacrificed themselves. Better if they had not tried to sacrifice the Court, too. Lacking faith in Congress, they broke faith with the Court. They forgot what Holmes feared they would forget, and what Stone, Brandeis, and Cardozo were vainly reminding them of. 'It must be remembered,' Holmes had said and Stone quoted, 'that legislators are the ultimate guardians of the liberties and welfare of the people in quite as great a degree as the courts.'

A spectator in the courtroom, after the decision was announced, said, 'It seemed to me the Court showed signs of the usual hangover after a lynching.'

Their victim, however, didn't stay dead. Congress promptly passed another act. They called it a Soil Conservation Act. It forbade the Secretary from making any agreement with the farmers; they had to reduce their acreage, in the interests of soil conservation, before they got their money. And the appropriation of the money was made out of general funds in the Treasury. It is a happy speculation whether the majority would have held that act unconstitutional. No one will ever know. It was never given the chance. For, Nature in her heedless way, aided ironically by the very abuse of the soil when the excessive surpluses had been piled up, reduced the crops herself. The A.A.A. and Nature, between them, had nearly doubled the farmers' earnings. How in 1937 fair weather produced more surpluses, and how Congress passed another A.A.A. in 1938, is another story.[128]

Coal Control

When the N.R.A. went overboard, Congress itself enacted a code for the soft coal industry. That is what the Guffey Coal Control Act amounted to. Soft coal was a key industry. It was also a depressed industry. Something had to be done about it.

The codes under the N.R.A. were enforced by making any violation of them a misdemeanor. The Guffey Coal

Control Act took a different line. It began by laying 'an excise tax' of 15 per cent on the sale price of all coal produced, unless the producer 'accepted' and 'acted in compliance with' the Act. If the producer accepted the Act, 90 per cent of the tax was remitted.

The Act had two parts. One concerned the prices to be charged for coal. The other concerned the wages to be paid to miners. Take the wage part first.

The President was to appoint a Labor Board with authority to settle disputes between the coal companies and the unions. Unions which were to be guaranteed the right of collective bargaining, just as they had been in the N.R.A. Whenever, in any district, maximum hours or minimum wages were agreed to between two-thirds of the companies, voting by tonnage, and one-half of the unions, voting by workers, those hours and those wages were to be compulsory on all other companies. If they did not comply, they were liable to this 15 per cent penalty on all the coal they produced. All this, of course, would take time.

On the other hand, the price part was to go into effect at once. It did not have to wait for agreements between the companies and the unions. District boards, as soon as they could be set up, were to classify coals and fix their respective prices, not too low to yield a return per net ton of the average of the total costs in the district, not so high that they would yield more than a reasonable profit. Prices had to be 'just and equitable.' If the companies thought they were not, they could get a review in the courts.

This, you will recall, was the act which President Roosevelt had urged Congress to pass notwithstanding any doubts of its validity. He had written to a member of the House Ways and Means Committee [129] saying, 'I hope your committee will not permit doubt as to constitutionality, however reasonable, to block the suggested legislation.'

You will remember, too, that the case in which the Court held the Act unconstitutional was Mr. Carter's suit against his coal company.[130] The next day after the President signed the Act [131] the Carter board of directors met and voted to accept the act, on account of the penalty, though they believed that it was unconstitutional and also 'economically unsound.' They then called a special meeting of their stockholders who voted to approve their action.[132] Then Carter, the president of the Company, brought suit to enjoin his company from paying the tax. Note, before we go further, that no injunction could issue unless the Court found the whole act invalid. If any of it was valid, the company's failure to comply with that part of it would prevent the remission of the 90 per cent. Carter had to kill the whole thing, if he was to get his injunction.

The constitutional power on which Congress had relied was the power to regulate interstate commerce. For wherever soft coal is mined, almost all of it is shipped off into other States. That was true of over 97 per cent of what the Carter Coal Company mined in West Virginia. Congress thought this warranted a regulation of the wages of the West Virginia miners.

The Court thought quite otherwise. Sutherland wrote the opinion.

It was not hard to hold the wages provisions beyond the power of Congress, given the Schechter decision. There is a clear distinction, Sutherland said, between mining and commerce, 'Mining brings the subject matter of com-

merce into existence. Commerce disposes of it.' In the
Schechter case, he said, the poultry, although shipped
from another state, had come to rest in the state of its
destination, and was no longer in a current or flow of interstate commerce. 'There the flow had ceased. Here it had
not begun. The difference is not one of substance. The
applicable principle is the same.'

There remained the price-fixing provisions. Unless
they, too, were bad, Carter could not get his injunction.
And the majority did not say they were. They took another line. They said, 'The necessity of considering the
question of their constitutionality will depend upon
whether they are separable from the labor provisions so
that they can stand independently.'

Congress perhaps had foreseen, at any rate Congress
had tried to take care of, this eventuality. Section fifteen,
near the end of the Act, read, 'If any provision of this Act
. . . is held invalid, the remainder of the Act . . . shall not
be affected thereby.'

Yes, said Sutherland, but this is 'not an inexorable
command.' What was the intent of the law makers? he
asked himself, and answered, 'Perhaps a fair approach to
a solution of the problem is to suppose that while the bill
was pending in Congress a motion to strike out the labor
provisions had prevailed, and to inquire whether in that
event the statute shall be so construed as to justify the
conclusion that Congress, notwithstanding, probably
would not have passed the price fixing provisions of the
code.' Please mark the *probably*.

Sutherland then examined the act, and continued,
'Thus, the primary contemplation of the act is stabiliza-
tion of the industry through the regulation of labor *and* the

regulation of prices; for, since both were adopted, we must conclude that both were thought essential. The regulations of labor on the one hand and prices on the other furnish mutual aid and support; and their associated force — not one or the other but both combined — was deemed by Congress to be necessary to the end sought. The statutory mandate for a code upheld by two legs at once suggests the improbability that Congress would have assented to a code supported by only one.' And he concluded, 'The two are so woven together as to render the probability plain enough that uniform prices, in the opinion of Congress, could not be fairly fixed or effectively regulated, without also regulating these elements of labor which enter so largely into the cost of production.'

Please continue to keep one eye on the 'probability.' For Sutherland went on, 'What authority has this court, by construction, to convert the *manifest* purpose of Congress to regulate production by the mutual operation and interaction of fixed ways and fixed prices into a purpose to regulate the subject by the operation of the latter alone? The conclusion is *unavoidable* that the price-fixing provisions of the code are so related to and dependent upon the labor provisions as conditions, considerations or compensations, as to make clearly probable that the latter being held bad, the former would not have been passed. The price-fixing provisions of the code are thus disposed of without coming to the question of their constitutionality.' [133]

These are Sutherland's words, but the italics are not Sutherland's. They indicate how he stepped himself up to the point where he did not have to answer the question whether the price-fixing provisions were constitutional.

The fact is, they were constitutional. The minority,

Hughes, Cardozo, Stone, and Brandeis made that clear in their dissenting opinions. Cardozo went to some pains, Hughes was all but abrupt in his demonstration.

Accept the judgment of the majority that the wages provisions were invalid. The minority did not deny they were. Accept the opinion of the minority that the price-fixing provisions were valid. The majority would not say they were not, and four years later the Court rested the validity of the Act of 1937 on what Hughes and Cardozo here said.[134] But people did think that Congress, if it chose, could enact one without the other. Congress did its best to do just that. Congress said that if any provision of the Act was held invalid the rest should not be affected. It would be hard to speak more plainly. Cardozo said, the lawmakers 'announced with all the directness possible for words that they would keep what they could have if they could not have the whole.'[135] Hughes said, 'I do not think that the question of separability should be determined by trying to imagine what Congress would have done if certain provisions found to be invalid were excised. The question does not call for speculation of that sort but rather for an inquiry whether the provisions are inseparable by virtue of inherent character — by reason of an inextricable tie.'[136]

The two parts were certainly not inextricable. Take railroad rates. Their regulation has never been thought to carry with it the necessity of fixing wages. Moreover, here prices and wages were to be regulated by different bodies, and in different ways. More than that, they were to go into effect at different times. The district boards were to start fixing prices at once, hours and wages were left to abide the agreement of two-thirds of the companies and the unions. That would take time. They might even never be. There might never be two-thirds in agreement. In the meantime the price-fixing would be going on and prices fixed.

How do you suggest Congress could have persuaded the majority that it meant what it said?

Minimum Wages

It was a bit ironical that in the battle between the Old Court and the New Deal the Court's lines should break over what was not New Deal at all. It was not surprising. For it would be a great mistake to think of the New Deal as really new. The bulk of its strength lay in the past, in the great head of long overdue reforms backing up behind it. The Old Guard in the Court had been fighting maximum hours and minimum wages for a generation. When they held the New York minimum wage act unconstitutional, in June, 1936, just before the conventions met for the elections to be held that coming autumn they won their last fight. Indeed, because they won that fight, at that particular time, their line broke. They had stretched a rubber band too far.

Why is a statute fixing a minimum wage unconstitutional? Properly told, that is a story which would contain most of the constitutional facts of life. Briefly, it is like this.

The Fifth Amendment laid the prohibition on the Federal government that 'no person shall be deprived of life, liberty, or property, without due process of law.' To everybody at that time, including the fathers and founders, this meant fair and traditional methods of procedure, your right to a hearing, your right to have notice of the hearing, your right to a fair trial, etc. It still means that. In the Fourteenth Amendment, which was adopted after the Civil War, in 1868, the same prohibition was laid upon the state governments. And then Due Process of Law began to mean something more, no less than all the natural inalienable rights that man is heir to, our absolutes, and among them, one of them, was the right to pursue your trade or calling as unmolested as possible in this bright and bustling world.

The era of Big Business was beginning, an era of competition among powerful and capable men who did not want to be interfered with. They were very successful and they were very sure of themselves. Their ideology was Darwinian, not Eighteenth Century. Darwinism, said Henry Adams in his *Education*, in the chapter by that name and dated 1867–1868, 'was the very best substitute for religion; a safe, conservative, practical, thoroughly Common-Law deity.' Darwinism and Evolution. If man belonged to the animal kingdom, he, too, was subject to its laws. Not only subject to them, but best ruled by them, and by them alone. If the world was wicked, there was nothing to do about it. You could not change its nature. If it was ill-arranged, it could best arrange itself. A sound religion for successful men.

Spencer became their intellectual tutor. As he said himself, his two best friends in this country were Andrew Carnegie and a publicist named Edward Livingston Youmans.[137] The Darwinism which Spencer expounded gave new grounds for your right to pursue your lawful business, the less molested the better by people who thought they knew more than Nature had taught you or you Nature.

John D. Rockefeller put it very neatly in one of his little Sunday-school sermons. 'The growth of a large business is merely the survival of the fittest. The American Beauty rose can be produced in the splendor and fragrance which bring cheer to the beholder only by sacrificing the early buds which grow up around it. This is not an evil tendency in business. It is merely the working out of a law of Nature and a law of God.' [138]

To Rockefeller this was an eminently fitting subject for a Sunday-school talk, or a sermon for that matter. To him and his co-religionists it was a law of God as well as a law of Nature, divine as well as zoölogical and botanical, which was working itself out in him, and his success in business and his monopoly in oil was its flower, its American Beauty. Its divine attribute was the contribution of the Puritans, to whom all of life, including business, was an opportunity which it was a man's moral and religious duty to exploit. Through the Puritans, business had taken over the name of a virtue, industry.[139] Profits were our human measure of the fulfillment of that duty. No doubt Rockefeller made his money with the same religious zeal with which later, in a different season of opinion, he gave it away. Of course he had to be as free to do one as the other. Liberty of contract was freedom to worship God as well as to sign a legal document. If you had suggested that it was as irrational, and perhaps even as wrong, to take acquisitiveness for your basic instinct as it would have been to accept sex, Rockefeller would not have agreed with you.[140]

In 1905 came the Lochner case.[141] A New York statute fixed maximum hours for bakers. The Court held it unconstitutional, five to four, because New York was interfering with Liberty of Contract, the right of the baker to work more than sixty hours a week. It was here that those who did not agree first became articulate. Holmes in this case gave the great dissent. If ever a dissent was in fact a precedent, it is this one. Here is all of it, dropping only the few citations.

'I regret sincerely that I am unable to agree with the judgment on this case and that I think it my duty to express my dissent.

'This case is decided upon an economic theory which a large part of the country does not entertain. If it were a question whether I agreed with that theory, I should strive to study it further and long before making up my mind. But I do not conceive that to be my duty, because I strongly believe that my agreement or disagreement has nothing to do with the right of a majority to embody their opinions in law. It is settled by various decisions of this Court that State constitutions and State laws may regulate life in many ways which we as legislators might think as injudicious or, if you like, as tyrannical as this, and which equally with this interfere with the liberty to contract. Sunday laws and usury laws are ancient examples. A more modern one is the prohibition of lotteries. The liberty of a citizen to do as he likes so long as he does not interfere with the liberty of others to do the same, which has been a shibboleth for some well-known writers, is interfered with by school laws, by the Post Office, by every State or municipal institution which takes his money for purposes thought desirable, though he likes it or not. The Fourteenth Amendment does not enact Mr. Herbert Spencer's *Social Statics*. The other day we sustained the Massachusetts vaccination law. United States and State statutes and decisions cutting down the liberty to contract by way of combination are familiar to this Court. Two years ago we upheld the prohibition of sales of stock on margins or for future delivery in the constitution of California. The decision sustaining an eight-hour law for miners is still recent.

'Some of these laws embody convictions or prejudices which judges are likely to share. Some may not. But a constitution is not intended to embody a particular economic theory, whether of paternalism and the organic relation of the citizen to the State or of laissez-faire. It is made for people of fundamentally differing views, and the accident of our finding certain opinions natural and familiar or novel and even shocking ought not to conclude our judgment upon the question whether statutes embodying them conflict with the Constitution of the United States.

'General propositions do not decide concrete cases. The decision will depend on a judgment or intuition more subtle than any articulate major premise. But I think that the proposition just stated, if it is accepted, will carry us far toward the end. Every opinion tend to become a law. I think that the word liberty in the Fourteenth Amendment is perverted when it is held to prevent the natural outcome of a dominant opinion, unless it can be said that rational and fair man necessarily would admit that the statute proposal would infringe fundamental principles as they have been understood by the traditions of our people and our law. It does not need research to show that no such sweeping condemnation can be passed upon the statute before us. A reasonable man might think it a proper measure on the score of health. Men whom I certainly could not pronounce unreasonable would uphold it as a first instalment of a general regulation of the hours of work. Whether in the latter aspect it would be open to the charge of inequality I think it unnecessary to discuss.'

During the next twenty years the Lochner decision was allowed to earn what Holmes later called 'a well-earned repose.' A ten-hour law for women in Oregon was not held void.[142] That was the Muller case, in which Brandeis presented his factual brief. In the Bunting case time and a half for overtime over ten hours was upheld.[143] Then, in 1923, came the Adkins decision, in a subtle transition from maximum hours to minimum wages.

This Adkins case concerned the District of Columbia minimum wage statute for women, passed five years before in 1918. It fixed wages for women at rates which were adequate 'to supply the necessary cost of living, to maintain them in good health, and to protect their morals.' It was held unconstitutional. Brandeis was on the Court, but he took no part because he had been preparing the case for argument when he was appointed. Frankfurter took over the completion of another of Brandeis' long briefs on the facts. Holmes dissented, of course. Taft dissented, and when Taft dissents, that is news.[144] He could see no constitutional difference between minimum wages and maximum hours, and also he thought the Bunting decision controlled the case.

One paragraph from Sutherland's opinion for the majority will be peculiarly pertinent to us. 'The feature of this statute which, perhaps more than any other, puts upon it the stamp of invalidity is that it exacts from the employer an arbitrary payment for a purpose and upon a basis having no causal connection with his business, or the contract or the work which the employee engages to do. The declared basis is not the value of the services rendered but the extraneous circumstances that the employee needs to get a prescribed sum of money to insure her subsistence, health, and morals. *A statute to pay the value of the services rendered, even to pay with fair relation to the extent of the benefit obtained from the service, would be understandable.* But a statute which prescribes payment without regard to any of these things and solely with relation to circumstances apart from the contract of employment, the business affected by it, and the work done under it cannot be allowed to stand under the Constitution of the United States.'

Sutherland did not italicize the next to the last sentence, but it is necessary to do so, because some sixteen state legislatures immediately took it as a hint that a minimum wage law based on the fair value of the services rendered would be held valid. Of course, they were wise to try it, but they were a little simple if they thought that Sutherland meant that he would hold constitutional anything he could understand. They thought he was using 'understandable' as a synonym for 'reasonable.' Of course, he meant no such thing. Do you think Spencer would have said that the 'value' of anything, services included, could possibly have been determined by statute, or by anything but the law of supply and demand? It was an unfortunate remark and it later proved slightly embarrassing to the Court.

Twice during the next dozen years, once in 1925 and again in 1926, without giving reasons, the Supreme Court held acts invalid which simply fixed a minimum amount for women's wages. Arizona forbade anyone to employ a female in any store, office, shop, restaurant, laundry, or manufactory at a weekly wage of less than $16. Arkansas declared it unlawful to pay any female worker with six months' experience less than $1.25 a day, and inexperienced females less than $1.00 a day. Both these statutes were held invalid by the Court without more comment than a reference to the Adkins decision. And, as we have noted, Holmes joined without further dissent, respecting the precedent that had been established.

That was the situation in 1935, when Joseph Tipaldo, who ran the Spotlight Laundry in Brooklyn, was caught making false entries in his time-book. His idea was to make it appear that he was paying his women the minimum wage in New York for women who worked in laundries. Tipaldo was indicted on both counts — for the false entries and also for paying his women less than the minimum wage. He protested that the minimum wage law was unconstitutional. He simply referred to the Adkins decision in the United States Supreme Court which in 1923 had held the District of Columbia minimum wage void as a violation of the Due Process Clause.

New York was one of those who had taken the hint and its minimum wage law for women began by a declaration against any wage for women which was 'both (1) less than fair and reasonable value of the services rendered and (2) less than sufficient to meet the minimum cost of living necessary to health.' If the wages in laundries were enough to live on but below what the work was worth, that was legal. If they were not enough to live on, but yet all the work was worth, that was legal too. But, if they were neither, then they were 'oppressive and unreasonable' and illegal.

A Wage Board of three employers, three employees, and three disinterested persons were to fix minimum wages for the different industries and localities and the wage it fixed — mark this — was to be 'fairly and reasonably commensurate with the value of the service or class of service rendered.' That was what Sutherland had said 'would be understandable.'

Tipaldo was convicted, and appealed to the Court of Appeals, the highest court in New York. There he won four to three. The four simply followed the decision in the Adkins case. They said, 'We do not see wherein this act differs materially from the act of Congress ruled upon in *Adkins* v. *Children's Hospital*, wherein it was held that the Minimum Wage Act of 1918 was an unconstitutional interference with liberty of contract. The interpretation of the Federal Constitution by the United States Supreme Court is binding upon us; we are in duty bound to follow its decisions unless they are inappropriate. We find no material difference between the act of Congress and this act of the New York State Legislature.'

You will notice that the New York court had made a mistake. In fact, there was a material difference, just the difference which Sutherland had said would make a minimum wage 'understandable,' between the test for the minimum wage in the Adkins case and the test by which the Labor Board was to fix the minimum wage. The Board had to fix a wage that was fairly and reasonably commensurate with the service rendered. That did not have to be a living wage. The New York court had misconstrued its own statute.

Tipaldo's case came up on *certiorari* and was argued on April 28 and 29, 1936. The Court heard his attorney and

the attorneys for the State of New York. It allowed Dean
Acheson, now Under Secretary of State, to appear on behalf of the States of Connecticut, Illinois, Massachusetts,
New Hampshire, New Jersey, and Rhode Island, for they
had similar statutes to defend.

On June 1, 1936, it was decided, five to four, that the
New York minimum wage law was unconstitutional.
Butler wrote the opinion for the majority, and this is how
he did it.[145]

This appeal, Butler said, was sought on the ground that
the New York statute could be distinguished from that
which had been held invalid in the Adkins case. That was
the only question, therefore, before the Court. 'No application has been made for reconsideration of the constitutional question there decided.' The State of New York 'is
not entitled and does not ask to be heard upon the question whether the Adkins Case should be overruled.'

We've got to examine that. For if Butler was right,
the majority could duck the main issue, which was simply
this — should the Adkins decision be overruled?

What New York's petition for review had said was this:
'The circumstances prevailing under which the New York
law was enacted call for a reconsideration of the Adkins
Case in the light of the New York act and conditions
aimed to be remedied thereby.' Is not that asking for 'a
reconsideration of the constitutional question' decided in
the Adkins case?

But suppose the lawyers had been stupid enough not to
ask the Court to overrule this thirteen-year-old decision.
The validity of the laws of sixteen states was in issue. Is
the Court to be bound to continue in error until the next
case comes up because the lawyers have not asked the

Court to correct it? Perhaps yes, if we are dealing with private litigation. Then counsel has simply mishandled the case for his client. It may be that in private litigation, the plaintiff should himself and alone decide what issues he wants tried. For he is the litigant and it is his litigation. But here we are dealing with something more than private litigation. When what the Court is really doing amounts in fact to a determination of governmental policy, it is preposterous to let Tipaldo's choice of a lawyer frame the issue. Two years later the Court took quite a different attitude. In the Tompkins case [146] it overruled a hundred-year-old decision which neither party had even questioned, far less argued. Then it was Butler and McReynolds who protested and asked for a rehearing, and were denied.[147]

Butler's ruling narrowed the issue to a purely technical question. Could this New York statute be distinguished from the District of Columbia statute which had been held void in the Adkins case? As we have seen, it could. But the New York court had misconstrued the New York law. It had said there was 'no material difference.' This Court, Butler said, is without power to put a different construction upon a state enactment from that adopted by the highest court of the state. The meaning of the statute as fixed by the decision of the New York court must be accepted, he said, just as if that meaning had itself been expressed in the statute. 'We are not at liberty to consider petitioner's arguments based on the construction repudiated by that court.'

So, not having been asked to overrule the Adkins decision, the Court simply followed it and held the New York statute void.

They had to say something. They couldn't brush off so

easily the four dissenting Justices who were going to attack the Adkins decision, which was almost their own decision. Sutherland had written the opinion. Van Devanter, McReynolds, and Butler had all been on the Court and voted for it. McKenna, who had made the fifth then, was dead. Roberts was taking his place. So Butler was a little on the defensive and he went on to defend it. We don't need to follow him.

Hughes and Stone both wrote dissents, and Brandeis, Stone, and Cardozo joined in both of them. Perhaps Hughes did not want to join in what Stone said, because Stone, as he had in the A.A.A. case, again spoke bitterly. His dissent is too long to give in full. It is too good not to give some of it. Skip if you must, but not the last sentence.

'There is grim irony in speaking of the freedom of contract of those who, because of their economic necessities, give their service for less than is needful to keep body and soul together. No one doubts that the presence in the community of a large number of those compelled by economic necessity to accept a wage less than is needful for subsistence is a matter of grave public concern, the more so when, as has been demonstrated here, it tends to produce ill health, immorality and deterioration of the race.

'The fact that at one time or another Congress and the Legislatures of seventeen States, and the legislative bodies of twenty-one foreign countries, including Great Britain and its four Commonwealths have found wage regulation is an appropriate corrective for serious social and economic maladjustments growing out of inequality in bargaining power, precludes, for me, any assumption that it is a remedy beyond the bounds of reason.

'It is difficult to imagine any grounds, other than our

own personal economic predilections, for saying that the contract of employment is any the less an appropriate subject of legislation than are scores of others, in dealing with which this court has held that Legislatures may curtail individual freedom in the public interest.

'In the years which have intervened since the Adkins case we have had opportunity to learn that a wage is not always the resultant of free bargaining between employers and employees; that it may be one forced upon employees by their economic necessities and upon employers by the most ruthless of their competitors. We have had opportunity to perceive more clearly that a wage insufficient to support the worker does not visit its consequence upon him alone; that it may affect profoundly the entire economic structure of society and, in any case, that it casts on every taxpayer, and on government itself, the burden of solving the problems of poverty, subsistence, health and morals of large numbers in the community. Because of their nature and extent these are public problems. A generation ago they were for the individual to solve; today they are the burden of the nation.

'It is not for the courts to resolve doubts whether the remedy by wage regulation is as efficacious as many believe, or is better than some other, or is better even than the blind operation of uncontrolled economic forces. The Legislature must be free to choose unless government is to be rendered impotent. The Fourteenth Amendment has no more embedded in the Constitution our preference for some particular set of economic beliefs than it has adopted, in the name of liberty, the system of theology which we may happen to approve.'

Here was another nut Congress could not crack, another

block in the road round which there was no detour. For, like the distinction between direct and indirect, liberty of contract was an abstraction. Theological, Stone called it. There was no circumventing that until the Court was de-Darwined and un-Spencered. These two abstractions were insoluble in any legislative liquid. And the theory on which the A.A.A. had been held unconstitutional seemed to be insoluble in any liquid at all. For there the Court had said, simply, that it was against the spirit of the Constitution. That was that, so long as that spirit could keep its feet.

The Election of 1936 and the President's Court Plan

While the Justices were deliberating minimum wages, the Party Leaders were deliberating the coming campaign. It was the election of 1936. Soon after the Court announced its decision on minimum wages, which was on June 1, it adjourned and the Justices scattered to their summer homes, to which sacks of *certiorari* petitions, next year's cases, would soon be following them. Already the Republican leaders were moving toward Chicago and preparing for the convention.

It was clear that they would have to support the Court, and defend what the majority had done. A loyal opposition, loyal to the spirit of opposition as well as to their country, they could do no other. 'The New Deal,' the Republican platform said, 'has insisted on the passage of laws contrary to the Constitution. The integrity and authority of the Supreme Court has been flouted.' But those who drafted the platform must have started their work before June 1 when the minimum wage decision came down. For they had said, 'We pledge ourselves to support the adoption of state laws to protect women and children with respect to maximum hours, minimum wages, and working conditions. *We believe that this can be done within the Constitution as it now stands.*'

Unless this was written before the Court's decision, anticipating a different result, either they were committing the party to a court plan of its own or their dreams betrayed them. Landon knew better. As soon as he was nominated he telegraphed the Convention, 'I hope the opinion of the Convention is correct that the aims which you have in mind may be attained within the Constitution as it now stands. But if that opinion should prove to be erroneous, I want you to know that if nominated and elected, I shall favor a constitutional amendment permitting the states to adopt such legislation as may be necessary adequately to protect women and children in the matter of maximum hours, minimum wages, and working conditions.'

President Roosevelt and the Democrats, on the other hand, made it quite clear that the New Deal was going to go on. In the keynote speech at the Democratic Convention Senator Barkley quoted from Lincoln's first inaugural. Let me repeat one sentence. 'If the policy of the Government on vital questions affecting the whole people is to be irrevocably fixed by the decisions of the Supreme Court the instant they are made in ordinary litigation between parties in personal actions, the people will have ceased to be their own rulers, having to that extent practically resigned their government into the hands of that eminent tribunal.'

The fact is, the Court had created more of a situation

than Landon's amendment could cure. In addition to the legislation that had already been invalidated, there was the Social Security Act and the National Labor Relations Act. Both had already been enacted, already on their way to the gallows. For it was pretty plain that this majority in the Court would spare neither of them. When they did come before the Court later, that was amply verified, but in dissenting opinions. And there was more, too, on the New Deal program that had not yet been enacted. There was the Wages and Hours Act. The President was to send it to Congress in the coming May, 1937, saying that 'goods produced under conditions which do not meet the rudimentary standards of decency should be regarded as contraband and ought not to be allowed to pollute the channels of interstate trade.' To make it constitutional not only these decisions but also an eighteen-year-old case, *Hammer* v. *Dagenhart*, which had set aside a Child Labor Act, would all have to be reversed. For the Wages and Hours Act would include the old Child Labor Act, and go further, not only abolish child labor but set minimum wages and maximum hours for nearly all labor.

The old suggestion was made again that the Constitution should be amended to give Congress the power to override the Court's decision, like overriding a presidential veto. This had been Theodore Roosevelt's remedy. Chief Justice Marshall, as we know, had gone so far as to suggest it, as preferable at any rate to impeachment.

Lloyd Garrison, then dean of the Wisconsin Law School, suggested a further grant of power to Congress over all matters of 'general economic welfare.' But what did that mean? It was an outsize phrase, which would call for the exercise of great self-restraint by Congress, and anyhow, as Professor Corwin asked, 'What would be the point in adding "new" powers to Congress by constitutional amendment, if these powers were to be exposed to the same principles of construction that made them necessary?' [148]

Had the country best wait until one or two of the justices died? The difficulty there was Brandeis. He was so old he might be the first. And Stone was then ill. Or should the country simply suffer it out until one of them changed his mind?

On October 12, a few weeks *before* the election, the Court denied a motion to reargue the New York Minimum Wage decision.[149] Within two weeks *after* the election there was a division in the Court which gave some reason to think that the Court might have had a change of heart.[150]

It was in a case involving the New York Unemployment Compensation Act, which had been argued the day *after* election, November 11, 1936. When the decision came down on November 23, Stone was still ill. So there were only eight Justices left to vote. The Chief Justice announced that the Court was evenly divided. All the Court said, all it could say, was 'Affirmed by an equally divided court.' There was no opinion because there was no majority, and so no decision. The decision below in the Court of Appeals of New York, which had been five to two in favor of the Unemployment Act, therefore stood.[151] But it showed that one of the five had shifted. Otherwise, with Stone absent, the vote would have been five to three. Who was it? Why was it? The election returns? Or some subtlety of legal distinction? No one knew and few had the wit to guess. Meanwhile, the President was worrying over the problem. Finally he lost patience. On

February 5, 1937, he suddenly announced his court plan.

The Constitution does not say how many judges there shall be. That is left to Congress to say, from time to time. Congress has power to enlarge the Court, as Congress pleases, as freely as the British King can make peers and enlarge the House of Lords. There is no doubt about that.

The President's plan was that when a judge had served ten years on the Court and had passed the age of seventy, he could retire on full pay, but if he didn't retire, a new judge should be appointed, up to a total Court of fifteen. This was an invitation to six of them, all but Roberts, Stone, and Cardozo.

To see precisely what the plan amounted to, put yourself in the seat of one of the majority justices. You are over seventy and you have served for more than ten years. You can retire on full pay. If you don't, you are to be given an associate, whose mind, you are well assured, will not chime with yours. If you do, he will take your place. Your feelings are hurt, but aren't your feelings your own concern?

What was it that prevented our Chief Executive and our Chief Justice from talking over a matter which so strongly concerned the nation? Is there any other country in the world where the highest judicial officer cannot talk to the head of the government? Surely in England the Prime Minister and the Lord Chancellor would already have had long talks about any such proposal. Then they would have sent for the Lord Chief Justice to join them.

Why, here in the United States, would it have been naïve to suggest that the Chief Justice go to the President and say, 'Mr. President, my court, as we both well know,

is performing a governmental as well as a judicial function.
I find it as difficult as you do to get it to perform both
functions. You have lost your temper, and I don't blame
you. But no more than I, do you want to impair its dignity. There is no more reason why we should not consult
upon the best interests of this country than any other two
public officials with a sense of responsibility. Let us consult about a reconstruction of the Court. If you will give
me your thoughts on new appointments as candidly as I
will give you my thoughts on resignations, perhaps we
may be able to bring this Court, our Court, which is as
much yours as it is mine, into a position where its duty
will be better done and its dignity better secured. You
have made this harder for me to do by forcing the issue.
I had already recognized it. But the question whether I
should have come to you or you to me is trivial in comparison with the occasion. What can you and I now do?'

The impropriety of the President's Court Plan stands on
precisely the same basis as the impropriety of such a conference between the President and the Chief Justice. It
would be dirty business to pack a Court for the purpose of
getting a reversal of a decision between private parties.
But when the Court, in the course of private litigation before it, asserts and exercises governmental functions, then
its business is political and may properly be so regarded
and properly so treated. Can we have it both ways? Can
we wish governmental functions on a law court and yet
insist that it remain nothing but a law court?

No such conversation took place. Hughes had the situation in hand. He had no more reason to go to the President than the President had to propose his plan, and that
was why the President's plan failed. This was fortunate,

for the event was to give a better solution than its success ever could have. In the event, the country found itself in the happy position of one who had eaten his cake and had it, too. The country had its way and it still had its Court. Arguably it might be even a stronger Court. For as the old majority yielded and the country got what it wanted, the new majority took over what was no less a law court now shining with the flattery which the opponents of the plan had been showering on it. It was the old majority that took the blame for the offending decisions. They were glad to do it, for they were proud of them, though few of the opponents of the President's plan tried to defend them. What they were defending was the Court, not five men, not nine men, but the sanctity of a court of law.

This happy event was the fruit of what must have been a good deal of meditation on the part of one man. The Court owes a great deal to Roberts. There is no need of assuming that he had laid down his conscience as other men had laid down their lives, for his country. He had quite simply reverted to his former attitude in the Nebbia case three years before.

It is not the first time in history that the welfare of a country has depended upon the conscience and wisdom of one man. The defeat of the President's plan was plainly due to Roberts's shift, and his new loyalty to the new majority which he made. It is true that the plan might have been passed by the Senate if Senator Wheeler had not held it up. That was early, before the fact of the shift and the new majority had become clear. It is true that the delay gave the opponents of the plan time to prepare, time for the American Bar Association to organize an opposition, time for the big New York law firms to open an office in Washington and pool their juniors to gather statistics and write up briefs, time for the Senate Committee to hold enough public hearings. For there was a tremendous amount of opposition. It is true also that the President did not introduce his plan as candidly or as forcefully as he should have or could have. He admitted so later himself. That was a mistake, and it set the Chief Justice to writing a letter to the Senate Committee, in which Brandeis joined. Nor did he put the bill into the best hands at the start. When he finally persuaded Senator Robinson to take charge of it, Senator Robinson died suddenly and tragically of a heart attack. By then it was all but too late, the plan had all but collapsed. By that time it was becoming clearer that nothing had to be done. The situation was taking care of itself. The fact is, the Court had been taking care of itself ever since the election, and that is what the Chief Justice should have told the President.

In the middle of December, 1936, another minimum wage law, this time from the State of Washington, was argued. This was the Parrish case.[152]

The Washington statute was an old one. It had been in force for twenty-three years. How it had got by for so long is a wonder. It had been drafted ten years before Sutherland had dropped the hint in the Adkins case that a minimum fixed at the fair value of the service was constitutionally 'understandable.' So, unlike the New York act, this Washington act unblushingly required its minimum wage to be adequate to supply the necessary cost of living and to maintain the workers in health. It was just as bad as it could be under the rule of the Adkins case. No use, then, in trying to distinguish it from the District of Columbia act.

The Court must have conferred on it the next Saturday, a couple of months before the President's announcement, but we do not know when it came to a final vote. Probably before February 5. If so, the plan had nothing to do with the decision. But something had. For there was a new majority, Hughes, Brandeis, Stone, Cardozo, and *Roberts*. And of course they held the Washington law valid. Hughes wrote the opinion.

'We think,' said he, 'that the question which was not deemed to be open in the Tipaldo case is open and is necessarily presented here. The importance of the question in which many states having similar laws are concerned, the close division by which the decision in the *Adkins* case was reached, and the economic conditions which have supervened, and in the light of which the reasonableness of the exercise of the protective power of the state must be considered, make it not only appropriate but, we think imperative that in deciding the present case the subject should receive fresh consideration.' [158]

Then the Chief Justice went directly to the point, freedom of contract. 'What is this freedom? The Constitution does not speak of freedom of contract. It speaks of liberty and prohibits the deprivation of liberty without due process of law. In prohibiting that deprivation the Constitution does not recognize an absolute and uncontrollable liberty. Liberty in each of its phases has its history and connotation. But the liberty safeguarded is liberty in a social organization which requires the protection of law against the evils which menace the health, safety, morals, and welfare of the people.'

He went on, 'There is an additional and compelling consideration which recent economic experience has brought into a strong light. The exploitation of a class of workers who are in an unequal position with respect to bargaining power and are thus relatively defenseless against the denial of a living wage is not only detrimental to their health and well-being but casts a direct burden for their support upon the community. What these workers lose in wages the taxpayers are called upon to pay. The bare cost of living must be met. We may take judicial notice of the unparalleled demands for relief which arose during the recent period of depression and still continue to an alarming extent despite the degree of economic recovery which has been achieved. It is unnecessary to cite official statistics to establish what is of common knowledge through the length and breadth of the land.'

Thus the new majority. It was Sutherland who spoke for the old, in this their first open defeat. He and not Butler, for it was he who had delivered the Adkins opinion, thirteen years before. Symbolically, perhaps, to show that they had not budged. A satisfactory abstraction cannot budge, certainly not for supervening economic conditions.

'It is urged,' Sutherland said, 'that the question involved should now receive fresh consideration, among other reasons, because of "the economic conditions which have supervened."' And he went on to take the same position which his three colleagues, Van Devanter, McReynolds, and Butler had taken when zoning laws were upheld ten years before. 'The meaning of the Constitution does not change with the ebb and flow of economic events. We frequently are told in more general words that the Constitution must be construed in the light of the present. If by that is meant that the Constitution is made up of living words that apply to every new condition which they include, the statement is quite true. But to say, if that be intended, that the words of the Constitution mean today what they did not mean when written — that is, that they do not apply to a situation now to which they would have applied then — is to rob that instrument of the essential element which continues it in force as the people have made it until they, and not their official agents, have made it otherwise.'

Sutherland turned on Stone's assertion that self-restraint was the only check on a judge. Stone had implied the old majority lacked it. Now Sutherland implied the new had no sense of duty. 'The suggestion that the only check upon the exercise of the judicial power, when properly invoked, to declare a constitutional right superior to an unconstitutional statute is the judge's own self-restraint, is both ill considered and mischievous. Self-restraint belongs in the domain of will and not of judgment. The check upon the judge is that imposed by his oath of office, by the Constitution and by his own conscientious and informed convictions; and since he has the duty to make up his own mind and adjudge accordingly, it is hard to see how there could be any other restraint.' [154]

Though it was obvious that the Tipaldo case as well as the old Adkins decision had been overruled, Hughes had refrained from saying so. Taking advantage of Butler's saying that counsel had not asked for any reconsideration of Adkins, Hughes said, as we have seen, that that question had not then been deemed open. Roberts had done no more by joining with the ex-majority than to follow it as a precedent that was binding on him. No more, indeed, than Holmes himself had done, when he accepted Adkins in the two cases that had come up from Arizona and Arkansas shortly afterwards. And the Court now refrained from saying that Tipaldo had been overruled. Not for more than six years and then only by a casual reference in a footnote to one of Jackson's opinions was it ever referred to as having been overruled.[155] And the same is true of the other cases in which Roberts had participated and which had equally obviously by then been overruled. The new majority fully appreciated what they owed to Roberts and they were going to make him feel at home. They left it to Roberts himself to say that the Schechter case 'must be regarded as overruled.'[156] The Carter case has never, so far as I know, been overruled.[157] As for the Railroad Pensions case, once when it was mentioned four years later, Hughes simply changed the subject.[158]

One thing Bacon said in his essay 'Of Judicature' hits so precisely on the relation of the Court with the New Deal that it is hard to believe it did not spring from something similar in his own time. It is this. 'Judges ought above all to remember the conclusion of the Roman Twelve Tables, *Salus populi suprema lex;* and to know that laws, except they be in order to that end, are but things captious, and oracles not well inspired. Therefore it is an happy thing in a state when kings and states do often consult with judges; and again, when judges do often consult with the king and state: the one, when there is matter of law intervenient in business of state; the other, when there is some consideration of state intervenient in matter of law. For many times the things deduced to judgment may be *meum* and *tuum,* when the reason and consequence thereof may trench to point of state. I call matter of state, not only the parts of sovereignty, but whatsoever introduces any great alteration or dangerous precedent, or concerns manifestly any great portion of people. And let no man weakly conceive that just laws and true policy have any antipathy: for they are like the spirits and sinews, that one moves with the other. Let judges also remember that Solomon's throne was supported by lions on both sides. Let them be lions, but yet lions under the throne.'

Sub Deo et Lege. Right. But *sub Republica,* too. The Court's allegiance is triple not dual.

11

A NEW COURT

Collective Bargaining

YOU COULDN'T CALL the Parrish decision a surrender to the New Deal. For one thing, minimum wage laws were not new; for another, the Republican party had indorsed them as well as the Democratic. The Parrish case cleared away the Adkins case, and let the Lochner decision go back to sleep again, this time we hope for good. When, however, the Court sustained the validity of the Wagner Act, it was not only exploding another obsolete abstraction, it was signifying its surrender to the New Deal. That came two weeks later, on April 12, 1937.

A group of cases had been argued together on the Tuesday following the President's announcement of his plan, on February 5. Perhaps the Court took them up in conference the next Saturday. That would be the twelfth, the morning General Motors recognized John L. Lewis's C.I.O., with a five cents an hour increase in wages. That, too, was a surrender, forced on General Motors by sit-down strikes in its key plants, and what was even worse, legally and judicially speaking, accompanied by the defiance of court injunctions. But we mistake the temper of the Court if we think either made any difference.

The Wagner Act had been passed on July 5, 1935, a few weeks after the Schechter case, right in the teeth of that warning, and in complete disrespect of the Court. If the N.R.A. was unconstitutional, how good was the N.L.R.A.? For all it did was re-enact the labor provisions out of the N.R.A., and set up a board with authority to enforce them. Would the Court reverse its unanimous ruling in the Schechter case? Would the Court, moreover, reverse the Carter Coal Company case, in which within eight months, it had held unconstitutional the labor provisions in the Guffey Coal Act? If Congress could not regulate labor relations in the critically depressed coal-mining industry, how could the Court say that Congress had power to regulate all labor relations 'affecting interstate commerce?'

There was the case of the Jones and Laughlin Steel Corporation, the fourth largest producer of steel in the country, whose nineteen subsidiaries owned and operated coal and limestone mines, lake and river transportation, and terminal facilities and railroads, located in many more than one state. Its selling agencies made sales in twenty cities. Its headquarters were in Pennsylvania and out of that state about three-quarters of its product was shipped, to be sold all over the country. Did its unfair labor practices obstruct, or would collective bargaining with it favorably affect, interstate commerce?

Then there was the Fruehauf Trailer Company, which manufactured and sold trailers. It was the largest concern of its kind. Its plant was located in Detroit, and it had sales offices in twelve different states and distributors and dealers in all principal cities. Into its plant in Detroit came its raw materials from many states. There the trailers were manufactured and distributed throughout the country. Did its rejection of the union and its discharge of men for joining the union obstruct interstate commerce?

The Friedman-Harry Marx Clothing Company made men's clothing at Richmond, Virginia. More than 99 per cent of its raw materials came from other states; more than 80 per cent of its manufactured products were sold to customers outside of Virginia. Would its discharge of employees for engaging in union activities obstruct or affect interstate commerce?

A fourth was the Washington, Virginia and Maryland Coach Company, which ran motor buses between the District of Columbia and Virginia, but there was really no doubt about that being interstate commerce.

The fifth was the Associated Press. To digress for a moment, the A.P. had a special defense of its own, the freedom of the press; and the new minority, who thought the Act transcended the power over interstate commerce anyhow, delivered a dissent in support of the freedom of the press which is unique. Freedom of the press had always been invoked in defense of the position that even if I hate every word you say, yet I will defend with my life your right to say them. Here the A.P. invoked the right of Poyns, the right to keep in the middle of the highway. Sutherland argued that the A.P., in order to preserve its impartiality on the news of the nation, had a constitutional right to fire a rewrite editor solely because he belonged to a union. He said the Constitution authorized the A.P. to regard only non-union men as truly neutral in the controversy between labor and capital. We will not go into that now. We are concerned with the extent of the power of Congress to regulate interstate commerce.[159]

Mrs. Hughes had appeared in the courtroom when the Parrish minimum wage opinion was handed down. Her appearance two weeks later on this Monday, the day when decisions are announced and opinions are read, was an intimation that the decision on the constitutionality of the Wagner Act was coming. On this Monday, the twelfth of April, 1937, in a courtroom crowded with cherry-blossom tourists, Mrs. Hughes watched her husband's incisive gestures, emphasizing a sentence by taking off and shaking his eyeglasses, as he read the long opinion of the majority, and I dare say a smile of satisfaction spread over the face of Solicitor General Reed at the table reserved for counsel.

You will recall the 'necessary and well-established distinction between direct and indirect effects' which Hughes had used in the Schechter case to determine how far the federal government could go in controlling intrastate transactions on the ground they 'affected' interstate commerce. It was 'a fundamental one, essential to the maintenance of our constitutional system.' You will recall how the Court, Sutherland speaking, relied on it in the Carter case to invalidate the Guffey Coal Act. 'The extent of the effect bears no logical relation to its character. The distinction between a direct and an indirect effect turns, not upon the magnitude of either the cause or the effect, but entirely upon the manner in which the effect has been brought about. If the production by one man of a single ton of coal intended for interstate sale and shipment, and actually so sold and shipped, affects interstate commerce indirectly, the effect does not become direct by multiplying the tonnage or increasing the number of men employed, or adding to the expense or complexities of the business, or by all combined. It is quite true that rules or law are sometimes qualified by considerations of degree, as the government argues. But the matter of degree has no bearing upon the question here, since that question is not — What is the *extent* of the local activity or condition, or the *extent* of the effect produced upon interstate commerce? but — What is the *relation* between the activity or condition and the effect?' [160]

Sutherland now made the point again in the course of the oral argument. Here is what he asked Stanley Reed and what Reed replied.[161]

> *Mr. Justice Sutherland:* 'Before you pass to that point, what is the primary effect of a strike in a steel mill? Is it not simply to curtail production?'
>
> *Mr. Stanley Reed:* 'Certainly; that is one of the effects.'
>
> *Mr. Justice Sutherland:* 'Isn't that the primary effect, the immediate effect?'
>
> *Mr. Stanley Reed:* 'Well, I should say it was the first effect. I do not mean to split hairs. Of course, that is one of the primary effects of it.'
>
> *Mr. Justice Sutherland:* 'That is the primary effect, to curtail production, and then the curtailment of production in its turn has an effect upon interstate commerce; isn't that true?'
>
> *Mr. Stanley Reed:* 'As *I* understand it, no. The strike is something that instantaneously and at the same time that it stops production stops interstate commerce. It is a single thing that happens, and that stoppage of works stops interstate commerce right at that instant.'
>
> *Mr. Justice Sutherland:* 'It affects interstate commerce just as the cessation of work in a coal mine. The primary effect of that, as suggested in the *Carter* case, was to curtail the production and then the secondary effect which came from the curtailment of production was the effect upon interstate commerce.'

Turn now to Hughes's opinion for the new majority. It
was long, as befitted the importance of the occasion, but it
was simple enough. One short sentence gives the heart of
it, 'The question is necessarily one of degree.' He shook
his eyeglasses, and went on, 'In view of respondent's far-
flung activities, it is idle to say that the effect would be
indirect or remote. It is obvious that it would be immediate and might be catastrophic. We are asked to shut our
eyes to the plainest facts of our national life and to deal
with the question of direct and indirect effects in an intellectual vacuum. Because there may be but indirect and
remote effects upon interstate commerce in connection
with a host of local enterprises throughout the country, it
does not follow that other industrial activities do not have
such a close and intimate relation to interstate commerce
as to make the presence of industrial strife a matter of the
most urgent national concern. When industries organize
themselves on a national scale, making their relation to
interstate commerce the dominant factor in their activities, how can it be maintained that their industrial labor
relations constitute a forbidden field into which Congress
may not enter when it is necessary to protect interstate
commerce from the paralyzing consequences of industrial
war? We have often said that interstate commerce itself
is a practical conception. It is equally true that interfer-
ences with that commerce must be appraised by a judgment that does not ignore actual experience.'

And then Hughes turned to the immediate point. 'Experience has abundantly demonstrated that the recognition of the right of the employees to self-organization and
to have representatives of their own choosing for the purpose of collective bargaining is often an essential condition

of industrial peace. Refusal to confer and negotiate has been one of the most prolific causes of strife. This is such an outstanding fact in the history of labor disturbances that it is a proper subject of judicial notice and requires no citation of instances.'

Such was the opinion in the Jones and Laughlin case, a great steel business, but Hughes and this new majority reached the same conclusion in the other cases, though there the companies involved were comparatively small. You could hardly say that the activities of the Friedman-Harry Marx Clothing Company of Richmond were 'far-flung' or that the effect of its discharge of eight of its employees 'might be catastrophic.' The same result, however, was reached. How could the Act be invalid for a big company and yet valid for a little one, invalid for a big violation, valid for a little one? The law must be the same for the little as well as for the big.

How does that go logically with a doctrine which is supposed to rely, not on the relation, but only on the *extent* of the effect on interstate commerce? This was the point McReynolds made when he spoke for the four dissenters, Van Devanter, Sutherland, Butler, and himself. He spoke extemporaneously, and in a loud voice.

In the Jones and Laughlin case, he said, ten men out of ten thousand were discharged; in the other cases only a few. 'The immediate effect in the factory may be to create discontent among all those employed and a strike may follow, which, in turn, may result in reducing production, which ultimately may reduce the volume of goods moving in interstate commerce. By this chain of indirect and progressively remote events we finally reach the evil with which it is said the legislation under consideration undertakes to deal. A more remote and indirect interference with interstate commerce or a more definite invasion of the powers reserved to the states is difficult, if not impossible, to imagine.' [162]

'If a man who raises cattle regularly delivers them to a carrier for interstate shipment, may Congress prescribe the conditions under which he may employ or discharge helpers on the ranch? May a mill owner be prohibited from closing his factory or discontinuing his business be-cause so to do would stop the flow of products to and from his plant in interstate commerce? May employees in a factory be restrained from quitting work in a body because this will close the factory and thereby stop the flow of commerce? May arson of a factory be made a Federal offense whenever this would interfere with such flow? If the business cannot continue with the existing wage scale, may Congress command a reduction? If the ruling of the Court just announced is adhered to these questions present some of the problems certain to arise.'

McReynolds applied this to the case before him. 'It is gravely stated,' he said, 'that experience teaches that if an employer discourages membership in "any organization of any kind in which employees participate, and which exists for the purpose in whole or in part of dealing with employers concerning grievances, labor disputes, wages, rates of pay, hours of employment, or conditions of work," discontent may follow and this in turn may lead to a strike, and as the outcome of the strike there may be a block in the stream of interstate commerce. Therefore Congress may inhibit the discharge! Whatever effect any cause of discontent may ultimately have upon commerce is far too indirect to justify congressional regulation. Almost anything — marriage, birth, death — may in some fashion affect commerce.' [163]

Logically, was not McReynolds quite right? But cannot the national legislature regulate the affairs of the nation, though a state is also interested, or even though a state is more interested? McReynolds is dead. Were he still alive, there is no reason why he should not answer a civil question. We might ask him what he thinks of the Court's recent decision on the Fair Labor Standards Act of 1938, where the Court allowed Congress to fix the overtime pay of window cleaners in an office building in Detroit because most of the windows were in offices of tenants whose business was the production of goods for interstate commerce.[164]

Hughes had treated the precedents somewhat delicately out of regard to Roberts's feelings. He had distinguished the Schechter and the Carter cases — thus, 'In the Schechter case, we found that the effect there was so remote as to be beyond the federal power. To find "immediacy or directness" there was to find it "almost everywhere," a result inconsistent with the maintenance of our federal system. In the Carter case, the Court was of the opinion that the provisions of the statute relating to production were invalid upon several grounds. These cases are not controlling here.'

'Not controlling.' To the ex-majority they were very distinctly controlling, and if not followed they must be overruled. Yet Hughes did not say they were overruled, and you will have noticed that what he quotes from the Schechter case is Cardozo's concurring opinion, not the opinion of the majority, though he himself had written it. Does not that show how far the Court had moved? If, indeed, there was any precedent left, it was what Cardozo had said, not what Hughes had written for the Court and what he had been unable to persuade Cardozo and Stone to subscribe to.

When Cardozo died and the bar moved resolutions to his memory, Hughes said in his reply for the Court, 'For Justice Cardozo the distrust of concept was the beginning of wisdom.' The new majority had made that beginning. They had broken the old concept of a relation between the activity and its effect and replaced it with a new one, the concept of the extent of its effect on interstate commerce, and that was a different sort of concept, because it was a matter of degree. It was a ramp, with no convenient landings for a logical mind, slightly out of breath, perhaps, to rest on.

That was one thing, but not the only thing that had happened. The majority had also shifted the point of reference, the zero point. Coming down to sea-level, so to speak, the boiling point of unconstitutionality was higher. Butler and McReynolds could not understand this, because their altitude, their zero point, had remained unchanged. They were afraid for the future, because this new concept was one of degree, which had no logical stopping place. That is why they feared the 'serious impairment of the very foundations of our federated system,' and even worse, the decision would 'give potency to the efforts of those who apparently hope to end a system of government found inhospitable to their ultimate designs.' To them it was 'subversive doctrine.' True enough for Justices who perform their duties under the sole compulsion and domination of logic. Not true for those who know how to handle matters of fact and matters of degree in fact. As the power to tax is logically the power to destroy, so the power of Congress to regulate commerce is logically the power to obliterate the state's power over its industries. Elbowing its way through their anxieties for the society they had been bred to, loved, and in which they had been so successful, was the apprehension of the logical consequences of what the Court had said. Why shouldn't a judge trust his successors, quite as much as he trusts himself, not to slip on the easy slopes of logic?

Social Security

The 1936–1937 term was not yet over. Some six weeks after collective bargaining came, social security was made constitutionally possible in the United States. On May 24, 1937, the Court took up state and national unemployment insurance.

The Court first sustained the Alabama Unemployment Compensation Act.[165] You will recall that the New York Act had been allowed to stand by an evenly divided Court, four to four, the previous autumn.[166] Roberts, we thought, had shifted to make it four to four, Stone being out sick. This now became apparent, for we find Roberts with the new majority and only the Old Guard dissenting. Dissenting, and saying that the Alabama statute was like the New York statute; with only this small difference, McReynolds would not join his three colleagues, he dissented alone and without opinion. Sulking?

What was the matter with a state unemployment compensation law? Nothing, except the way Alabama, like New York, had gone about doing it. The contributions of the employers — and of the employees, too, though they were not objecting — were all put into one big fund, and out of that fund the compensation was distributed to employees out of a job. This had been one of the troubles with the Railroad Pension Act, you will recall. Alabama had been guilty of 'the same unfairness, in an aggravated form,' Sutherland said. For obviously if the employers paid their quota into the fund per the number of employees working for them and it was paid out to all the employees they discharged, the employers who didn't discharge so many, were going to bear the burden of paying the discharged employees of a competitor who had let more of them go. That offended the equal protection of the laws guaranteed by the Fourteenth Amendment, Sutherland said. Anyhow, here was Roberts confirming the position he had taken the autumn before, and holding good what he had said was bad in the Railroad Pensions case.

Then the Court turned to the Federal act.[167]

Until this Social Security Act of 1935, only a few states had unemployment insurance. Indeed, before the Social Security Act was in the offing, only one, Wisconsin, whose statute was adopted in 1931. In 1935, just before the Act was adopted, four more states followed, Massachusetts, California, New Hampshire, and New York; and after it was passed thirty-eight more. The reason was clear enough — no state wanted to put itself into a position of economic disadvantage as compared with its neighbors and competitors. Take Massachusetts, whose act was passed on August 12, 1935, two days before the Social Security Act. It provided that it should not become operative unless the federal bill was enacted or unless at least eleven of her industrial rivals imposed similar burdens on their employers. Alabama worked it another way. It candidly provided that its statute should 'become void' if the Federal Social Security Act were held unconstitutional.

Even if the states could constitutionally set up unemployment insurance, paying the benefits from a single fund to which all employers contributed, could the national government make it practically possible for the states to do this? That was a different question. The New Deal proposed to do it this way.

All employers of more than eight persons know what that was. A tax was laid on their payrolls, to be paid into the federal treasury, but they were to get a credit up to 90 per cent on the federal tax if they paid a similar tax to their own state government for an approved unemployment scheme.

Such a conditional tax was not novel. Congress had passed a similar estate tax in 1926. Congress may even have had its eye upon Mr. Justice Sutherland, for it was he who had written the unanimous opinion of the Court which sustained that tax.[168] There four-fifths of the tax was remitted if the state imposed the same tax. Florida had complained. For its Constitution prohibited all inheritance taxes, admittedly as a lure to wealthy settlers. Florida argued, 'The federal government has no power by taxation or otherwise to control the internal affairs of the state in any matter not in conflict with the powers delegated to the United States or inhibited to the states by the Constitution.' That was ten years before the A.A.A. case, and ten years too soon, for the argument fell flat, so flat indeed that Sutherland did not even mention it in his opinion.

Could an argument not even worthy of mention then be

now controlling? If the federal government could tax inheritances in the states that would not tax them, could it not levy a tax on all employers of eight or more persons in states that would not have unemployment compensation?

This was the converse of the A.A.A. If the United States could not constitutionally *bribe* farmers to restrict their crops because that was something only the states could make them do, could the United States *penalize* all employers of eight employees with a tax unless their state passed unemployment compensation laws?

Certainly not, McReynolds said. The Act unduly interferes with the orderly government of the State by her own people and otherwise offends the federal Constitution, which, he said, quoting from an opinion of Chief Justice Chase in 1869, 'looks to an indestructible union composed of indestructible states.' This decision now, he said, 'opens the way for practical annihilation of this theory; and no cloud of words or ostentatious parade of irrelevant statistics should be permitted to obscure that fact.' Then with a grim sense of humor, if any, he went on to quote, through nine long pages, a veto message which President Franklin Pierce had sent to the Senate in 1854. Perhaps its subject made it seem relevant. Pierce was speaking of a bill making a grant of public land for the benefit of the indigent insane.

Sutherland and Van Devanter couldn't quite take that. They could not say that the states were coerced. But the Act seemed to them to invade the governmental powers of the states reserved to them by the Tenth Amendment, which says, 'The powers not delegated to the United States by the Constitution, nor prohibited by it to the

States, are reserved to the States respectively, or to the people.' They concluded that 'the federal agencies are authorized to supervise and hamper the administrative powers of the state to a degree which not only does not comport with the dignity of a quasi-sovereign state — a matter with which we are not judicially concerned — but which denies to it that supremacy and freedom from external interference in respect of its affairs which the Constitution contemplates — a matter of very definite judicial concern.' 'If we are to survive as the United *States* — this is their emphasis — the balance between the powers of the nation and those of the state must be maintained. There is grave danger in permitting it to dip in either direction, danger — if there were no other — in the precedent thereby set for further departures from the equipoise. The threat implicit in the present encroachment upon the administrative functions of the state is that greater encroachments, and encroachments upon other functions, will follow.'

Butler agreed with what all three had said. Their objections were 'well taken.' He, too, felt the stair carpet slipping. 'The Constitution grants to the United States no power to pay unemployed persons or to require the states to enact laws or to raise or disburse money for that purpose. The provisions in question, if not amounting to coercion in a legal sense, are manifestly designed and intended directly to affect state action in the respects specified. And, if valid as so employed, this "tax and credit" device may be made effective to enable federal authorities to induce, if not indeed to compel, state enactments for any purpose within the realm of state power and generally to control state administration and state laws.'

Lay aside what McReynolds said, for he gave signs of losing his temper, and let us strip this argument on the Tenth Amendment and see what it means. Does it add anything? If a power is granted, it has not been reserved. If it has not been granted, it is reserved. It's the two sides of the same silver dollar. What's not on one side, is on the other. If it's not tails, it's heads. It seems to me a sterile argument.

Stone burned away a lot of fog about the Tenth Amendment in the Darby case [169] when he said that it 'states but a truism that all is retained which has not been surrendered. There is nothing in the history of its adoption to suggest that it was more than declaratory of the relationship between the national and state governments as it had been established by the Constitution before the amendment or that its purpose was other than to allay fears that the new national government might seek to exercise powers not granted, and that the states might not be able to exercise fully their renewed powers.'

What then do they mean, these Justices? They must be sucking something from this express reservation of ungranted powers which it does not logically contain. For they are laying the weight of the Tenth Amendment against almost the whole of the rest of the Constitution, including the fact that the Constitution created a nation. That is the equipoise that Sutherland referred to. These Justices were appalled by their responsibility for our federalism, and they were taking comfort from express language that expressed no more than was already implied.

Cardozo spoke for the other five Justices. There is no need here to parade their 'irrelevant statistics' as to the number of unemployed, which had reached sixteen million. But they seemed to these other five Justices to show that the states were unable to give the requisite relief, that the problem had become national in area and dimensions, and that there was need of help from the nation if the people were not to starve. 'It is too late today,' Cardozo said, 'for the argument to be heard with tolerance that in a crisis so extreme the use of the moneys of the nation to relieve the unemployed and their dependents is a use for any purpose narrower than the promotion of the general welfare.'

And what was that but Hamilton's theory, which had been adopted in the A.A.A. case? Cardozo cited that decision.

He went on, 'In the presence of this urgent need for some remedial expedient, the question is to be answered whether the expedient has overleapt the bounds of power. The assailants of the statute say that its dominant end and aim is to drive the state legislatures under the whip of economic pressure into the enactment of unemployment compensation laws at the bidding of the central government. Supporters of the statute say that its operation is not constraint, but the creation of a larger freedom, the states and the nation joining in a co-operative endeavor to avert a common evil.'

'Who then is coerced through the operation of this statute? Not the taxpayer. He pays in fulfilment of the mandate of the local Legislature. Not the state. Even now she does not offer a suggestion that in passing the unemployment law she was affected by duress. For all that appears she is satisfied with her choice, and would be sorely disappointed if it were now to be annulled.'

Cardozo continued, 'The difficulty with the petitioner's contention is that it confuses motive with coercion. Every tax is in some measure regulatory. To some extent it interposes an economic impediment to the activity taxed as compared with others not taxed. In like manner every rebate from a tax when conditioned upon conduct is in some measure a temptation. But to hold that motive or temptation is equivalent to coercion is to plunge the law in endless difficulties. The outcome of such a doctrine is the acceptance of a philosophical determinism by which choice becomes impossible. Till now the law has been guided by a robust common sense which assumes the freedom of the will as a working hypothesis in the solution of its problems. The wisdom of the hypothesis has illustration in this case. Nothing in the case suggests the exertion of a power akin to undue influence, if we assume that such a concept can ever be applied with fitness to the relations between state and nation. Even on that assumption the location of the point at which pressure turns into compulsion, and ceases to be mere inducement, would be a question of degree — at times, perhaps, of fact.'

This April 12 wound up with the decision on old age pensions.[170]

A shareholder of the Edison Electric Illuminating Company of Boston had brought suit to restrain that corporation from making the payments called for by the Act. He said that the company had decided to obey the Act in spite of his protest and that the deductions from the wages of the employees were producing unrest among them and would be followed, he predicted, by demands that their wages be increased. The company, he said, and its shareholders, among them himself, would suffer irreparable loss, not only directly from the payments, but also in the value of their shares.

Was there no grant of power to Congress that would save old age pensions from being 'reserved to the States respectively, or to the people'? Yes, the spending power for the general welfare, and that in the Hamiltonian sense. Here again there was virtue, then, in the Court's adoption of Hamilton's view in the A.A.A. case. It had not been academic historial research. Sutherland and Van Devanter had subscribed to it, and they were not going back on it now. McReynolds and Butler dissented alone.

'Nor,' Cardozo was writing the opinion, 'is the concept of the general welfare static. Needs that were narrow or parochial a century ago may be interwoven in our day with the well-being of the Nation. What is critical or urgent changes with the times. The purge of nation-wide calamity that began in 1929 has taught us many lessons. Not the least is the solidarity of interests that may once have seemed to be divided. Unemployment spreads from State to State, the hinterland now settled that in pioneer days gave an avenue of escape. The hope behind this statute is to save men and women from the rigors of the poorhouse as well as from the haunting fear that such a lot awaits them when journey's end is near.'

Cardozo was answering the question of the first rugged individualist, Am I my brother's keeper? Who else would dare ask God such a question?

But Cardozo had not finished his answer. 'Counsel has recalled to us the virtues of self reliance and frugality. There is a possibility, he says, that aid from a paternal government may sap those sturdy virtues and breed a race of weaklings. If Massachusetts so believes and shapes her laws in that conviction, must her breed of sons be changed, he asks, because some other philosophy of government finds favor in the halls of Congress? But the answer is not doubtful. One might ask with equal reason whether the system of protective tariffs is to be set aside at will in one state or another whenever local policy prefers the rule of laissez faire. The issue is a closed one. It was fought out long ago.' [171] And Cardozo happily referred not only to nullification in South Carolina but to the Hartford Convention, about which he suggested, by a citation, the attorney from Massachusetts might read in chapter eight of Henry Adams's *History*.

Post Mortem

When the court term closed that next week, Van Devanter retired. It was June, 1937. A week or so later the Senate Committee reported against the President's plan, as 'a needless, futile, and utterly dangerous abandonment of constitutional principle.' Certainly it was needless, and therefore futile. If it had not been, it would have been necessary, dangerous or not.

The rest is anti-climax. Senator Robinson had taken over the fight for the plan in the Senate. On July 14 he died suddenly of a heart attack. The next day the President told Senator Barkley that the fight must go on, and it took nearly a week to persuade the President that he could not win in the Senate, because he had already won in the Court. On July 22, 1937, the bill was killed with only twenty votes in its favor.

The bar, of course, were pleased, but they were not at all satisfied with the result, for their Court had been converted.

Two years later Frank J. Hogan, the President of the American Bar Association, told the members at their annual convention what many of them had been thinking and saying. Hogan's comment was both acute and just, 'The conclusion to be drawn from all of this may, I think, be stated simply: It is that reliance against the exercise of arbitrary power must be placed by the people henceforth in the legislative rather than in the judicial department of the national government. Legislative independence and legislative wisdom are now America's almost sole reliance for the continuance of that security of the blessings of liberty for which the Constitution was framed and the Government of the United States of America created.'

It would be difficult to put it better, except for the 'now' and 'henceforth.' It had always been so. What Mr. Hogan viewed with such apprehension in 1939, Chief Justice Marshall had foreseen with complete equanimity in 1824. 'The wisdom and discretion of Congress, their identity with the people, and the influence which their constituents possess at elections, are in this as in many other instances the sole restraints on which they have relied, to secure them from its abuse. They are the restraints on which the people must often rely solely, in all representative governments.' [172] If we did not know better, Mr. Hogan might have been quoting Marshall. Or Holmes, who had said, you will recall, 'It must be remembered that legislators are the ultimate guardians of the liberties and welfare of the people in quite as great a degree as the courts.' [173] And Stone had said the same thing in his A.A.A. dissent. Hogan and Stone — two hearts with but a single thought, but they did not beat as one.

Mr. Hogan, nevertheless, was optimistic. He went on,

'Upon the graves of the old constitutional doctrine new ones were erected, monument-like in present appearance, but, if history repeats itself, of doubtful durability. The day must come when the future chronicles of our judicial history, in according unstinted praise to the rugged sturdiness of McReynolds and Butler, shown in their courageous efforts to preserve landmark after landmark of the law, will likewise record that their ringing dissents in this day became rules of decision in a later generation.'

The bar did not like to see these landmarks go. Some, because they liked them for their own sake. They had got used to them. Others did not want to have to learn new ones. Some few because they thought any was better than none at all, which would come hard to deny.

Mr. Hogan put it this way, 'Those who think lightly of shifts in constitutional doctrines must think lightly also of the importance of knowing what the law is. Is it to be a movable thing, changing and changeable after each reconstruction in the membership of courts? Is it to vary with the shifting currents of political will? Or is it to be something certain, steadfast and enduring, upon which reliance can safely be placed? The plain result of all this is that no lawyer can safely advise his client what the law is; no business man, no farmer, can know whether or not he is breaking the law, for if he follows established principles he is likely to be doing exactly that.'

How far is a lawyer professionally entitled to be able to advise his clients whether a statute is unconstitutional? If a court of law is going to make the decision, a lawyer ought to be able, at least profess to be able, to give an opinion. The businessman and the farmer can read a statute or their lawyers will read it for them and tell them what it says. But the bar wants more than that. They want, and they claim they are entitled to be able to tell their clients with some degree of authority that they can break a law with as much impunity as the Court is in duty bound to ignore it. Earl F. Reed, counsel for the Weirton Steel Company, is quoted as having said, in happier days, 'I feel perfectly free to advise a client not to be bound by a law that I consider unconstitutional.' [174]

Now this is as it should be, if Hogan's 'established principles' are really legal principles, and not governmental policies which are called legal only because a court of law has been dealing with them. A lawyer should be able to advise his clients on their titles, on their rights under their contracts, on their civil and criminal liabilities, and on some questions covered by the Constitution, certainly. That is matter of law, which a lawyer is trained for. That is what he professes to know. But has he any special competence to tell his clients whether an act of Congress is constitutional? Is the stuff out of which constitutional law is made legal or political? Test it on these decisions we have been discussing.

Look back over the problems which were presented to the Old Court — agriculture, labor, the coal industry, minimum wages. Think of the reasons they gave, the distinctions they made, and see if you can believe that the Court would have been willing to act itself on any of those reasons.

Take the A.A.A. Is it suitable for a great country to hinge its decision on how to rehabilitate its agriculture on the difference between an agreement and a condition, or, as the lawyers would put it, on the difference between a bilateral and a unilateral contract? Or even in the margin of distinction between a tax and a penalty?

Take the extent of the power over interstate commerce.
Can the reconciliation of labor and industry suitably be
made to depend on a metaphor and Congress be made to
sit and watch the race of the argument from the banks of
'the stream of commerce'? Or should it depend on the
dialectical difference between direct and indirect? Better
by indirection find direction out. It is a poor mind that
cannot recognize a matter of degree when it is thrust in its
face. And it is worse than nonsense to make the validity
of compulsory railroad pensions depend on a distinction
that puts loyalty on one side and gratitude on the other.
The propriety of minimum wages does not require aspira-
tions toward an ideal liberty, half zoölogical, half religious.

When Holmes said, 'Judges are apt to be naïve, simple-
minded men and they need something of Mephistophe-
les,' [175] he was contradicting something Plato had said in
the *Republic*.[176] There Plato argued that unlike physi-
cians, who would prove most skillful if from childhood up
they had familiarized their bodies with sickness by having
all the diseases themselves, judges had best not have
grown up with evil. For that is a sickness of the soul, and
they use their souls in their work. They had better be
simple-minded and easily deceived, Plato thought, than
have patterns of evil in their souls. Yet Holmes and Plato
were not so far apart as this would make it seem. For
Plato goes on to say that a good judge will be a late learner
of the nature of evil, training himself to understand it, but
as a thing alien to himself, by knowledge and not from
personal experience. Certainly these Justices were no
more naïve and simple-minded than they were evil-
minded. They were good men who had just such an
objective knowledge of evil as Plato required of good
judges.

It is absurd to think that these Justices would have reasoned as they did to us in these opinions, if they had been asked to give, not judicial opinions, but solutions of our national problems. Put these Justices into a committee room in Congress in executive session. These are not the arguments they will make that a proposed bill is unconstitutional. Let them be members of a Joint Committee to resolve differences between the two Houses. Ask them to follow up their arguments in a speech on the floor. They will talk sensibly enough. Why then do they talk to us in this way? The Legal Tradition makes it very difficult, almost impossible to talk sensibly about these questions by expecting, almost prescribing that a court treat them as purely judicial questions.

There are several points which can be made in any debate or discussion on the difference between legislative and judicial action. One, however, runs very deep, the difference between the man who does his thinking in order to put its conclusions to work, knowing that they are going to be put to work, and the man who does his thinking for his own satisfaction and his own justification, the discharge of his duty. The legislator's conclusions are going to be put into operation. What he has been thinking is going to be what men will be doing. The judge, on the other hand, is thinking about undoing a kink in the past, and the effect on the future is only a consequence, not the object of what he does. His thinking is not the prelude to action, but the unveiling of justice. So, while the reasoning of the legislators is factual, the reasoning of the judge is essentially casuistical.

Perhaps it is only putting the same thing in another way to say that the Tradition required these Justices, or so they thought, to argue empirical problems as if they were analytic, as if the predicate they were seeking could be spun wholly out of what was implied in the subject, that is, the constitutional doctrines they had been brought up on. But they were dealing with matters of political experience. They had had political experience. No wonder they were frustrated and talked a good deal of nonsense when they were expected to work with intellectual tools wholly unsuited to the material they were dealing with. It was like using a knife to divide an orange without spilling any juice. You can do that only with your fingers.

12

RECONSTRUCTED OR CONVERTED?

THE PRESIDENT made no appointment to Van
Devanter's place until August, 1937. Then he appointed Senator Hugo Black, to the consternation
of the bar. Black was just over fifty, a Southerner of the
New South, from Birmingham, Alabama, and a graduate
of the University of Alabama Law School. Like Miller, he
had thought of medicine, but turned to the law. Starting
from police judge and prosecuting attorney, he had
reached a large and successful practice in Alabama. Since
1927 he had been United States Senator, succeeding Underwood and defeating Bankhead. The most unaffected,
democratic of men, there was no more experienced, no
more expert legislator in the country. In 1937 he appeared on the Court a legislator among lawyers, an author
among critics.

Black spent the winter settling into his seat, and filing a
series of lone dissents. Most of the bar regarded him as if
he were filled with new wine; others, and with them the
people agreed, as one who had fed on wild honey. Indeed,
he was raising his voice in what must have seemed to him
a wilderness of legislative nonsense. Cardozo was the
closest to him, but Cardozo was taken ill in December and
never returned to the bench.

Halfway through the winter, in January, 1938, another of the Four, Sutherland, retired and the President advanced Solicitor General Reed to the Court. He had led for the government in the arguments for much of the New Deal legislation, the N.R.A., the A.A.A., and the Labor Board cases. He was greeted with joy by the bar. After Black, what might they not expect? Whatever his views, they said, Reed is a good lawyer, and so he was. He was fifty-four, born in Kentucky, educated at Yale, law at the University of Virginia and Columbia. He had practiced at the Kentucky bar. He had served in the Kentucky legislature. Then he became general counsel for a series of governmental agencies, the Federal Farm Board, the R.F.C., and finally Solicitor General of the United States from 1935 until his appointment. There was no question of his talents as a lawyer, nor of his devoted and distinguished public service.

Cardozo died in the following July, 1938. But it was not until January, 1939, that the President filled his place. It was Felix Frankfurter who then took the seat that had long been warm under Curtis, Gray, Holmes, and Cardozo.

Frankfurter was fifty-seven. He had come to America from Vienna when he was twelve. College of the City of New York; Harvard Law School. Then he worked for Stimson in the U. S. Attorney's office in New York and in the War Department. In 1914 he became Professor of Law at Harvard. During the First World War he worked under the Secretary of War on labor relations, witness his report on Mooney. In 1927 he was the most powerful of the defenders of Sacco and Vanzetti, witness his article on their case. In 1932 he preferred his professorship to a seat on the Massachusetts Supreme Court. And all the while, before and since, he has been training and exciting young men for public service. As Black was the expert legislator, here was the expert in public service, in whom learning, courage, and loyalty were felicitously blended.

Then Brandeis retired, in February, 1939. An old man who had wisely served his people, the citizens of his country; an Isaiah whose fervor had no need of vehemence. The President replaced him with the Chairman of the Securities and Exchange Commission, William O. Douglas.

Douglas was only forty-one. From the State of Washington, educated at a local college, law at Columbia, where later he lectured while he practiced in New York. Then he taught law at Yale. He directed the S.E.C.'s investigations into bankruptcy in 1934. Since 1936 he had been Chairman of the S.E.C.

By 1939, then the Court had been 'reconstructed,' as Frankfurter put it,[177] but it had already been converted, and it was not so much these new Justices as its conversion which was to fix the character of the Court.

A conversion is an upsetting experience. Almost the first thing the New Court did was to overrule a doctrine which had nothing to do with the New Deal and which had been an established part of our federal jurisprudence for a hundred years. This doctrine of *Swift* v. *Tyson* is almost exclusively of interest to lawyers, and we need not go into its merits. Suffice it that a good many, perhaps most, of the bar agreed that the Court was well rid of it. The point is the way it was done. You recall Butler's insistence that the Court could not reconsider the Adkins case because counsel had not asked it to do so. In this case, which came before the Court in the winter of 1937–38,[178] no one had even suggested overruling *Swift* v. *Tyson.* Quite contrary, one of the attorneys had said, 'We do not question the finality of the holding of this court in *Swift* v. *Tyson.*' The other assumed its finality and referred to it as 'now elementary.' Yet the Court overruled it. Butler and McReynolds in their dissent made it clear that they had asked for a reargument on the point and had protested against the Court's overruling such an ancient precedent on its own motion and without argument.[179] But the Court would not listen.

It was in this spirit that the New Court proceeded to clear away the last obstacles to the progress of the New Deal. We must finish that story before we go on.

Is it a valid regulation of interstate commerce when Congress uses its power for what are called ulterior motives? Can the power be used, say even at the expense of that commerce, for the sake of something else? When the Court blocked Congress's use of the spending power to do something for agriculture, Congress turned to its power over commerce. If it could not make grants to farmers and growers who agreed to produce less, could Congress penalize the grower who marketed more, by cutting him off from interstate commerce? Likewise Congress had proposed a Wages and Hours bill, which would keep out of interstate commerce what Roosevelt called 'the product of ruined lives.'

The power of Congress to exclude a commodity from interstate commerce had been first recognized in 1902, when the Court upheld the power of Congress to prohibit sending lottery tickets out of a state.[180] The decision had created a great stir, and the Court had been hesitant. They said, a majority of the Court, 'We should hesitate long before adjudging that an evil of such appalling character, carried on through interstate commerce, cannot be met and crushed by the only power competent to that end. It is a kind of traffic which no one can be entitled to pursue as of right.' [181]

They made it very clear that the decision must not be understood to uphold a general right to exclude any article at all from interstate commerce. The Court expressly confined its decision to things of 'such appalling character' as lottery tickets. The decision itself appalled the more discerning members of the bar. A writer in the *American Law Review* noted the far-reaching consequences. 'The Court,' he said, 'has unfolded a vast power wrapped up in the commerce clause.' [182]

Congress had unwrapped its new-found power like a Christmas present. Diseased animals, impure foods, immoral women, intoxicating liquors, stolen automobiles, convict-made goods, and kidnapped persons were one after another regarded as sufficiently appalling to be excluded from interstate commerce. But the Court felt Congress had gone too far when it tried to exclude the products of child labor, and said so, in the case of *Hammer* v. *Dagenhart*.[183]

Child labor did not appall them. You were entitled to employ children if your state law did not stop you, and so far as your national government was concerned, you were entitled to sell what children had made.

Holmes had dissented, and when the President sent the Wage and Hour bill to Congress, on May 24, 1937, he not only based its constitutionality on Holmes's dissent, but borrowed his phrase, 'the product of ruined lives.'

'I had thought,' said Holmes, 'that the propriety of the

exercise of a power admitted to exist in some cases was for the consideration of Congress alone and that this court always had disavowed the right to intrude its judgment upon questions of policy or morals. It is not for this court to pronounce when prohibition is necessary to regulation if it ever may be necessary — to say that it is permissible as against strong drink but not as against the product of ruined lives.'

'The act does not meddle with anything belonging to the states. They may regulate their internal affairs and their domestic commerce as they like. But when they seek to send their products across the state line they are no longer within their rights. If there were no Constitution and no Congress their power to cross the line would depend upon their neighbors. Under the Constitution such commerce belongs not to the states but to Congress to regulate. It may carry out its views of public policy whatever indirect effect they may have upon the activities of the states. Instead of being encountered by a prohibitive tariff at her boundaries the state encounters the public policy of the United States which it is for Congress to express. The public policy of the United States is shaped with a view to the benefit of the nation as a whole. The national welfare as understood by Congress may require a different attitude within its sphere from that of some self-seeking state. It seems to me entirely constitutional for Congress to enforce its understanding by all the means at its command.'

If Holmes was wrong, some of this power to regulate commerce, which must admittedly have existed in the states before the Constitution, had dropped between the slats. For surely, if Congress had got all the power there was over such commerce, all the states had had, then the character of the commodity Congress wished to exclude from interstate commerce made no odds. For the Court to make the validity of the regulation depend on the evil character of the commodity to be excluded, was simply trying to decide whether Congress ought to regulate it. It was saying that the evil must be so noxious, in the view of the Court, that it ought to be prohibited. In 1902, it required an evil of such appalling character as a lottery ticket to win the Court's approval. Since then the Court had become more and more sophisticated.

How sophisticated? Up to the point that a man had no right to traffic in surplus crops, more than the market would take at a good price? Up to the point that a man had no right to sell goods produced under conditions that seemed to Congress something short of rudimentary standards of decency?

In the Agricultural Adjustment Act of 1938, Congress abandoned the method of making grants under the spending power and turned, as I have said, to its power to regulate interstate commerce. The purpose of the new A.A.A. was to keep the objectionable surplus out of the interstate and foreign market. The means chosen was to penalize any farmer who offered more than his fair share for sale. Wallace, then Secretary of Agriculture, was given power, when it seemed to him that an oversupply of a crop threatened prices, to fix the quota, state by state. This he was to do in November. Then he was to hold a referendum of producers and growers. If two-thirds of them voted in favor of his quota, it was to become effective and apportioned among the farmers by local committees. If a farmer did not like what was allotted to him, he could appeal to the courts. The force of the Act thus lay in a penalty instead of an inducement. If a farmer marketed more than his allotment, the warehouseman who conducted the auction at which his crop was sold — that was the way tobacco was sold — had to pay over to the Secretary one-half of the price of the excess, which he then could deduct from the sum that became owing to the farmer after the auction. There was no limit, mind you, to what the farmer might grow if he chose. This penalty applied only to what he sent to market.

Roberts wrote the opinion, as he had for the Act of 1933, perhaps by way of penance.[184] The statute, he said, does not control production. It sets no limit upon the acreage which may be planted or produced and imposes no penalty for the planting and producing of tobacco in excess of the marketing quota. It was solely a regulation of interstate commerce, he concluded.

Was that being very naïve? Deliberately? Obviously Congress was striking at production through marketing. The farmers grew their tobacco in order to sell it, not to smoke it themselves.

What still remained of the Old Court, Butler and McReynolds, in their dissent pointed this out. It seemed to them, from a mere inspection of the statute and the Secretary's regulations that the unmistakable purpose of the act was to raise price by lessening production. Whatever may be its declared policy or appearance, they said, the enactment operates to control quantity raised by each farmer. It seemed to them wholly fallacious to say that the penalty was not imposed upon production. The farmer raises tobacco only for sale. To punish him for selling tobacco was the exact equivalent of punishing him for raising the tobacco. So the Act seemed to them wholly invalid.[185]

What is there to be said to that? Wasn't that the common-sense position to take? Was not the new majority turning their head away from the facts? The very things they took such care and such pride in perceiving?

There was only one answer and Roberts had it. Any rule, he said, such as that embodied in the Act, which is intended to foster, protect, and conserve that commerce, or to prevent the flow of commerce from working harm to the people of the nation, is within the competence of Congress. The motive of Congress, he said, in exerting the power, is irrelevant to the validity of the legislation.

Roberts must have heard, as one member of the bar remarked, 'a peal of mellow laughter from the skies.' Surely Holmes had been listening.

The Fair Labor Standards Act of 1938 did not reach the Court until after Butler and McReynolds had retired. So it was unanimously sustained. Stone would be scarcely human if he did not enjoy writing the opinion.[186]

'The motive and purpose of a regulation of interstate commerce,' he said, 'are matters for the legislative judgment upon the exercise of which the Constitution places no restriction and over which the courts are given no control.' He referred to the century and more which had elapsed since the decision of *Gibbons* v. *Ogden* and to those principles of constitutional interpretation which had been so long and repeatedly recognized by the Court as applicable to the Commerce Clause, and thought there would be little occasion for repeating them again — were it not for the decision twenty-two years ago in *Hammer* v. *Dagenhart*. Then he referred to 'the powerful and now classic dissent of Mr. Justice Holmes setting forth the fundamental issues involved.

'*Hammer* v. *Dagenhart* has not been followed. The distinction on which the decision was rested that Congressional power to prohibit interstate commerce is limited to articles which in themselves have some harmful or deleterious property — a distinction which was novel when made and unsupported by any provision of the Constitution — has long since been abandoned. The thesis of the opinion that the motive of the prohibition or its effect to control in some measure the use or production within the states of the article thus excluded from the commerce can operate to deprive the regulation of its constitutional authority has long since ceased to have force.

'The conclusion is inescapable that *Hammer* v. *Dagenhart* was a departure from the principles which have prevailed in the interpretation of the Commerce Clause both before and since the decision and that such vitality, as a precedent, as it then had has long since been exhausted. It should be and now is overruled.'

'Long since?' It was less than two years since Holmes's peal of laughter had been heard. Until then, for all the bar had been told, *Hammer* v. *Dagenhart* was still part of the Constitution.

13

THE NEW COURT

THE RECONSTRUCTION of the Court had been proceeding. After two of the Old Guard retired, Van Devanter and Sutherland, and two of the old minority, Cardozo and Brandeis, died, they had been replaced by Black, by Reed, by Frankfurter, and by Douglas. Butler and McReynolds were not left for long. First Butler died, then McReynolds retired. Hughes, too, retired, and President Roosevelt appointed Stone to fill his great shoes as Chief Justice. The three vacancies were filled by Murphy, Byrnes, and Jackson. They were all appointments from other fields of the public service. Murphy and Jackson were promoted from the office of Attorney General. Byrnes was taken from the Senate.

Frank Murphy was a Michigan man of about fifty, unmarried and a Catholic. He had taught a little law in a night school, gone into the United States Attorney's office, sat for a little in a police court, and then been elected Mayor of Detroit. From there he had risen through a distinguished political career, Governor General of the Philippines, Governor of Michigan at the time of the sit-down strikes, Attorney General of the United

States. He was appointed to the Court in January, 1940.

James F. Byrnes came from Charleston, South Carolina. He was admitted to the bar in 1903. After serving as the official court reporter, he went to Congress for a dozen years, and then practiced law in Spartansburg for half a dozen. In 1931 he was elected to a distinguished career in the Senate, from which Roosevelt took him in June, 1941. It was the Senate's loss. It was the Court's loss in the autumn of 1942 when Roosevelt took him from the Court and made him Assistant President. For the Court got only one term's worth of his wisdom.

Robert H. Jackson was another man in his early fifties. He came from upstate New York, Chautauqua County. In Jamestown he had been counsel for the street railway, the telephone company, the bank, and the city itself, and then in 1934, with the incoming New Deal, general counsel for the Bureau of Internal Revenue. In 1936 he had moved over to the Department of Justice, as assistant attorney general, Solicitor General, and Attorney General. He joined the Court with Byrnes in July, 1941. In 1945 he went to Nuremberg to prosecute the Nazi war criminals.

When Byrnes was taken to be Assistant President, Wiley Rutledge took his place. Rutledge came from Kentucky, had gone to college in Wisconsin and to law school in Colorado. Then he taught law for fifteen years, until Roosevelt appointed him to the Circuit Court of Appeals for the District of Columbia. His promotion to the Court gave the law professors a majority (Stone from Columbia, Roberts from the University of Pennsylvania, Frankfurter from Harvard, Douglas from Yale, and Rutledge from Colorado, Washington University, and Iowa State), which only shows that law professors were in public service, not that the Court was going academic. When Roberts retired in 1945, President Truman appointed Senator Harold H. Burton of Ohio. Burton was born near Boston and educated in Bowdoin and the Harvard Law School, but he left New England for Cleveland, where he practiced law and then served as mayor. He was elected Senator from Ohio in 1941.

That this New Court would be unanimous or harmonious was scarcely to be expected. To be sure, a single President had appointed them, all but Burton, but Roosevelt had not picked his nominees for like-mindedness. Anyone could see that. Acceptance of the New Deal, even devotion to it, was not a dominating philosophy. And the New Deal was now successful and those who had fought for it could now break ranks. Deeper than this, there was the Court's reorientation away from the Legal Tradition and conceptual thinking of all sorts toward the pertinence of facts. That made individual differences easier. Each Justice was going to speak up more for himself, instead of simply joining others, whether in majority or minority. Yet there were more than individual divisions. If the New Court was not bipolar, it was bifocal. Black, Douglas, and Murphy, more often than not, were seeing eye to eye. You could add Rutledge. On the other hand, Stone, Roberts, Frankfurter, Jackson, and Byrnes, while he was there, were looking at things in a similar way and from about the same distance. Certainly the division was not so simple a matter as conservative and radical, if that be simple.

14

FEDERALISM

State over Nation

NOTHING is said about federalism in the Constitution, nothing explicit. Stronger than that, it is implicit. The powers of the national government are delegated. All the other powers of government are reserved by the Tenth Amendment to the states and the people. It became the Court's business to keep the equipoise. We have seen the Court throw its weight against the national threat of the New Deal. When the nation was new, it was the other way about. The tender shoot had to be protected from the power of the states.

In particular, the new nation had to be protected from the states' power of taxation. The states retained that power undiminished, except in one respect, duties on foreign imports and exports.

There was nothing in the document to prevent the states from killing the new nation by taxation; nothing but mutual prudence and reciprocal forbearance, Hamilton said.[187] If this were not enough, it seemed up to the Court to do something about it.

The question first presented itself in the form of the constitutional right of the State of Maryland to tax a branch of the Bank of the United States. Since the leisure of the times permitted long opinions, you will have to permit four paragraphs of Marshall's. 'But,' Marshall said, 'let us resume the inquiry whether this power can be exercised by the respective states consistently with a fair construction of the Constitution. *That the power to tax involves the power to destroy*, that the power to destroy may defeat and render useless the power to create, that there is a plain repugnance in conferring on one government a power to control the constitutional measures of another, which other with respect to those very measures is declared to be supreme over that which exerts the control, are propositions not to be denied. But all inconsistencies are to be reconciled by the magic of the word "confidence." Taxation, it is said, does not necessarily and unavoidably destroy. To carry it to the excess of destruction would be an abuse which would banish that confidence which is essential to all government.

'But is this a case of confidence? Would the people of any one state trust those of another with the power to control the most insignificant operations of their state government? We know they would not. Why, then, should we suppose that the people of any one state should be willing to trust those of another with the power to control the operations of a government to which they have confided their most important and most valuable interest? In the Legislature of the Union alone are all represented. The Legislature of the Union alone, therefore, can be trusted by the people with the power of controlling measures which concern all with the confidence that it will not be abused. This, then, is not a case of confidence. We must consider it as it really is.

'If we apply the principle for which the State of Maryland contends to the Constitution generally, we shall find it capable of changing totally the character of that instrument. We shall find it capable of arresting all the measures of the government and of prostrating it at the foot of the state. The American people have declared their Constitution and the laws made in pursuance thereof to be supreme, but this principle would transfer the supremacy in fact to the states.

'If the states may tax one instrument employed by the Government in the execution of its powers, they may tax any and every other instrument. They may tax the mails, they may tax the Mint, they may tax patent rights, they may tax the papers of the Custom House, they may tax judicial process, they may tax all of the means employed by the Government to an excess which would defeat all the ends of government. This was not intended by the American people. They did not design to make their government dependent on the state.' [188]

The Court, dazed by Marshall's reasoning, quite forgot that this was a tax on all banks, and lay as heavily on state banks as it did on the branch of the Bank of the United States. There was no discrimination against the United States. It was a clear case of the fallacy of resting your decision solely on the logical consequences. We are warned that the machine dominates man in this machine age. Here an abstract principle was dominating its masters.

The first important judicial protest came from Judge Holmes in 1928. Though he agreed that the imposition of a uniform state tax on gasoline sold to the Coast Guard was invalid as a practical matter, he declined to accept

Marshall's reasoning. 'It seems to me,' Holmes said, 'that the State Court was right. I should say plainly right, but for the effect of certain dicta of Chief Justice Marshall which culminated in or rather were founded upon his often quoted proposition that the power to tax is the power to destroy. In those days it was not recognized as it is today that most of the distinctions of the law are distinctions of degree. If the States had any power it was assumed that they had all power, and that the necessary alternative was to deny it altogether. But this Court which has so often defeated the attempt to tax in certain ways can defeat an attempt to discriminate or otherwise go too far without wholly abolishing the power to tax. The power to tax is not the power to destroy while this Court sits.' [189]

There is no way of stopping logical consequences. By January of 1937, the Court had gone so far as to hold unanimously that the general counsel of the Panama Railroad need pay no New York income tax, simply because all that company's stock was owned by the United States, which made it 'a federal instrumentality.' [190]

Holmes's protest went unheeded until March, 1939, the New Court was asked whether New York could tax the income of one of the examining attorneys of the Home Owner's Loan Corporation.[191] All its stock was owned by the Federal Government. Plainly it was a federal instrumentality. Nevertheless, said the New Court, New York can do just that.

Butler and McReynolds, of course, protested. 'Futile indeed are the vague intimations that this court may protect against excessive or destructive taxation. Where the power to tax exists, legislatures may exert it to destroy, to discourage, to protect or exclusively for the purpose of raising revenue.'

Pure Marshall, as you will recognize and as Frankfurter, in a concurring opinion, pointed out. He deemed it appropriate, he said, to add a few remarks, going back 'to the early healthy practice whereby the justices gave expression of individual opinions. But the old tradition still has relevance when an important shift in constitutional doctrine is announced after a reconstruction in the membership of the Court.

'For one hundred and twenty years this Court has been concerned with claims of immunity from taxes imposed by one authority in our dual system of government because of the taxpayer's relation to the other. The basis for the Court's intervention in this field has not been any explicit provision of the Constitution. The States, after they formed the Union, continued to have the same range of taxing power which they had before, barring only duties affecting exports, imports, and on tonnage.

'But, as is true of other activities of the State and national governments, the fact that we are a federalism raises problems regarding these vital powers of taxation. Since two governments have authority within the same territory, neither through its power to tax can be allowed to cripple the operations of the other. Therefore, State and federal governments must avoid exactions which discriminate against each other or obviously interfere with one another's operations. These were the determining considerations that led the great Chief Justice to strike down the Maryland statute as an unambiguous measure of discrimination against the use by the United States of the Bank of the United States as one of its instruments of government.'

'The arguments upon which *McCulloch* v. *Maryland* rested had their roots in actuality. But they have been distorted by sterile refinements unrelated to affairs. These refinements derived authority from an unfortunate remark in the opinion in *McCulloch* v. *Maryland*. Partly as a flourish of rhetoric and partly because the intellectual fashion of the times indulged a free use of absolutes, Chief Justice Marshall gave currency to the phrase that "the power to tax involves the power to destroy."'

'This dictum,' Frankfurter went on, 'was treated as though it were a constitutional mandate.' But it was not. It was only a 'seductive cliché.' Until recently, he said, we have been moving in the realm of what Lincoln called 'pernicious abstractions.' 'The judicial history of this doctrine of immunity is a striking illustration of an occasional tendency to encrust unwarranted interpretations upon the Constitution and thereafter to consider merely what has been judicially said about the Constitution rather than to be primarily controlled by a fair conception of the Constitution. Judicial exegesis is unavoidable with reference to an organic act like our Constitution, drawn in many particulars with purposed vagueness so as to leave room for the unfolding future. But the ultimate touchstone of constitutionality is the Constitution itself and not what we have said about it.'

There was not only nothing in the Constitution that forbade the states from taxing the nation. There was no reason why they should not tax as they choose — up to the point where they really and actually interfered with the national government. A uniform tax did not do this. Only discrimination did this. The Court had been following an abstraction, a pernicious abstraction, dressed in a seductive cliché.

This lay all on the political side of federalism. It was a question of the relations of governments, the state governments against the national government, the power of the state governments over the officials of our national government. There is an economic side to our national life.

Are you and I, and the corporations to which we sell, from which we buy, for which we work, and in which we may hold stock — are we and they to have the advantages of belonging to a great nation? One of them is full freedom of trade. Freedom of trade *among* the states as well as freedom *within* each state, which taken together make up the great whole. We want both if we are to have a full measure. Each is competing, as we want them to compete, against the other: the local store against the chain, local production against national mass production, local sales against national distribution. At times our national trade has needed to be protected against local prejudice, just as the nation has needed protection against the states. Look at all this largely and you will see that constitutionally it is the same problem and so much more important that here the Constitution said something expressly about it.

The Constitution gave Congress power to regulate the national commerce, commerce *among* the states. Yet Congress has done little or nothing to prevent the states from interfering. The states could have taxed that commerce out of existence quite as effectively as a state might a federal agency. Unless something had been done, we should never have had any national commerce. Not a pretty picture. This, of course, would have been Congress's fault. However, since Congress did little or nothing, again it was the Court, and again the Court had no more express authority here than it had to prevent the states from taxing the national government itself.

Marshall had recognized that it was with the same problem he had dealt with in the case of the Bank of the United States. In the leading case, *Brown v. Maryland*, in 1827,[192] he said that the doctrine of *McCulloch v. Maryland*, the case of the tax on the Bank, was 'entirely applicable.' [193] Perhaps it never occurred to him that the facts which were going to have to be fitted into the doctrine were immeasurably more complicated. Commerce then was not what commerce is now. However, the point is, we are dealing with the same constitutional doctrine. There it was applied to the political relations between the national government and the states; here to the economic relations between national business and the states.

So here, too, the Court adopted the flat doctrine that the states could no more tax interstate commerce than the national government itself. Not even a uniform tax, not even if the same tax were laid on competing intrastate commerce. A State could tax its own local merchants, that was its own affair, but it could not tax the companies from outside the State with whom they were competing.

The result, of course, was to discriminate against local trade, but the Court had a clear idea of what it was doing. 'It is hardly within the scope of the present discussion to refer to the disastrous effects to which the power to tax interstate or foreign commerce may lead. If the power exists in the state at all, it has no limit but the discretion of the state, and might be exercised in such a manner as to drive away that commerce, or to load it with an intolerable burden, seriously affecting the business and prosperity of other states interested in it; and if those states, by way of retaliation, or otherwise, should impose like restrictions, the utmost confusion would prevail in our commercial affairs.' [194]

And under that doctrine we became the greatest single market in the world, so great that some people used to say that we did not need any foreign trade.

Black was the first to attack the doctrine, in one of the lone dissents he made in his first year in the Court, and he followed it up a year later with another.

Both involved the question of the validity of including in a gross receipts tax receipts from your interstate business as well as from the business you did within the state. Many states had been turning to a tax on gross receipts instead of on income. One of these cases involved the one per cent tax in Indiana on the business of the J. D. Adams Manufacturing Company, an Indiana corporation, which made road machinery and sold eighty per cent of it in other states.[195] The other was a Washington tax of one-half of one per cent on Gwin, White and Prince, a Washington corporation, whose entire business consisted in marketing apples and pears grown in Washington and Oregon and sold in other states.[196]

Was that such an interference with interstate commerce that the commerce clause by itself, Congress having done nothing, forbade it? The Court cited a dozen cases for the invalidity of such a tax as a burden on interstate commerce. Moreover, it was discriminating, because, said the Court, 'If Washington is free to exact such a tax, other states to which the commerce extends (these apples were sold in Washington) may, with equal right, lay a tax similarly measured for the privilege of conducting within their respective territorial limits the activities there which contribute to the service. The present tax, though nominally local, thus in its practical operation discriminates against interstate commerce, since it imposes upon it, merely because interstate commerce is being done, the risk of a multiple burden to which local commerce is not exposed.' [197]

That was what the Court said and it aroused Black. No, he said, this tax itself is not discriminatory, and it is not to be made so simply by the risk that the interstate business here taxed equally with the intrastate may be taxed again by another state. That, he said, is a hypothetical possibility, being taxed again. It is an apprehension that another state might lay another tax, but any such tax would be held equally unconstitutional and void. Multiple taxation can result only if another state passes a valid tax and under this decision it would be invalid. If all such other taxes do come before us and are held unconstitutional — the test of a rule lies in its universal application — this construction of the Commerce clause imposes an unfair and discriminatory burden, not on interstate but on *intrastate* commerce. For interstate business becomes relieved of all taxes. Intrastate bears the burden for both.[198]

So much for that. But Black went further. Why isn't this all matter for legislation by the Congress, he asked, not matter for judicial decision by the Court. Was not the Court taking upon itself what the Constitution intended Congress to do? Black went on, 'A Court may act to protect a litigant from unfair and unjust burdens upon the litigant's interstate business. Yet, it would seem that only Congress has the power to formulate rules, regulations, and laws to protect interstate commerce from *merely*

possible future unfair burdens. The control of future conduct, the prevention of future injuries and the formulation
of regulatory rules in the fields of commerce and taxation,
all present legislative problems.' [199]

Is he not quite right? The Court had suggested that the
state might have, and should have, apportioned the tax,
setting off interstate and taxing only intrastate business.
So it might, and if it had drawn the line nicely its resulting
tax on the business within its own borders might have
been valid. It is not, however, a simple thing to do. It is
not easy to draw the nice line between inter- and intrastate
commerce, not even for the Court itself. Every attempt
to make the apportionment would be subject to litigation
and ultimate approval or disapproval by the Court. Black
said, 'Only a comprehensive survey and investigation of
the entire national economy — which Congress alone has
power and facilities to make — can indicate the need for,
as well as justify, restricting the taxing power of a State so
as to provide against conjectured taxation by more than
one State on identical income. A broad and deliberate
legislative investigation — which no Court can make —
may indicate to Congress that a wise policy for the national
economy demands that each State in which an interstate
business operates be permitted to apply a non-discriminatory tax to the gross receipts of that business either because of its size and volume or practically to offset the
tendency toward centralization of the nation's business.
Congress may find that to shelter interstate commerce in a
tax exempt refuge — in the manner of the judgment here
— is to grant that commerce a privileged status over intrastate business, contrary to the national welfare.' [200]

Black concluded, 'It is essential today, as at the time of

the adoption of the Constitution, that commerce among the States and with foreign nations be left free from discriminatory and retaliatory burdens imposed by the States. It is of equal importance, however, that the judicial department of our government scrupulously observe its constitutional limitations and that Congress alone should adopt a broad national policy of regulation — if otherwise valid State laws combine to hamper the free flow of commerce. Doubtless, much confusion would be avoided if the courts would refrain from restricting the enforcement of valid, non-discriminatory State tax laws. Any belief that Congress has failed to take cognizance of the problems of conjectured "multiple taxation" or "apportionment" by exerting its exclusive power over interstate commerce, is an inadequate reason for the judicial branch of government — without constitutional power — to attempt to perform the duty constitutionally reposed in Congress. I would return to the rule that — except for State acts designed to impose discriminatory burdens on interstate commerce because it *is* interstate — Congress alone must determine how far it shall be free and untrammeled, how far it shall be burdened by duties and imposts and how far it shall be prohibited.' [201]

Black dissented alone in these two cases, but the next time, in 1940, two years after the first and a year after the second, Frankfurter and Douglas had joined the Court and they joined him. This was in the case of a gasoline tax on the Dixie Greyhound Bus Line.[202]

The Dixie Greyhound buses ran between Memphis, Tennessee, and Saint Louis, Missouri, which is a three hundred and forty-two mile run. Since a bus got only about five miles out of a gallon of gas, seventy gallons were taken on for the trip. Leaving Memphis, three miles out they hit the Arkansas border and a police officer stopped them and demanded the Arkansas tax of six and a half cents a gallon on each gallon they carried over twenty. It was a criminal offense in Arkansas to drive with more than twenty gallons unless this tax had been paid.

Since the Greyhound bus had by that time used up less than a gallon, it had to pay a tax on almost fifty gallons. But only about sixteen of those fifty gallons were going to be used on Arkansas roads. For it was only about eighty miles across Arkansas into Missouri. This, then, was a tax on gasoline that was not going to be used in Arkansas. It was a tax on gasoline that was, in fact, going to be used on Missouri roads. Could Arkansas tax it for the benefit of her highways?

No, said the Court, this tax cannot reasonably be regarded as proper compensation for using Arkansas' roads.

Black, Frankfurter, and Douglas dissented in a joint opinion. 'We take a different view,' they said. 'Congress, sole constitutional legislative repository of power over interstate commerce, has enacted no regulation prohibiting Arkansas from levying a tax — on gasoline in excess of twenty gallons brought into the State — in return for the use of its highways. The cost entailed by the construction and maintenance of modern highways creates for the forty-eight States one of their largest financial problems. A major phase of this problem is the proper apportionment of the financial burden between those who use a State's highway for transportation within its borders and those who do so in the course of interstate transportation. Striking a fair balance involves incalculable variants and therefore is beset with perplexities. The making

of these exacting adjustments is the business of legislation.' [203]

For them, this case again but illustrated the wisdom of
the Founders in placing interstate commerce under the
protection of Congress. The problem was not limited to
Arkansas, but was of national moment. 'Maintenance of
open channels of trade between the States was not only of
paramount importance when our Constitution was framed;
it remains today a complex problem calling for national
vigilance and regulation.' [204] 'Judicial control of national
commerce — unlike legislative regulations — must from
inherent limitations of the judicial process treat the subject by the hit and miss method of deciding single local
controversies upon evidence and information limited by
the narrow rules of litigation.'

'Spasmodic and unrelated instances of litigation cannot
afford an adequate basis for the creation of integrated
national rules which alone can afford that full protection
for interstate commerce intended by the Constitution.
We would, therefore, leave the questions raised by the
Arkansas tax for consideration of Congress in a nation-
wide survey of the constantly increasing barriers to trade
among the States.

'Unconfined by the narrow scope of judicial proceedings Congress alone can, in the exercise of its plenary constitutional control over interstate commerce, not only
consider whether such a tax as now under scrutiny is consistent with the best interests of our national economy, but
can also on the basis of full exploration of the many aspects
of a complicated problem devise a national policy fair
alike to the States and our Union.

'Diverse and interacting State laws may well have

created avoidable hardships.   But the remedy, if any is
called for, we think is within the ample reach of Congress.' [205]

So much for what these three said.   But Congress has
not reached.   Congress has done nothing.   The whole
matter has been left in the hands of the Court, and the
Court has been juggling it, so to speak, from one hand to
the other.   Certainly this was what the Court was doing in
the Northwest Airlines case,[206] which came up in the spring
of 1944.   The company's planes flew all over the North-
western states, stopping in one after another for passengers and re-fueling.   Minnesota taxed them.   Frankfurter
was persuaded that Minnesota could do this on the ground
that the company was incorporated there, which, he
thought, made Minnesota its 'domicile.'   Jackson concurred because he thought Saint Paul, Minnesota, could
be regarded as the 'home port' of the fleet, but he remarked, 'It seems more than likely that no solution of the
competition among states to tax this transportation agency
can be devised without legislative help.'   Four other Justices thought they had such a device and dissented on the
ground they wanted to see it used.   They would have sent
the case back to the state court for it to make a fair apportionment of the total tax among all the states concerned.   But this blinks the problem, which is national,
not state.   You do not decide whether Congress or the
Court is to handle the problem by throwing it back on the
states.   That would be like deciding the custody of a child
as between its parents by letting it be adopted.

Black's solution, as we have seen — and here he stuck
to it — was simply that this was none of the Court's business.   'The differing views of members of the Court in this

and related cases illustrate the difficulties inherent in the judicial formulation of general rules to meet the national problems arising from state taxation which bears in incidence upon interstate commerce. These problems, it seems to me, call for Congressional investigation, consideration, and action. The Constitution gives that branch of government the power to regulate commerce among the states, and until it acts I think we should enter the field with extreme caution.' [207]

Taxes are not the only way to burden commerce. Diverse local regulations could kill our national market quicker than it could be taxed out of existence. But the principle is the same, though local policies, for they and not simply the local tax rate are at stake, may make it harder to perceive. Taxes are only money. Local policies are the springs of good and evil.

Needless to say, there are a multitude of examples. One pair of cases points the matter up so well that it will be enough. Jim Crow cars have always troubled us, and they have been as obnoxious to some of us as they seem necessary to others. Shortly after the Civil War, in 1869, Louisiana passed an act that in no railroad, street car, steamboat, stagecoach, omnibus, or other vehicle should there be any discrimination 'on account of race or color.' Mrs. DeCuir, a colored lady, took passage on a steamboat plying between New Orleans and Vicksburg as far as Hermitage, and she was refused accommodations in a cabin specially set apart for white persons. She brought suit for her mental and physical suffering.

This statute had been passed under a provision in the reconstructed Constitution of Louisiana that 'all persons shall enjoy equal rights and privileges upon any convey-

ance of a public character.' That was all right. The
Court set the statute aside under the Commerce Clause,
because it interfered with the free flow of trade. 'A passenger in the cabin set apart for the use of whites without
the State must, when the boat comes within, share the
accommodations of that cabin with such colored person
as may come on board afterwards, if the law is enforced.
Commerce cannot flourish in the midst of such embarrass-
ments. No carrier of passengers can conduct his business
with satisfaction to himself, or comfort to those employing
him, if on one side of a State line his passengers, both
white and colored, must be permitted to occupy the same
cabin, and on the other be kept separate.' [208]

In 1946 the same case came up in reverse. A Jim Crow
law from Virginia came before the Court and was held
equally invalid.[209] Reed spoke for the Court. It was
simple enough. 'It seems clear to us,' Reed said, 'that
seating arrangements for the different races in interstate
motor travel require a single uniform rule to promote and
protect national travel. Consequently, we hold the Virginia statute in controversy invalid.' And he cited the
DeCuir case as precedent.

Black was in a bit of a dilemma. He did not want to be
misunderstood. This was none of the Court's business.
Congress, and not the Court, had to regulate interstate
commerce if it was to be regulated at all. 'The Commerce
Clause of the Constitution,' he said, 'provides that "Congress shall have power . . : to regulate commerce . . .
among the several States." I have believed, and still believe that this provision means that Congress can regulate
commerce and that the courts cannot.

'But in a series of cases decided in recent years this

Court over my protest has held that the Commerce Clause justifies this Court in nullifying state legislation which this Court concludes imposes an "undue burden" on interstate commerce.' Here he referred to the cases in which, as we have seen, he had been dissenting, Adams, Gwin, Dixie Greyhound. 'I think that whether state legislation imposes an "undue burden" on interstate commerce raises pure questions of policy, which the Constitution intended should be resolved by the Congress.

'I thought then, and still believe, that in these cases the Court was assuming the rôle of a "super-legislature" in determining matters of governmental policy. But the Court, at least for the present, seems committed to this interpretation of the Commerce Clause. So long as the Court remains committed to the "undue burden on commerce formula," I must make decisions under it. In view of the Court's present disposition to apply that formula, I acquiesce.'

He was agreeing to a truce, laying down his arms for a moment, to permit Jim Crow laws to be buried. A special concession to a burden on interstate commerce which seemed to him 'of a far more serious nature.'

Only Burton dissented. 'The Court recognizes,' he said, 'that it serves as "the final arbiter of the competing demands of state and national interests" and that it must fairly determine, in the absence of Congressional action, whether the state statute actually imposes such an undue burden upon interstate commerce as to invalidate that statute.' But Burton could not see there was need here of 'a single uniform rule.' The ten contiguous states around Louisiana had all made at least progress toward a uniformity by requiring racial separation. There was at least a regional uniformity. On the other hand, there were eighteen states which in one way or another made racial separation in public carriers unlawful. 'If the DeCuir case is followed,' he said, 'without weighing the surrounding facts, it would invalidate today statutes in New England states prohibiting racial separation in seating arrangements on carriers, which would not be invalidated under the doctrine stated in the Arizona case.'

Burton was referring to a recent case where the Court had held invalid an Arizona statute limiting freight trains to seventy cars. There the Court had meticulously compared the dangers of long trains with the dangers of shorter trains, examined the economics of operation, and weighed the burden on interstate commerce of a variety of state laws on the subject. Perhaps the Court had felt itself competent, having handled, as almost every Court has, enough employers' liability cases and enough rate cases to make a judge feel like something of an expert on such matters. Anyhow, the Court had been quite willing to go into the facts and had said flatly that 'state laws will not be invalidated without the support of relevant factual material which will afford a sure basis for an informed judgment.' Burton was ready enough to hold a Jim Crow law unconstitutional, but not on the strength of a precedent which, thereby confirmed, would likewise render unconstitutional the anti-discrimination laws of eighteen northern states, and discourage twenty more from following their good example. Certainly not unless he had the support of enough facts to afford a surer basis for judgment than he could discern here.

The Court as well as Black was in a dilemma. It would not follow Black, the genuine Black, and recant its power

over interstate commerce. There were cases in which it
felt bound to act like the national institution it was. But
by what authority?

Nation Over State

If the young nation needed protection from the state,
after the Civil War it was the other way about, and the
Court promptly adopted the reciprocal of Marshall's doctrine of the immunity of the nation from taxation by the
states. In *Collector* v. *Day* [210] the Court refused to let Congress tax the salary of a state official, in that case a Massachusetts probate judge. It was a straight application of
Marshall's reasoning that the power to tax involved the
power to destroy. 'The exemption,' the Court said, 'rests
upon necessary implication, and is upheld by the great law
of self preservation; as any government, whose means
employed in conducting its operations, if subject to the
control of another and distinct government, can exist only
at the mercy of that government.' But the Court was
misapprehending the very nature of a federal system. It
was confusing the relation of the whole with one of its
parts with the very different relation of a part with the
whole. Marshall's doctrine had no reciprocal, as he very
well knew. As he himself said, near the end of the second
paragraph quoted from his opinion in *McCulloch* v. *Maryland*, 'The legislature of the Union alone can be treated by
the people with the power of controlling measures which
concern all with the confidence that it will not be abused.'
Bradley told the Court in his dissent, 'It seems to me that
the general government has the same power of taxing the
income of officers of the State governments as it has of

taxing that of its own officers. It is the common government of all alike; and every citizen is presumed to trust his own government in the matter of taxation. No man ceases to be a citizen of the United States by being an officer under the State government. I cannot accede to the doctrine that the general government is to be regarded as in any sense foreign or antagonistic to the State governments, their officers, or people; nor can I agree that a presumption can be admitted that the general government will act in a manner hostile to the existence or functions of the State governments, which are constituent parts of the system or body politic forming the basis on which the general government is founded. The taxation by the State governments of the instruments employed by the general government in the exercise of its powers, is a very different thing.' [211]

And yet the Court continued to treat the two doctrines as if they were the same. In the spring of 1937 a majority told the chief engineer of the New York State Bureau of Water Supply that he did not have to pay any federal income tax, because a water supply was 'essentially governmental in character.' [212] But it was only a majority. Stone and Cardozo concurred on the ground that he was exempted anyhow, and Roberts and Brandeis dissented. They thought the tax was not unconstitutional. They said it could be unconstitutional only if it discriminated against the state official and in favor of private citizens, or if its burden was 'palpable and direct,' and not merely hypothetical and remote. They were disturbed. The importance of the case, they said, arises out of the fact that the claimed exemption may well extend to millions of persons employed by municipalities throughout the nation whose work no wise differs from that of their fellows in private enterprises. These exemptions are essentially unfair. They are unsound. Federal and state business ought to bear their proportionate share of taxation, in order that comparison may be made between the cost of conducting public and private business.

A year later, in May, 1938, came the case of construction engineer employed by the New York Port Authority, who claimed that he, too, was immune from the Federal income tax.[213] But he was dealing with a New Court which, though it refused to grasp the nettle of the 'century of precedents' which Butler and McReynolds insisted and protested it was overruling, made the engineer pay his income tax. There were cogent reasons, the Court said, why any constitutional restriction upon the taxing power granted to Congress, so far as it can be properly raised by implication, should be narrowly limited. If the tax considered in *Collector* v. *Day* upon the salary of an officer engaged in the performance of an indispensable function of the state which cannot be delegated to private individuals may be regarded as such an instance, this is not, they said, the case presented here. The New Court had not quite hit its stride. It was not until the next year that *Collector* v. *Day* was overruled, in the case of the attorney of the Home Owners' Loan Corporation.[214]

In all this, the Court was treating a state, what it is and what it does, in a very old-fashioned sense. This was well enough when a state's activities were restricted to what we used to be brought up to believe were proper governmental functions, but when a state twitched its mantle and went off into new pastures, what then? Marshall's pernicious abstractions, on which the Court had relied, having ignored his confidence in the national government, sprang from a time when 'asking one of the states to surrender part of her sovereignty was like asking a lady to surrender part of her chastity,' as John Randolph of Roanoke said.[215]

In 1905, the Court had to meet the question, Is a State still a State if she goes into trade? In this case it was the liquor business, and in that era it was as if one had been asked, Is a lady still a lady if she does something as ungenteel as that? In a state it was called socialism then. But it was enough to help the Court swallow its abstraction and stand back when the Federal government taxed the once genteel State of South Carolina when she took over a monopoly of the liquor trade. The Court stood aside and refused to heed South Carolina's protests at being taxed.[216]

Only three of the Justices were bold enough champions of the old abstraction to dissent. By this ruling, they said, and by the reasoning which sustains it, the ancient landmarks are obliterated and the distinct powers belonging to both the national and the state governments are reciprocally placed the one at the mercy of the other. Each, now, has the potency of destroying the other. So said White and Peckham and McKenna. A State then, they said, can tax national banks, or the Post Office, for they are no more governmental than a state's absolute control over the sale of intoxicating liquor.

Fortunately, the Court, prejudiced or not, was practical. The majority said that the framers of the Constitution were not mere visionaries, toying with speculations or theories, but practical men dealing with the facts of political life. It was equally true of themselves.

We are not going to exempt a state, they said, from being taxed if it goes into the liquor business. If we do,

what next? Mingling the thought of profit with the necessity of regulation a state may be induced to take posses-
sion in like manner of tobacco and all other objects of the
internal revenue tax. The whole internal revenue may
thus be stricken down. More than this, the States may
take over the public utilities. There is a large and growing movement to this end, they added. 'We may even go
a step further. There are some insisting that the states
shall become the owners of all property and managers of
all business, though, of course, that is an extreme view.'

There was no need of carrying their suppositions so far.
There was then no Federal income tax. Ten years before,
it had been held unconstitutional for good, and the Sixteenth Amendment was not adopted until 1913. So far as
the Court could then see, in 1905, the only available resources of the Federal government were excise taxes and
the tariff, and a good fourth of its entire income was derived from the excise tax on liquor. It would make a
pretty picture were the United States to have to rely only
on the tariff. Not that this would have hurt the sensibilities of some of the senators or some of the lobbyists. But
suppose the states were to start importing on their own
account, why would not even the tariff then become unconstitutional?

However far-fetched this may seem to us now, to these
Justices then it was no scarecrow, flapping its empty arms
in the winds of doctrine. We now, we the people of the
United States, can tax incomes and inheritances and a
good part of our government's income comes from that
source. Then we had no such resource. The majority
was being severely practical. If they were obliterating an
ancient landmark, it was under a truckload of the good
loam of fact.

But an abstraction is seldom or never stifled for lack of air. Twice since then there have been protests in the Court against taxing the sovereign majesty of a state which goes into trade; once by Butler and McReynolds in 1938, again recently by Black and Douglas in 1946. Both occasions may seem of small consequence to you, but an abstraction crystallizes on a matter of small immediate significance quite as readily as on things of greater moment. A word on each.

A good part of the income of the University of Georgia and so, too, of Georgia Tech, and of many another great educational institution, comes from their football teams. Certainly that was so in 1934, when the combined take of these two in Georgia was nearly one hundred and fifty thousand dollars. The Federal government taxed admissions to football games as well as theaters and prizefights, but these were both state institutions. Were they to be taxed? The State of Georgia protested. The Court was not impressed. Liquor stores and football games looked too much alike in a constitutional way. But Butler and McReynolds were troubled enough by notions of sovereignty to dissent. These athletic contests, they considered, were an integral part of the State's program of education, and they found it hard to understand how they could be brought down to the level of the sale of intoxicating liquors.[217]

When, eight years later, in 1946, New York went into the business of selling soft drinks at Saratoga Springs, it was Douglas and Black, instead of Butler and McReynolds, who took up the torch.[218] If football games were only education to them, selling Saratoga Spring water, with or without sweetening, was to Douglas and Black no

more than exploiting New York's natural resources. Any
activity in which a state may choose to engage, within the
limits of its powers, is an exercise of its sovereign power
and therefore immune from Federal taxation. Butler or
McReynolds may or may not have expected the torch to be
carried so far as that, but it was the same torch. They
had received it from White. White had gone back to Marshall for it. Listen to Douglas and Black:

'A tax is a powerful, regulatory instrument. Local
government exists to provide for the welfare of its people,
not for a limited group of stockholders. If the Federal
Government can place the local governments on its tax
collector's list, their capacity to serve the needs of their
citizens is at once hampered or curtailed. The field of
Federal excise taxation alone is practically without limits.
Many State activities are in marginal enterprises where
private capital refuses to venture. Add to the cost of
these projects a Federal tax and the social program may
be destroyed before it can be launched.

'In any case, the repercussions of such a fundamental
change on the credit of the States and on their programs
to take care of the needy and to build for the future would
be considerable To say the present tax will be sustained
because it does not impair the State's functions of government is to conclude either that the sale by the State of its
mineral water is not a function of government or that the
present tax is so slight as to be no burden. The former
obviously is not true. The latter overlooks the fact that
the power to tax lightly is the power to tax severely.'

Again pure Marshall, not only in their echo of his notion
that the power to tax is the power to destroy, but in their
deference to sovereignty. Their major objection, they

said, was that the Court 'disregards the Tenth Amendment, places the sovereign States on the same plane as private citizens, and makes the sovereign States pay the Federal government for the privilege of exercising the powers of sovereignty guaranteed them by the Constitution.' And to button that up, they quoted Hamilton in the Federalist and Marshall in *McCulloch* v. *Maryland*.

Sovereignty, like personality which goes so far as to regard itself as immortal, is a sticky abstraction. There always have been, perhaps there always will be, someone on the Court who will cherish it and speak for it in our federal system, just as there has been, and is, and perhaps always will be, its lovers in international relations.

Frankfurter wrote what appears in the reports as the judgment of the Court, though Rutledge was the only other who subscribed to it and he felt he had to write another opinion for himself, too. Frankfurter was not quite willing to ditch the idea of state sovereignty entirely. There is a Platonic strain in his thinking that clung to the essence, the very being, of sovereignty, which he put this way. 'There are, of course, State activities and State-owned property that partake of uniqueness from the point of view of intergovernmental relations. These inherently constitute a class by themselves. Only a State can own a Statehouse; only a State can get income from taxing. These could not be included for purposes of federal taxation in any abstract category of taxpayers without taxing the State as a State. But so long as Congress generally tags a source of revenue by whomsoever earned and not uniquely capable of being earned only by a State, the Constitution of the United States does not forbid it merely because its incidence falls also on a State.'

That, however, was as far as Frankfurter would go, and it is as far as the abstraction as an abstraction is true and usable. If you are going to perpetuate it at all, it must be in precisely that form. But even so much was too much for four of the Justices. If Black and Douglas seem to have a predilection for the abstract, these four had none.

Stone, Reed, Murphy, and Burton would not have anything to do with any abstraction. To them the question was a simple question of fact. The problem, they said, is not one to be solved by a formula; and they rejected even the distinction between a discriminating and a non-discriminating tax as infallible. 'We are not,' they said, 'prepared to say that the national government may constitutionally lay a non-discriminatory tax on every class of property and activities of States and individuals alike. A federal tax which is not discriminatory may nevertheless so affect the State, merely because it is a State that is being taxed, as to interfere unduly with the performance of its functions of government. That, then, is the only test. The taxing power of either government unavoidably has some effect upon the other. Either necessarily sets an economic limit to the practical operation of the taxing power of the other. Each must function with the minimum of interference from the other. Each must have a reasonable scope and neither may be unduly curtailed.'

When is a question judicial and when is it legislative? Aside now from the stringency of a situation where no one but the Court will undertake to answer it. The Old Court was willing to accept almost anything as judicial, because it had such confidence in the power of abstractions to solve any problem, or, and, because there was no one else to stick his finger in the hole in the dike. When is a question properly judicial? When it is fairly susceptible of conceptual treatment, fairly and practicably, too. It becomes legislative when there are no available and useful abstractions.

Abstract ideas are like women. We cannot do without them. Until we can think of something better, we have to do with them. So the question is, Is your abstraction useful? Does it get you anywhere you can stand on? Does the result make sense? We are dealing with quadrilateral equations and some of the answers may be square roots of negative numbers, like the gratitude-loyalty complex. The truth of the abstractions we are talking about is pragmatic and instrumental. John Dewey has given us the philosophy that we should adopt here. If it won't work, call in Congress.

In these cases, there are many of them, the New Court needs our sympathy. When the Court was young, a hundred years ago, it undertook what seemed then not too difficult. Indeed, it all looked simple enough then to be susceptible of judicial treatment. As time passed and life got more complicated, it began to look harder. Yet the Old Court was not dismayed, because it was still self-confident and also because it had got itself into the way of oversimplifying things, which made the problems still seem easy. But this was not true of the New Court, less under the spell of a Legal Tradition which regarded itself as omniscient and omnicompetent.

15

DELEGATED JUDICIAL LEGISLATION

O UT OF COURTESY and out of a respect for our federal form of government, the Court leaves the interpretation of state statutes to their own supreme courts. For to one brought up in the local law, 'varying emphasis, tacit assumptions, unwritten practice, a thousand influences gained only from life, may give to the different parts wholly new value, that logic and grammar never could have got from the books.' [219] But what a national Congress means is the business of a national Court, and a large part of its business. For the Court is offered many more chances to construe an act of Congress than the Constitution.

So far as the Constitution is concerned, we are agreed that an inquiry after the intent and meaning of the men who made it is worse than futile. For the attempt turns unawarely into introspection, and leads to day-dreaming and logical fantasy, instead of the practical decisions which those men expected us to make. The remedy, we agreed, was for the Court to accept candidly the delegation of power which those men made to the future. How does it stand with an act of Congress, which is usually much more recent and nearer to us and where search need not be so futile?

The Court really does try to ascertain Congress's intent. It is common to find long quotations from the debates in the Court's opinions. Recently, indeed, the Court had to laugh off in a footnote the contention of one lawyer that his client had been denied due process of law when a state court refused to hear individual legislators as witnesses to what they had meant by a recent statute.[220] Congress, naturally enough, responds to this by feeling quite free to make its intentions less plain. Why try to explain what you mean when you have standing beside you someone who tells you he can divine your thoughts? Especially when you find it embarrassing either to make up your mind or to come out with it? There is the Court ready and willing to take responsibility for decisions you'd sooner not make. It is often politically inexpedient to define a clear-cut policy. For example, Congress left to the War Labor Board the task of selecting the appropriate bargaining unit in each case as it arose. To do more would have been impracticable at a time when the issue of craft versus industrial unions was still an open one.[221] The result is that, just as the Founders deliberately left questions to the future decision of Congress or the Court, whichever had the hardihood to answer them, so Congress delegates quite as much power to the Court by the somewhat inscrutable process of expecting it to divine their undisclosed intentions. The result is the same, though the motives may be different.

'Nay,' said the Bishop of Bangor to George the First, 'Whoever hath an *absolute authority* to *interpret* any written or spoken laws, it is *he* who is truly the *Law-giver* to all intents and purposes, and not the person who first wrote or spoke them.' [222] Needless to say, the Bishop was a latitudinarian, and regarded as a heretic by the high church party, but here there is no escape. The less clearly and the less certainly Congress speaks out, the more power it gives to the Court. It is a delegation of legislative power to the Court. An unavoidable and necessary, often politic and advisable, sometimes careless and unfortunate, occasionally rather appalling, delegation of legislative power. At times, as I say, it is excessive, but it is always desirable that there be some, in order to give play to the joints and to keep a bearing free which otherwise would be frozen. A law is in good part a prophecy, and always the future plays you some tricks. The Court has blustered a little over the delegation of power when it was express and when it was made to bodies other than itself, but oddly it is not even called a delegation of power when the Court itself is the recipient.

We have seen what the Court was not willing to let Congress delegate to the President. See what the Court was willing to let Congress delegate to itself. The Sherman Act declares that every combination in restraint of trade is illegal. Those are the words of that act. They mean, as declared by the Court, that every combination is illegal 'which by reason of intent or the inherent nature of the contemplated acts, prejudice the public interests by unduly restraining competition or unduly obstructing the course of trade.' [223] If you are a lawyer and you are consulted about a contemplated course of conduct, you go to the Court's decisions. You will not waste your time rereading the act itself. If you are not a lawyer, you will appreciate that this is a delegation of the power of Congress over monopolies to the Court, and no more than the Court is willing to accept.

It is harder to believe that power should not be delegated when you are the one who will exercise it. The fact is, the Court is thinking not so much of the separation of powers in the government as the rights of the individual. When the delegation of power to the courts involves a criminal offense and is excessive, they hold it unconstitutional, as a violation of due process of law. It offends due process, for it fails to give you and me, as prospective lawbreakers, any intelligible standard of conduct. We cannot tell whether we have broken such a law until we are convicted. It gives us no warning of what a court may do to us. The nicest example is the Kentucky statute which forbade combinations in trade to fix prices at more than 'real value.' Holmes said neatly and sardonically that this was 'the price in an imaginary world.' [224]

Statutes and other serious communications are no place for such fancies. They belong in folk lore or fairy tales or advertising. This phrase, 'real value,' had a proper place in the advertisement which the National Association of Manufacturers in the spring of 1946 spread across newspaper pages in an attack on the O.P.A. 'Remove price controls on manufactured goods, and production will step up fast. Goods will then pour into the market and, within a reasonable time, prices will adjust themselves naturally and competitively, as they always have, in line with *the real worth of things*. This is the way you can get the goods you want at prices you can afford to pay.'

That, however, is not what we are now talking about, which is the part the Court plays in the process of legislation by reason of its authority, its duty, to interpret the acts of Congress. The perspicacious, polemical old Bishop of Bangor may well call it law-making, but it is important that we should recognize it as a judicial act. Interstitial, Holmes called it, molecular and not molar. For it has its limits. The Court must not trench upon Congress, but the Court does that only when it *mis*interprets. The extent to which the Court indulges itself is wholly up to Congress, who can always speak more precisely or speak further.

If Congress does not, is it any the less judicial? A natural feeling of self-satisfaction when Congress allows the Court's construction of its acts to stand has misled some of the Justices. When the Court held that the Commodities Clause of the Interstate Commerce Act, which forbade a railroad from hauling its own commodities, except, of course, for its own use, did not forbid it to haul coal mined by a subsidiary corporation whose stock it owned, and Congress did nothing to amend the law, McReynolds contentedly remarked, 'Notwithstanding the intent imputed to Congress by this opinion, announced in 1915, no amendment has been made to the Commodities Clause. We must, therefore, conclude that the interpretation of the Act then accepted has legislative approval.' [225] Right enough, but we find Roberts a few years later inclined to regard a proper feeling of satisfaction as if it were legal doctrine. For he referred, dissenting in a recent tax case, to 'the settled doctrine that the re-enactment of a statute so construed, without alteration, renders such construction a part of the statute itself,' and he called upon the Court not to ignore it.[226]

Does the meaning which the Court imputes to Congress become by Congressional inaction — for the re-enacted language is the same, without change — the act of Congress, 'part of the statute itself'? We were told that the Court's interpretation of the Constitution became an integral part of that document, so much so that it required a constitutional amendment to change it. Here the Court, by a process of divination, has discovered a Congressional intention that may or may not have existed. How can Congress, by a process of silent reflection of the Court's opinion, spread it on the statute books? Does it now require an amendment by Congress to change it? Suppose the Court changes its opinion. Has it lost the power it has over all its other mistaken decisions? The Court has never considered that *stare decisis* prevented it from correcting its own mistakes. Does the Court lose that power simply because Congress does not undertake to make any correction itself? In the same tax case in which Roberts dissented, Frankfurter wrote the opinion for the Court and said, 'It would require very persuasive circumstances enveloping Congressional silence to debar the Court from re-examining its own doctrines. To explain the cause of non-action by Congress when Congress itself sheds no light is to venture into speculative unrealities.' [227] If Roberts is right, the Court's judicial act has passed into legislation.

Take a recent case, for this is not footless theory. A Seventh Day Adventist in Stoneham, Massachusetts, applied for citizenship in 1940. One of the questions in the application read, 'If necessary, are you willing to take up arms in defense of this country?' He wrote in, 'No, (non-combatant) Seventh Day Adventist,' and to the examiner he added, 'It is a purely religious matter with me, I have no political or personal reasons other than that.' He made no claim to be exempted from the Selective Service, only from combatant duty. He was willing enough to serve in the army, as thousands of other Adventists were doing, but he would not bear arms. The judge was willing to admit him to citizenship, but the Circuit Court of Appeals, two to one, refused; bound, as the two believed, by three decisions of the Supreme Court in 1929 and 1930.

You will remember these decisions. The first concerned Rosika Schwimmer, who was memorable because she got Henry Ford on his Peace Ship to get the boys 'out of the trenches by Christmas' back in the First World War, and her case is memorable for Holmes's dissent, where he suggested 'that the Quakers have done their share to make the country what it is, that many citizens agree with the applicant's belief, and that I had not supposed hitherto that we regretted our inability to expel them because they believed more than some of us do in the teachings of the Sermon on the Mount.' A professor in the Yale Divinity School, Macintosh, provided the second. In the third, a Miss Bland, the daughter of an Episcopalian clergyman, who had been a nurse on the battlefields in France, was likewise denied citizenship, because she, too, was unwilling to bear arms. The Court had said, speaking through Sutherland, 'The words of the statute do not admit of the qualification upon which the applicant insists. For the Court to allow it to be made is to amend the Act and thereby usurp the power of legislation vested in another department of the government.' [228]

Though Sutherland's words breathe an air of assurance, all of these cases were decided over vigorous dissents. Holmes, Hughes, Brandeis, Sanford, and Stone all dissented to this interpretation of the act of Congress. But

Congress did nothing to change the act. There was a good deal of agitation. Hearings were held and speeches made in six successive Congresses in an attempt to change the law, but Congress did not do it, and when in 1940 the naturalization laws were revised, the part which related to an applicant's willingness to bear arms was re-enacted as it stood. The required oath scarcely seems explicit enough to warrant Sutherland's feeling that any other interpretation would 'usurp the power of legislation' vested in Congress. It reads, 'I do solemnly swear . . . to support and defend the Constitution and laws of the United States against all enemies, foreign and domestic, and bear true faith and allegiance to the same.'

Congress chose not to change the language of this oath. It was much the same that Congressmen themselves took, and all office holders. Did its re-enactment fasten into it the meaning which the Court had ascribed to it? That was the question on which depended Girouard's, the Stoneham Adventist's, citizenship. No, it did not, said the New Court. The Schwimmer, Macintosh, and Bland cases do not, a majority thought, state the correct rule of law, and 'the silence of Congress and its inaction are as consistent with a desire to leave the problem fluid, as they are with an adoption by silence of the rule of those cases.' [229]

There was a powerful dissent, written by Stone and joined by Frankfurter and Reed. Powerful because we can be quite sure that none of them agreed with the three decisions which were being held not to be correct. They made it clear that they dissented solely because, in their opinion, Congress had enacted into law the incorrect interpretation. 'For that reason alone.' 'It is not the function of this Court to disregard the will of Congress in the exercise of its constitutional power,' their dissent concludes. But had that will been expressed?

A man's function is determined by what he is expected to do by his associates with whom he is working as well as by what he is told to do by the boss. Might it not surprise Congress to find that by doing nothing or by repeating the same words it was requiring the Court to repeat its decision? Not, of course, that Congress would be surprised if the Court came to the same conclusion. That might well be just what Congress itself would have done in the Court's place. But I think Congress wants it to be the Court's deliberate choice. For it may want the Court to take the responsibility.

It seems to me plain that Congress was very happy to leave the whole agitation precisely where it lay, in the Court's lap, with the responsibility for doing anything about it on the Court. The obvious, if not the only, way Congress could achieve this was just what Congress did, do nothing, and, if the whole naturalization law was to be revised in other respects, take care to repeat the same language in this respect. Imagine what the Court would have said if Congress had tried to expressly delegate the matter to the Court. There are lots of things you can do implicitly and cannot do explicitly.

Congress cannot explicitly delegate its legislative power to the Court, but Congress can and often does simply say nothing at all that covers a point in issue. It is the case of a hole in the statute, where nothing is said on a question which must be decided, though only on that particular point is the statute silent, and the act is clear and workable enough in other respects. You cannot say it is wholly void, and the Court cannot hold up decision until Congress has broken its one small silence.

It is commonly observed, now that unions have gained the right to organize and to bargain with their employers, that the next phase is going to be the reconciliation of their rights as groups with the rights of individuals and of minorities.[230] The Wagner Act gave unions the legal right to organize and recruit without interference from employers and the power of collective bargaining. Elections are held by the government and the winner is made, by authority of law, the sole bargainer, for its members and for all the other employees of the company. But the act is completely silent on the question whether the bargaining unit, the union which has won the election, is free to discriminate. This includes racial discrimination as well as other kinds, and so it is possible to suspect that the complete failure of the act to say anything on the point was more than heedless. The Southern solons sulk when racial discrimination raises its dirty face.

While the Negro was a slave, he had a near monopoly of the labor market; involuntary, but nonetheless monopolistic. Thomas Nelson Page said, 'In 1865, when the Negro was set free, he held without a rival the entire field of industrial labor throughout the South.' A considerable exaggeration, Gunnar Myrdal adds,[231] but the fact is a good one to start from. When the slave was given legal and political freedom, he effectively lost his involuntary legal monopoly. It became purely economic, and precarious. He had to compete with the whites. When jobs increased the Negro got more, but when they decreased and as the work became technically and mechanically less menial and less onerous, he got less. The door which was opened was blown to in the wind of discrimination.

On the railroads there were once a few Negro engineers. There were more firemen, for that was considered dirty work. But with technical improvements it became less dirty, more attractive, and more and more whites took it over. This progress was facilitated by the Brotherhood of Locomotive Firemen and Engineers, which excluded Negroes and dominated the situation.[232] Under the Railway Labor Act the Brotherhood became the sole and exclusive bargaining representative of the craft of firemen, and in that capacity the Brotherhood made agreements with the southern railroads, acting as representative of all firemen. Negroes who were excluded from the union as well as those in the union, were equally bound by the agreements.

In 1940 the Brotherhood notified the roads that it wished to amend the agreements to provide that only white men should thereafter be employed as firemen. This demand was compromised, but in February, 1941, the agreements were amended so that ultimately not more than half the firemen should be Negroes and until this ratio between whites and Negroes was reached all vacancies were to be filled with whites. The Brotherhood, moreover, reserved its right to negotiate for even further restrictions.

A couple of months later the mileage on a run on which a Negro fireman named Steele was working was reduced, his job was declared vacant, and it was given to a white man who was a member of the Brotherhood. Steele brought suit against both the Brotherhood and the road — it was the Louisville and Nashville — to enjoin them from carrying out their agreement. The Supreme Court of Alabama thought that the Brotherhood was authorized by the Act to make the agreement and that the Act had given the

Brotherhood plenary power, and no obligation to protect minorities from discrimination or unfair treatment.

Why should the white Brotherhood treat Negroes better just for being their 'representative'? White men had always represented Negroes. Negroes were an inferior race, the white men's burden, and their responsibility from long ago; the Act, by making them the representative of the Negro, made no change in their duties. So ran the opinion of the Alabama court. Otherwise, indeed, the privilege conferred by the Act would be a disadvantage which the Brotherhood had accepted to its cost. Every job a Negro kept, a white man lost; every seniority a Negro retained made a white man his junior. Congress had said nothing to the contrary. The representative of the Brotherhoods in Washington would have had much to say to Congressmen if it had. Consequently Steele's petition was dismissed and he appealed to the Court.

Chief Justice Stone wrote the opinion for a unanimous Court, except that Murphy thought they did not go far enough.[233]

All Stone had to go on in the Act was this. It said, 'Employees shall have the right to organize and bargain collectively through representatives of their own choosing. The majority of any craft or class of employees shall have the right to determine who shall be the representative of the craft or class for the purposes of this Act,' and the representative designated by the employees shall 'act for them.' The purposes of the Act were stated to be the avoidance of 'any interruption to commerce or to the operation of any carrier engaged therein' by 'the prompt and orderly settlement of all disputes concerning rates of pay, rules, or working conditions.'

'These purposes,' Stone said, 'would hardly be attained if a substantial minority of the craft were denied the right to have their interests considered at the conference table and if the final result of the bargaining process were to be the sacrifice of the interests of the minority by the action of a representative chosen by the majority. The only recourse of the minority would be to strike, with the attendant interruption of commerce, which the Act seeks to avoid.' [234]

True. Congress should have required just that of the representative of the majority, for the act to be effective. If the union represented only the majority, the Act would fail of its purpose.

Stone continued, 'Unless the labor union representing a craft owes some duty to represent non-union members of the craft, at least to the extent of not discriminating against them as such in the contracts which it makes as their representative, the minority would be left with no means of protecting their interests or, indeed, their right to earn a livelihood by pursuing the occupation in which they are employed. While the majority of the craft chooses the bargaining representative, when chosen it represents, as the Act by its terms makes plain, the craft or class, and not the majority.' [235]

It is not plain. Indeed there is no language in the statute, as we have seen, one way or the other. Stone had to fall back on general principles, which he did. 'It is a principle of general application,' he said, 'that the exercise of a granted power to act in behalf of others involves the assumption toward them of a duty to exercise the power in their interest and behalf, and that such a grant of power will not be deemed to dispense with all duty toward those for whom it is exercised unless so expressed.'

I would emphasize the phrase, 'It is a principle of general application.' For this is what the Court did, read into the Act a part of the American creed as a principle of general application, which Congress had omitted, deliberately, unless you believe that Congress took it for granted and thought it unnecessary to express it. So what have we? We have the Court enforcing as matter of law the American creed of equal opportunity and no discrimination. All right. Jews? All right. Aliens? All right. Employees who do not join the union, men of their own kind except they won't join? Members of a rival union that has been defeated in the election? Ah, but spies, suspects, Communists, racketeers? Can't a union discriminate against them? Future troubles, which the Court is expected to take care of one way or the other.

Where does the Court get any authority to tell the union how it shall behave toward non-members, toward employees, that is, who do not belong to it? By imputing to Congress what Congress did not choose, or did not dare, to express for itself. What the Court is doing is anticipating Congress's wish, in the confidence that Congress would wish things to be done that way, so long as others take the responsibility.

Murphy, in a concurring opinion, tried to rest the decision upon the Constitution. He said, 'The Constitution voices its disapproval whenever economic discrimination is applied under authority of law against any race, creed, or color.' [236] He refused to believe that Congress could have meant to authorize the representative union to ignore rights mentioned by the Constitution. If it had, he said, the Act would be unconstitutional under the Fifth

Amendment. 'For that reason I am willing to read the statute as not permitting or allowing any action by the bargaining representative in the exercise of its delegated powers which would *in effect* violate the constitutional rights of individuals.' [237]

Of course, a statute must always be construed, if any way possible, tortured, if necessary, into a constitutional meaning. But here it is not necessary to construe the Act to forbid discrimination in order to avoid unconstitutionality. It is certainly as constitutional for Congress to leave the unions free to discriminate, that is, to do nothing about their discriminating — which is precisely what Congress did — as it would be to forbid them. It would be a violation of the Fifth Amendment, to which Murphy appeals, to authorize and sanction such conduct. But that is no ground for reading the statute as forbidding it. The statute can be quite easily, more easily, construed as doing nothing at all about it. No, this is the Court's doing, and though slightly marvelous, it is good.

Congress can take over if it chooses. It is just what Congress has encouraged the Court to do about state interference with interstate commerce. The only difference is that here the Court is protecting personal, intimate personal rights and there, in interstate commerce, it was the rights of commerce. In both cases the people who need protection are those who have no say in the matter.

Come to the next question. Is the union, which has won the election and become the sole bargaining agent, free to exclude anyone it chooses from membership and so deny them a voice in its policy? Is it to be sole and free judge of its own membership? Must it not only represent others, but admit them to its councils and to the determination of its policies? Any group, to be a group, first recruits members, but it is not truly a group until it has some right of exclusion. It must circumscribe itself or it has no self. What limits, if there are any limits, are there to its exclusiveness?

The Court has really not yet had to face this question, but it is breathing down the Court's neck. Can a union which is the sole and exclusive bargaining agent exclude minorities from participation in its own councils and determinations?

In 1936 the War Labor Board said, 'It is preferable that the Board should not interfere with the internal affairs of labor organizations. Self-organization of employees implies a policy of self-management. The rôle that organizations of employees eventually must play in the structure established by Congress through that act is a large and vital one. They will best be able to perform that rôle if they are permitted freely to work out the solutions to their own internal problems. In its permanent operation the act envisages cohesive organizations, well constructed and intelligently guided. Such organizations will not develop if they are led to look elsewhere for solutions to such problems.' [238]

This was all very well said and wise in its day, which was 1936. Perhaps it is still. What Brandeis said about public utility commissions in the Saint Joseph Stock Yards case [239] is as true of unions as it is about every other body of men, Responsibility is the great developer. What unions most lack and most need, and what we ought above all things to see that they get is discipline, but it is self-discipline, and that comes best and soonest by way of responsibility. But to whom? To Congress? To the

Court? The kind of responsibility that Brandeis had in mind is responsibility to themselves and the public. Are there any limits, and, if so, who shall set them? There has been one case that very nearly and not quite raised this question.[240]

The Wallace Corporation was a small wood products concern — two hundred employees — in West Virginia. In 1941 the C.I.O. started to organize it, and the company sponsored an independent union. The two unions engaged in a running fight for supremacy. Finally, toward the end of the year they agreed to hold an election under the auspices of the Labor Board, on condition, said the C.I.O. 'that when we prove a majority and become the exclusive bargaining agency for all your employees, that as a condition of employment all eligible employees must become members of Local Union 129, U.C.W.O.C.' It was an election, approved by the Labor Board, with a closed shop for the winner, closed to the loser.

The election was held early in 1942 and the Independent Union, which was what the union sponsored by the company called itself, won, 98 to 83. The C.I.O. filed no objections and the Board certified the Independent as the sole bargaining agent for all the employees. It was not slow to claim the stake. It wrote to the company, a little breathlessly, 'The "Closed Shop" will, therefore, give us some control in preventing the hiring of additional employees who are unfavorable to our interests and who would further jeopardize our majority. It would also provide us with a legal means of disposing of any present employees, including Harvey Dodrill whom our members have declared by unanimous ballot that they will not work with, whose presence in the plant is unfavorable to our interests because those who are so unfavorable will not be permitted to become members of our organization and without such membership they would not be permitted to work in the plant under a closed shop contract which we respectfully insist that we *must* have.'

The company complied. A closed shop agreement was signed. Then the Independent demanded the dismissal of forty-three men, because they were not its members. They were C.I.O. members. Thirty-one had applied for membership in the Independent, to be rejected. Twelve had not even applied. The company expostulated and tried unsuccessfully to get the union to take the men in and let them keep their jobs.

At that point the Labor Board, holding that the discharge of these men was unfair, ordered the company to take them back and disestablished the Independent as bargaining agent. This ruling was sound enough, and so the Court held, but only if the Independent was dominated by the company, enough so that its refusal to accept the C.I.O. men was done in collaboration with the company. What if the union had done this on its own and for its own advantage?

Let Jackson say what he, Stone, Roberts, and Frankfurter thought. 'Neither the National Labor Relations Act nor any other Act of Congress expressly or by implication gives to the Board any power to supervise union membership or to deal with union practices, however unfair they may be to members, to applicants, to minorities, to other unions, or to employers. This may or may not have been a mistake, but it was no oversight. We suppose that there is no right which organized labor of every shade of opinion in other matters would unite more strongly in demanding than the right of each union to control its own admissions to membership. Each union has insisted on its freedom to fix its own qualifications of applicants, to determine the vote by which individual admissions will be granted, to prescribe the initiation or admission fees, to fix the dues, to prescribe the duties to which members must be faithful and to decide when and why they may be expelled or disciplined. The exclusion of those whose loyalty is to a rival union or hostile organization is one of the most common and most understandable of practices, designed to defend the union against undermining, spying, and discord, and possible capture and delivery over to a rival. Some unions have battled to exclude Communists, some racketeers, and all to exclude those deemed disloyal to their purposes. There are those who think that the time has come when unions should be denied this control over their own affairs. However this may be, we only know that Congress has included no such principle expressly in the Act.'

Suppose the question arises before Congress does express itself. It will be up to the Court in its infinite wisdom to apply general principles.

The problem of the responsibility of groups is a necessary introduction to personal liberties. It pleases the Court, and may reassure it, to think that it is sitting in judgment between an individual and a somehow hostile state. Often that is true, but more often it is doing nothing of the kind. It is adjusting or rearranging the relation between the state and the groups of which it is composed. For when an individual asserts or exercises a right guaranteed to him by the Constitution, it is more likely to be as a member of a group or even avowedly in its behalf than as an isolated individual. Then it is really the group which is enjoying the right. This is as it should be and as we expect it to be. We cultivate groups and we encourage co-operation within them as well as competition between them. We cannot have the one without the other, and some of these rights, freedom of speech, for example, are as indispensable to the formation and development of a group as they are to the development of individual personality.

The Court then is dealing with groups, and it is well to recognize that this is so. The Constitution recognizes it where superficially we should least expect it. Freedom of religion, which we are inclined to regard as the most intimately personal of personal rights, is treated by the Bill of Rights as the right to maintain 'religious establishments.' That is the phrase in the First Amendment. No man ever had to claim his constitutional rights in order to be alone with his God.

The myth of the lone individual is not unimportant. How else could anyone continue to believe that he is the center of the universe? But for us it is important to know that the Bill of Rights may be protecting the interests or the demands of a group under the guise of an individual, because groups are different and behave differently. A group is an abstraction from the individuals who compose it and belong to it of their one particular common interest, money making for a business corporation, some particular benefit or reform or sentimentality for a philanthropic organization. To think that groups behave like individuals is to make the same mistake that confuses abstractions with life. The theory of free enterprise, which is based on the assumption of the existence of that fictitious and disagreeable individual, the reasonable economic man, would have much to say for itself if we were all business corporations; perhaps this is why they take so kindly to that theory. Groups are almost always single-minded monomaniacs, and we had better recognize each as the embodiment of no more than its particular mania, if we are to deal either wisely or safely with them when they assert a nominally individual and personal right, as when a bank or a corporation defends itself as if it were Thoreau or a professor exercising academic freedom.[241]

16

PERSONAL LIBERTIES

W E HAVE GOT into a habit of assuming that personal and individual liberty is the rule and social discipline the exception. This is not the complacent error of taking liberty as a matter of course. We make this assumption in our active thinking about liberty. It is a good thing that we do, for it keeps us in the way of regarding encroachments on our liberties as needing justification. It puts the burden of proof on necessary abridgments if we think of them as exceptions to a rule that men should be free, as free as possible. We make this assumption because our ideology is still that of the eighteenth century. The Declaration of Independence, our Constitution, the Bill of Rights, all date from the eighteenth century. Their ideology is still alive here, more alive than it is anywhere else on earth. The French Revolution, which took so much of its thinking from ours, means more to us in the United States than it does anywhere else, more to us than it does to the French.

However, and whatever the reason, it is a good assumption and we should be grateful that we have got into the habit of making it. It is like the presumption we make in criminal law that a defendant is innocent until he is proved guilty, though in fact no one who has been indicted and formally charged with crime is really presumed innocent by anyone but his friends or well-wishers or someone who happens to know that the government was wrong. Yet no one would discard the presumption because it is wrong in fact. That would mistake its whole purpose, which is to combat the fact and put its weight against the facts. Ideologies are not scientific hypotheses, to be proved true or false as they conform or do not conform with fact. They are part of our law, which has the quite different purpose of controlling our behavior. It is a poor law which simply conforms to the facts.

Likewise the assumption that freedom is the rule and discipline the exception is, as it had better be, false, false now in comparison with the facts. Only in a world of abstractions, a make-believe world of unrealities, is individual freedom the rule and its encroachment by social discipline the exception. Man is by nature a social animal, said Aristotle, in his *Politics*, and an individual who is unsocial naturally and not accidentally is either beneath our notice or more than human. Anyone who either cannot lead the common life or is so self-sufficient as not to need to, and therefore does not partake of society, is either a beast or a god.

If you doubt Aristotle, ask yourself. Follow yourself through the day. What prevents or hinders you from speaking your own mind? To begin with, of course, you may not have one which is really your own. Yours may be a mimeographed copy of what you have not had the time nor the ability to make your own. But pass that. Good manners and the ruts of convention. Your aversions if you follow them up. Respect, perhaps a sound sensible fear of your boss, just as he has for his, as well as the respect you both share for the customer. Your wish to be respected yourself by people who want you to respect them. Your concern for your children's future, as you see it. Your affection, or whatever feeling you have, for your colleagues, fellow-workers, other union members, friends, almost everyone you have anything to do with. Do you feel as free when you are sober as you do after a couple of drinks? See for yourself if Aristotle wasn't right.

This is a social discipline, imposed on you, not by the state, not by governmental process of law, but by your fellows, by the organizations you belong to, by the corporations you work for, by the social group you live in. The Bill of Rights, and its application by the Court, is better understood, if we recognize that it does not forbid any of these social abridgments of your liberty. It forbids only governmental encroachments. Thus in the First Amendment it is Congress who shall 'make no law respecting an establishment of religion, or prohibiting the free exercise thereof; or abridging the freedom of speech, or of the press.' And the Fourteenth reads, 'nor shall any *State* deprive any person of life, liberty, or property, without due process of law; nor deny to any person within its jurisdiction the equal protection of the laws.'

The Bill of Rights, then, protects you only in that clearing of freedom which you have already made for yourself in society and protects you there, not against the encroachments of the forest, but only against the forest rangers.

But what, as a matter of fact, does that mean? Government in a democracy, the democratic process, does not usually act on its own initiative. A totalitarian state, which has arrogated to itself the whole discipline, social as well as legal, is different. A democracy acts at the instance of interested groups. So what the Bill of Rights does, and pretty much all it does, is prevent a dominant or temporarily powerful group, whether a majority or a minority is beside the point, from enlisting the aid of government against you. What a private group can do to discipline you, using only social processes, is a matter between you and it.

The democratic process, you see, demands a great deal of self-reliance from the individual. Freedom in a democracy is not given you, or even guaranteed to you, by the state. All that you get is what you get for yourself, and all that the democratic process guarantees to you is that the state will not help anyone take it away from you.

Freedom of Speech

Some day the Court may stand at Armageddon for personal liberties, but it has not done so yet. For one reason or another, the Court has never yet thrown itself for better or worse into that battle, as we have seen it do more than once for the rights of property. When in the Dred Scott case it threw its weight into the impending struggle, it was on the side of property as well as the South. In the Income Tax cases it had held the bridge against socialism, then approaching in the guise of a two per cent tax on incomes, and held it for fifteen years, 1895 to 1909, and it took a constitutional amendment to dislodge it. In 1935 and 1936 it fought off the New Deal for a couple of years. Perhaps some day the Court will be equally valiant for personal liberties. Better that it should never have to be.

It was the same Chief Justice Taney who led a majority of the Court in the Dred Scott case that four years later fought just as gallantly alone for the right of *habeas corpus* in the Merryman case. What he did shows what perhaps some day the Court may have to do. It was just at the outbreak of the war, in 1861. Picture him, Taney, the old man, magnificently going to Baltimore the day after Merryman had been arrested there by the military for destroying a railroad bridge — necessary for the passage of federal troops — and there sitting alone. Instead of the circuit judge, for Taney wanted the sole responsibility. Issuing his writ of *habeas corpus*, and then the next morning coming to court on the arm of his grandson and receiving, not Merryman, but an officer with red sash and sword and a courteous declination from the commanding general. The writ of attachment is handed to the marshal, who presently returns to report that he had presented his card at the Fort, but had been refused admission and therefore could not make service of the writ. There was nothing more for Taney to do, nothing much more he could do. He filed his opinion and directed the clerk to send a copy to the President.[242]

That was Taney alone. The Court did not have to pass on the issue until after the war, which, it seems, we owe to the discretion of the Attorney General, Bates. He was wiser than Stanton, the Secretary of War, and refused to accede to Stanton's suggestion that one out of the many *habeas corpus* cases that soon followed ought to be advanced for hearing. The Court was in no hurry for them, and they had to wait till they were duly reached on the docket.[243] And when the Vallandigham case threatened to bring the thing to a head, Lincoln in his own and inimitable way turned a perfectly promising case of *habeas corpus* into nothing more than *certiorari*, something much less acute. As we all know, Lincoln commuted Vallandigham's sentence of death for treason into banishment across the Confederate lines, with the result that there was no body to produce. Then there was nothing for counsel to do but ask that a writ of *certiorari* issue to the court-martial which had found their client guilty. This was easy, for, as the Court unanimously and promptly held, it had no authority to issue that writ to a military court-martial.

So the formidable issue, whether Taney was right and Lincoln's suspension of *habeas corpus* wrong, did not reach the Court until almost a year after Appomattox, not until April, 1865, when the war was over. This was the Milligan case. And it was not argued until nearly a year later, on March 5, 1866. Then, when it was too late to be of more than juristic importance, it was promptly decided.

Taney by himself had been single-minded, the Court could now be safely unanimous. Milligan's court-martial had been held in Indiana, far from the theater of war, and there Milligan had been tried and convicted of treason and sentenced to death in spite of the fact that the civil courts were open and available. The Justices all held that this was unconstitutional. The Executive had no power to set up court-martials and try citizens in such circumstances. Taney was right. Lincoln's suspension of *habeas corpus* in Baltimore had been unjustified. In fact, the Court was so far from sustaining Lincoln that it split over the question whether Congress could even have authorized him to do what he did. Five to four the Court held that Congress, though it had not, could not. But by that time the war was over.[244]

In the First World War, the lower courts acted hysterically enough to put the Court on its mettle, but again by the time the appeals came before it, the war was over.

The first was the Schenck case on March 3, 1919.[245] The Justices all agreed that Schenck's conviction for obstructing the draft had to stand, but Holmes, speaking for all of them, laid down a rule. It is the clear and present danger rule, and it is so useful, and so tempting to use, that the great question is when not to use it. It is like a lovely curve on a graph, so lovely that you extrapolate it. Holmes said, 'We admit that in many places and in ordinary times the defendants in saying all that was said in the circular would have been within their constitutional rights. But the character of every act depends upon the circumstances in which it is done. The question in every case is whether the words used are used in such circumstances and are of such a nature as to create a clear and present danger that they will bring about the substantive evils that Congress has a right to prevent. It is a question of proximity and degree. When a nation is at war, many things that might be said in time of peace are such a hindrance to its effort that their utterance will not be endured so long as men fight and that no court could regard them as protected by any constitutional right.'

By the next year, 1920, a 'red' panic had overcome the country and this time the Court as well as a great many other people lost their heads. It was no Armageddon. Quite the contrary. Perhaps the panic of an illusion, like fear in a dream, is harder to control than the fear of actual danger.

Abrams was one of a small group of four men and a girl who back in 1918, while the war was still on, had scattered leaflets off a roof in New York City. They were Russian born. They were pacifists. They were convicted. In 1920, after the war was over, now frighted with false fire, the Court sustained that conviction.[246]

Holmes dissented, and Brandeis agreed with him. This is what Holmes said. 'Persecution for the expression of opinions seems to me perfectly logical. If you have no doubt of your premises or your power and want a certain result with all your heart you naturally express your wishes in law and sweep away all opposition. To allow opposition by speech seems to indicate that you think the speech impotent, as when a man says that he has squared the circle, or that you do not care wholeheartedly for the result, or that you doubt either your power or your premises. But when men have realized that time has upset many fighting faiths, they may come to believe even more than they believe the very foundations of their own conduct that the ultimate good desired is better reached by free trade in ideas — that the best test of truth is the power of the thought to get itself accepted in the competition of the market, and that truth is the only ground upon which their wishes safely can be carried out. That at any rate is the theory of our Constitution. It is an experiment, as all life is an experiment. Every year if not every day we have to wager our salvation upon some prophecy based upon imperfect knowledge. While that experiment is part of our system I think that we should be eternally vigilant against attempts to check the expression of opinions that we loathe and believe to be fraught with death, unless they so imminently threaten immediate interference with the lawful and pressing purposes of the law that an immediate check is required to save the country. I regret that I cannot put into more impressive words my belief that in their conviction upon this indictment the defendants were deprived of their rights under the Constitution of the United States.' [247]

The best comment on these espionage cases is Holmes's own, in a letter to his friend, Sir Frederick Pollock, 'I hope we have heard the last, or nearly the last, of the Espionage Act cases. Some of our subordinate Judges seem to me to have been hysterical during the war. It is one of the ironies that I, who probably take the extremest view in favor of free speech (in which, in the abstract, I have no very enthusiastic belief, though I hope I would die for it), that I should have been selected for blowing up.'

'A free trade in ideas — the best test of truth is the power of the thought to get itself accepted in the competition of the market.' But note that the wares Holmes is bringing to market are 'fighting faiths' as well as 'imperfect knowledge.' 'Words,' Learned Hand says, 'are not only the keys of persuasion, but the triggers of action.' [248] The ideas which Holmes would wish to have bought and sold are the very essence and substance — Cardozo called them the matrix — of the democratic process. Take them away and there is nothing left. For free speech is the binder between thought and action. Without it they fall apart, and we become either solitary thinkers or no more than men of action, fighting without faith.

Herein lies the significance of Holmes's skepticism to Pollock. The reason why he is in favor of free speech — in which he had no very enthusiastic belief, though he would die for it — is not merely philosophic doubt. He identifies free speech with the democratic process, and he reads the duty and function of the Court in the light of that fact.

It is not Holmes the skeptic but Holmes the judge who is speaking. We know what he believed his function as a judge to be. Recall what he said in the Lochner case. The Constitution was for people of fundamentally differing views and the accident that a judge might find legislation novel or even shocking ought not to conclude his judgment, or bring it into conflict with the Constitution. He must be skeptical, or self-restrained, call it as you please.

That then is the situation here, but with a difference. Here it is not merely a conflict between Congress and the Constitution, it is between Congress and the democratic process itself. Here is a fundamental right, the liberty of free speech, which the Constitution says shall not be abridged. Congress shall make no law abridging it. We cannot be naïve about it, and yet we cannot be quite satisfied by just being reasonable about it, for free speech is essential and fundamental. Holmes is insisting that Congress shall treat this essential part of the democratic process precisely as the Court treats Congress, with equal restraint and equal respect. Congress must treat the expression of opinions which it loathes and fears in the same way the Court must treat legislation which is shocking to it.

In the Schenck case, when Holmes was speaking for the Court, the rule ran, 'The question in every case is whether the words used are used in such circumstances and are of such a nature as to create a clear and present danger that they will bring about the substantive evils that Congress has a right to prevent.' Holmes went further when he was speaking only for himself and Brandeis, in the Abrams case, 'unless they so imminently threaten immediate interference with the lawful and pressing purposes of the law that an immediate check is required to save the country.'

There is an exuberance about Holmes and Brandeis speaking for themselves, and at the same time it is the proper reaction to a majority in a panic. 'To save the country' is better than 'the substantive evils that Congress has a right to prevent.' Freedom of speech takes its place above what Congress may deem wise to do, and second to only one thing, the salvation of a country which would be equally well lost without it.

Frankfurter later forgot that Holmes and Brandeis had said this. 'The clear and present danger to be arrested may be danger short of a threat as comprehensive and vague as a threat to the safety of the Republic or "The American way of life." Neither Mr. Justice Holmes nor Mr. Justice Brandeis nor this Court ever suggested in all the cases that arose in connection with the First World War, that only imminent threats to the immediate security of the country would authorize courts to sustain legislation curtailing utterance. Such forces of destruction are of an order of magnitude which courts are hardly designed to counter.' [249]

Frankfurter is soberly right, those two were not wrong. There were people then in as much fear for the state when they saw a red flag coming down the street as they would have been if it had been a black cat crossing in front of them.

The nineteen-twenties were not an heroic age. This must be clear even to those who did not live through them. Nor was the Court, at any rate a majority, in any heroic mood, confirming jail sentences for saying no more than what Holmes and Brandeis believed the defendants had as much right to say 'as the Government has to publish the

Constitution of the United States now vainly invoked against them.' [250] It is odd, therefore, that right in the middle of that decade, in 1925, the Court should extend its jurisdiction over personal liberties so that it could reach at will any violation, not only by Congress, but by any governmental action anywhere in the United States, by state, city, or town, by anyone acting in an official capacity. It was done, too, in a quiet, almost casual way. It was like this.

Gitlow was a Communist. He had been a member of the New York Assembly. He wrote a pamphlet. It was commonplace communism, such things as, 'The Communist International calls the proletariat of the world to the final struggle!' As Holmes recognized, Gitlow's pamphlet 'had no chance of starting a present conflagration,' and he and Brandeis were for quashing his conviction under the New York Criminal Anarchy Act, which had been passed back in 1902 under the stress of McKinley's assassination by an anarchist. The Court, however, affirmed it. That is not the point. It is what they said, 'For the present purposes we may and do assume that freedom of speech and of the press — which are protected by the First Amendment for abridgment by Congress — are among the fundamental personal rights and "liberties" protected by the due process clause of the Fourteenth Amendment from impairment by the States.' [251]

Now that had not been the law as late as three years before. As recently as 1922 the Court had said just the contrary, that the due process clause imposed no restrictions on the states concerning freedom of speech.[252] Now, in 1925, the Court says it does. Quietly, all but casually. I do not believe we can find anything that happened either inside or outside the Court which had caused this complete, sudden, and really revolutionary change. The water had been rising for a hundred and thirty odd years, until in 1925 it lapped quietly over the sill.

Mr. Madison's Proposal

In the spring of 1789 Madison was sitting in Philadelphia waiting for a quorum of the first House of Representatives to gather. He was a member from Virginia, and he had charged himself with the business of presenting the amendments to the Constitution which so many of the states had demanded when they adopted the new government. He had himself been one of the leaders in the Convention. Improvements had been demanded. He was there to see to it that they were improvements. What they were to be, he wrote to his friend and fellow Virginian, Thomas Jefferson.[253] 'A Bill of rights, incorporated perhaps in the Constitution will be proposed, with a few other alterations most called for by the opponents of the Government and least objectionable to its friends.' There had been no Bill of Rights in the original Constitution. The Convention had unanimously rejected any.[254] Why? Mistakenly, because the states had demanded one.

A quorum gathered slowly. Though the new Government had been supposed to start on March 4, it was not until April that they were there, and, as sometimes happens when neighbors come to dinner, the last to arrive were those who lived nearest. Then there was the necessary business of revenue and of organization. It was not till June that Madison had an opportunity to lay a Bill of Rights before the House.

In two important respects, Madison's proposals differed from the Bill of Rights as we have it.

One is that Madison's applied to the States as well as to Congress. The other difference you will notice is that Madison left out freedom of speech. Madison proposed that neither Congress nor the States shall violate 'the equal rights of conscience, or the freedom of the press, or the trial by jury in criminal cases.' Why should Madison have left out freedom of speech? Because it was not then recognized as one of the fundamental freedoms, not at any rate in the large sense we now give it quite as a matter of course. We are better off than our forefathers were in this respect. We claim more of this freedom. None of the states then had it in their constitutions.[255] All they insisted on was freedom of the press, and that was all that Madison put in. That was all that Massachusetts had, for example, that and the right of the people's representatives to speak their minds and their grievances freely enough on the floor of their legislatures. And even the liberty of the press, we must remember, had a touch of the disreputable about it, just as there had been about its most vigorous champion, Wilkes, among whose distinctions was the fact that Casanova coveted his mistress and failed to get her.

Madison had been too prudent about freedom of speech. The committee to which his proposals were referred added it in and when its report came before the House, the only opposition was to the other point, that Madison's proposals applied to the States. Mr. Thomas Tudor Tucker of South Carolina protested that it went to the alteration of the constitutions of the particular states. It would be much better, he apprehended, to leave the State Governments to themselves, and not to interfere with them more than we already do; and that is thought by many to be rather too much. But the record reads, 'Mr. Madison conceived this to be the most valuable amendment of all'; and, perhaps due to Mr. Madison's insistence, it passed and went to the Senate with the rest.

But there it failed. The Senate would agree to, and did agree to the inclusion of freedom of speech, but it would not agree to applying the amendments to the States. Mr. Tucker had his way. The Bill of Rights was addressed only to the new Government, only to Congress. Madison was disappointed. He wrote to Edmund Pendleton on September 14, 'The Senate have sent back the plan of amendments with some alterations, which strike, in my opinion, at the most salutary articles.' And he added, 'The difficulty of uniting the minds of men accustomed to think and act differently can only be conceived by those who have witnessed it.'

A Bill of Rights was something five of the states — and a respectable company, New York, Virginia, New Jersey, South Carolina, and Georgia — did not have. They adopted theirs later. What's more, this new one for a new nation was far stricter, far more idealistic than any the states had. The states' revolutionary constitutions were correcting the vices they saw and felt in the behavior of governments, contemporary and particular vices, and the safeguards they put in their constitutions were no more than they considered necessary. But now when the states came to setting up a new national government for the future they went beyond the immediately necessary into the idealistic. Also they were looking a little askance at their new creation. They were not certain it might not turn out to be a rival for the loyalty of their own citizens. Every item they added to the bill of rights which they imposed on this new government was a restriction upon its powers over their own citizens. As often, anyhow, you have a higher standard for another than you have for yourself. The States did not find it hard to make the new Bill of Rights better than any of their own.

Before we leave the contemporary history of the Constitution, there is a question of attitude which often silently determines our whole approach to the Bill of Rights. It was neatly exposed by Elihu Root the elder once in conversation with his partner Grenville Clark. He gave Clark a copy of the Constitution and asked him to turn to the Preamble, 'We, the People of the United States, in order to form a more perfect union, establish justice, insure domestic tranquillity, promote the general welfare, *and secure the blessings of liberty to ourselves and our posterity*, do ordain and establish this Constitution for the United States of America.' 'That word "secure",' Root said, 'is one of the most important words in the Constitution. If you take it to mean "obtain," your attitude toward the Constitution will be that it conferred new liberties not theretofore possessed. If, on the other hand, you take it to mean "make safe," you will view the Constitution as merely confirming rights which antedated 1789 and had a firm foundation in the preceding centuries of American and English history. Your sympathy with the liberties guaranteed by the Constitution may well be strongly affected one way or the other, according to whether you consider them as novel experiments or as the result of ages of trial and error,' and he went on to say that so far as he knew, the word 'secure,' as used at the time the Constitution was adopted, probably was intended to mean 'make safe.' [256]

To complete the story, Clark put what Elihu Root had told him years before into his brief for the American Bar Association in the Hague case.[257] Hague had tried to make a point, of which I cannot make sense, claiming that this same word, *secure*, in a section of the Judicial Code [258] meant 'created,' and in reply to that claim Clark added a footnote to his brief that it meant 'make safe.' Stone, in his opinion, picked up the suggestion and said, 'The preamble proclaiming the establishment of the Constitution in order to "secure the Blessings of Liberty," used the word "secure" in the sense of "protect" or "make certain."' [259]

Why cannot the word carry both meanings? An ambiguity is not necessarily an alternative, an either-or, either this or that. There is no good reason why a word cannot mean two compatible things at the same time. It is either this or that or both of them. The Constitution was at once summing up the past and opening a new chapter. In the process of life, every end is a beginning. And the preamble, do not forget, speaks in the first person, 'We, the People,' We here and We now, as well as, and as truly as, We then.

At any rate, to go back to our story, nobody could very well doubt that these amendments — the first eight, which are usually referred to as the Bill of Rights — were not intended to run against the states. It is difficult to think that any contemporary lawyer could have had much hope of persuading the contemporary Supreme Court to rule that they did. The bar, however, are irrepressible people — they are paid to be — and in 1833 the Court, then still under the leadership of Marshall, had to make a formal ruling.[260]   Marshall based his obvious conclusion upon the structural incongruity, the architectural impropriety of the presence in the Constitution of any restrictions on the states for the benefit of their own citizens. The Federal Government was something Marshall took a great deal of pride in, and he thought of it as a logically symmetrical structure, which, due so much to his efforts, it was.   The Constitution, Marshall said, was ordained and established by the people of the United States for themselves and for their own government, not for the government of the individual States.   Each State, he said, had established a constitution for itself, and had, in that constitution, provided such limitations and restrictions on the powers of its particular government as its judgment dictated.   Others should interfere no further than they have a common interest.

This is resplendent reasoning.   The federal government through the federal courts can interfere in the relations between a state and its individual inhabitants only when all the people of the United States are concerned, and under the Constitution it seemed to Marshall this was only in respect of matters which the people had delegated to the new United States government.   Persuasive and neat. Too neat.   There was a crack in Marshall's reasoning; and there was considerable pressure behind that crack.   How about the guarantee 'to every state in this union of a Republican form of government' which appeared in Article IV, Section 4?   Perhaps this was thought of only as a protection to the states, for it was coupled with protection against invasion and domestic violence.   But was it not also for the benefit of the new United States?   Free speech, liberty of conscience, and the orderly processes of law are the necessary ingredients of a republic. This had been the thought behind Madison's proposal, and it was going to be the thought which would be pressed on the Court until finally it prevailed. And the more the country became a single nation, the more inconvenient it would be to have intolerance, suppression, and disorder prevailing anywhere.

The Civil War gave us the Fourteenth Amendment, which so far as it concerns us now, reads,

'No State shall make or enforce any law which shall abridge the privileges or immunities of citizens of the United States; nor shall any State deprive any person of life, liberty, or property, without due process of law; nor deny to any person within its jurisdiction the equal protection of the laws.' The State, just as Madison had wanted to apply the Bill of Rights.

At first the bar made the mistake of insisting upon the words 'the privileges and immunities of citizens of the United States.' These are not, the Court replied, the fundamental rights you are asserting. They are only your rights as a United States citizen, which are limited to the part the United States plays in your lives. This provision, the Court said, prevents the states from interfering in any way with your relations with the United States, but no more than that. It does not touch your relations with your state. Thus the Court was giving the bar the converse of what they had got from Marshall. The United States does not meddle with your relations with your state. Your state cannot meddle with your relations with the United States.

This decision was made in the Slaughterhouse Cases.[261] Some butchers in New Orleans had protested against the monopoly which had been given to one slaughterhouse. They contended that their business was one of these privileges and immunities, fundamental rights that belonged to the citizen of every free government. In the course of the argument Bradley gave the bar a tip. This right, he said, to choose the lawful vocation of slaughtering is a portion of their liberty; their occupation is the property.[262] Not a privilege of citizens, but liberty and property under the second provision, 'nor shall any State deprive any person of life, liberty, or property, without due process of law.' Now a corporation could not very well be a citizen, but might it not be a 'person'?

The ruling by which a corporation was held by the Court to be a 'person' under the due process clause of the Fourteenth Amendment has always stuck in the throats of many people. Maury Maverick calls it prestidigitation, as you can read in his *In Blood and Ink*.[263] Forty-odd years after the event, Black, in one of his lone dissents in his first year on the bench, urged that the ruling be reversed.[264]

Roscoe Conkling is the man who should get much of the credit for what the Court now proceeded to do. He was of counsel for the Southern Pacific when it appealed to the Court about a tax assessment in San Mateo County in California. This was in 1882. Conkling had been a member of the Joint Committee on Reconstruction of the Congress which had proposed this Fourteenth Amendment. What he did was to misquote to the Court the secret journal of that Committee to show that it had intended to include corporations in the word 'person.'

It was not a very gross misquotation. It was only a little one, but it seemed to serve. It was this. He told the Court that the Committee had had before it, which it had not, a draft which secured life, liberty, and property only to *citizens*, and that they had deliberately substituted *persons*. And, Conkling argued that the reason for this change must have been to include corporations. He invited the Court to make the most of a small falsehood, and the Court did.[265]

It was a great triumph for the railroad lawyers, but they were not sowing for themselves alone. For whatever they did for the rights of property had to be equally true of life and liberty. These two words stood next to, indeed ahead of, property, in the phrase which the railroad lawyers were pressing on the Court, and if corporations were persons, so too are you and I.

What these lawyers accomplished ran far beyond what Madison had vainly urged. Madison's proposal was no more than to give the Federal Government the power of requiring the States to respect the scruples of conscience, the rights of free speech and press, and trial by jury. What these corporation attorneys persuaded the Court to do was nothing less than require the states to be just and fair in their dealings with all men as well as their clients. It is a story that calls for a book by itself, a tale of persistence, tact, eloquence, and fees. And they were so successful that when they were done they did not know how successful they had been, and they were appalled. What they had erected, as Charles Warren who was the first to perceive it said, was 'a tremendous engine for attack on State legislation — an engine which could not have been conceived possible by the framers of the first Ten Amendments or by the framers of the Fourteenth Amendment itself.' [266]

All hinged on the meaning of the phrase, Due Process of Law, which is the pinion of both the Fifth and the Four-

teenth Amendment.   It stems from Magna Charta no.
39, 'by the law of the land, that is,' Coke said, 'to speak it
once for all, by the due course and process of law.' [267] And
down to about 1890 that is all that it meant.   Certainly
that was what it meant to Madison and the other framers
of the Fifth Amendment.   Story is the best of witnesses,
and in the first edition of his book on constitutional law he
said due process meant no more than 'the right of trial
according to the process and proceedings of the common
law.'

The great tradition, then, of due process of law, from
Magna Charta down to the eighteen-nineties, raised and
settled only matters of proper legal procedure.   The courts
took the law they administered from the legislature.   They
applied the statutes to the cases before them and they did
not question the right of the legislature to tell them what
the law was, except when the legislature tampered with
their judicial methods of procedure, in which, naturally
enough, they were great believers.   When that was followed, they had no doubt of the justice of the result, but
only when it was followed.   If the established judicial
process was tampered with and the courts required to proceed in other ways, even that was a different matter.   It
was really a corollary from the separation of powers.   You
keep your hands off our procedure.   We'll keep ours off
your statutes.

This was the traditional meaning of Due Process.   The
one exception to it in the Court's opinions, before the Civil
War and the Fourteenth Amendment, proves the rule.
Taney, in the Dred Scott case,[268] in 1856, remarked, 'And
an Act of Congress which deprives a citizen of the United
States of his liberty or property merely because he came

himself or brought his property into a particular territory of the United States and who had committed no offense against the laws could hardly be dignified with the name of due process of law.' A casual remark, hardly enough to start an argument.

The break ironically came in a case where a board of commissioners had fixed too low a rate for another railroad, the Chicago, Milwaukee, and Saint Paul.[269]

It was not the first case in which the Court's attention had been invited to the activities of states setting rates for railroads and other public utilities. But in this case the Illinois legislature left the rates to be set by a board, which was a sort of pseudo-court, something like a court and yet not wholly a court, and quite lacking in the dignity of a court. So a majority of the justices were willing to scrutinize not only the procedure of this pseudo-judicial tribunal, but the result it had reached. If the Illinois legislature had set the rates itself, the Court might have declined to hear any appeal from it, on the ground that it was a legislative and not a judicial matter. But, since the legislature had chosen to act in a semi-judicial manner, the Court was lured into treating it as wholly judicial.

Three Justices, Bradley, Gray, and Lamar dissented. What they said makes it clear what the Court had done. 'Injustice,' they said, 'may take place in all tribunals. All human institutions are imperfect — courts as well as commissions and legislatures. Whatever tribunal has jurisdiction, its decisions are final and conclusive unless an appeal is given therefrom. The important question always is, what is the lawful tribunal for the particular case? In my judgment, in the present case, the proper tribunal was the legislature, or the board of commissioners which it created for the purpose.'

What the Court had done, over this dissent, for better, for worse, was take a legislative matter, that is, a question which our scheme of government had left to the legislature, and treat it like a judicial matter. This board was not a court. It was the legislature. The fixing of rates had not been a judicial matter. Now it was. And now what was not? At any rate so far as property rights were concerned. The railroad lawyers had done a good job.

There is no need here of counting their triumphs, only of indicating the path they were following, for on that path, further along, the property of a corporation turned into the liberty of an individual. The railroads and other corporations were claiming protection for their *property* against excessive taxes and unjust rates. Not *liberty*, at least not in the proper sense. But property, inert property was not enough. Corporations, like any business, had to be free to acquire more property. They had to be free to go out and get more business. In brief, they had to be protected in the liberty of enjoying an acquisitive way of life. That was their business, their only reason for being. Hence liberty at least of contract. So it followed that New York in the Lochner case was depriving them of *property* when it passed a law limiting the hours of employment in bakeries to sixty a week and ten a day.[270] Nor could Kansas in the Coppage outlaw yellow dog contracts, by which your employee agreed not to join a union.[271] For labor relations, too, were property rights. We are straddling the margin between property and liberty.

It was the cue Bradley gave in his Slaughterhouse dissent, the right to choose your lawful vocation, 'their occupation is property.' No narrow static notion of property in that era would have made any sense. The country was not much interested then in inherited fortunes. Your property was what you made it, your liberty to make it was your property. As the Court said in the Coppage case, 'Included in the right of personal liberty and the right of private property — partaking of the nature of each — is the right to make contracts for the acquisition of property.'

You will note that the Court's philosophy was profoundly egalitarian. This was no privilege of the wealthy, not in the eyes of the law, but of every man, rich or poor. The strong arm of the Due Process clause reached down to protect the humblest. As the Court went on to say in the Coppage case, 'Chief among such contracts is that of personal employment, by which labor and other services are exchanged for money or other forms of property. If this right be struck down or arbitrarily interfered with, there is a substantial impairment of liberty in the long-established constitutional sense. The right is as essential to the laborer as to the capitalist, to the poor as to the rich; for the vast majority of persons have no other honest way to begin to acquire property, save by working for money.' [272]

You and I and the other fellow are 'persons,' too, and we have other liberties than the making of contracts, even if corporations, being a special kind of person, are confined to their business of making money. What the Court had done to protect them, the Court could equally well do to protect us. How about freedom of speech?

In 1907, Harlan said, 'I go further and hold that the privileges of free speech and of a free press, belonging to every citizen of the United States, constitute essential parts of every man's liberty, and are protected against violation by that clause of the Fourteenth Amendment forbidding a State to deprive any person of his liberty without due process of law. It is, I think, impossible to conceive of liberty, as secured by the Constitution against hostile action, whether by the Nation or by the States, which does not embrace the right to enjoy free speech and the right to have a free press.' [273] And a dozen years later, another judge from Kentucky, Brandeis, said, 'I cannot believe that the liberty guaranteed by the Fourteenth Amendment includes only liberty to acquire and enjoy property.' [274]

Apparently they made no impression. You might have thought the Court had not heard. Indeed, two years later, in 1922 — now we are only three years from Gitlow — the Court remarked, 'But, as we have stated, neither the Fourteenth Amendment, nor any other provision of the Constitution of the United States imposes upon the States any restriction about "freedom of speech" or "the liberty of silence."' [275] The water was rising, though the Court seemed unaware of it.

What do you say of teaching? Is that a property right, a gainful occupation, or is it a liberty, as we imply when we speak of academic freedom? It is both, of course, but which do you say it is constitutionally, when you are considering the right of a teacher to teach, and not to be deprived of his teaching under the due process clause? The next year, in 1923, the Court considered a Nebraska statute which forbade the teaching of any modern language till after the eighth grade. The bar argued this case as a property right, contesting this statute as violative of the teachers' constitutional right to engage in the practice of their chosen profession or calling. And McReynolds, who wrote the opinion, took the same approach.[276]

The opinion is in McReynolds's best style. Plato is quoted, but not about teaching, only the part about having wives in common and no one knowing his own child. Spartan ideals are carefully differentiated from American. And by implication, the true American is delineated. He is the one to whom the Constitution vouchsafes the right 'to contract, to engage in any of the common occupations of life, to acquire useful knowledge, to marry, to establish a home and bring up children, to worship God according to the dictates of his own conscience, and generally to enjoy those privileges long recognized at common law as essential to the orderly pursuit of happiness by free men.' Like the advertisements of the young couple leaning on the fence looking at the real estate improvement, or the one in the cellar, where Mrs. shows Mr. the automatic oil furnace. It is a sound, healthy, happy, idealized picture that McReynolds draws of American manhood and womanhood.

So the Court concluded that the Nebraska statute was unconstitutional, because it deprived teachers of their livelihood, tinctured with a feeling that education belonged to the parents and a sentiment in favor of the home.

Holmes dissented. Not, Heaven knows, because he would not have German taught in the schools of Nebraska! But because he could not believe that it was any of his business, any of the Court's business. As, Drew Pearson reports, Holmes once put it to Stone, 'Young man,' said Holmes to his sixty-one-year-old friend, 'about seventy-five years ago I learned that I was not God. And so, when the people of the various states want to do something I can't find anything in the Constitution expressly forbidding them to do, I say, whether I like it or not, "Goddammit, let 'em do it!"' [277]

As Holmes put it when he was dissenting here, 'It is with hesitation and unwillingness that I differ from my brethren with regard to a law like this but I cannot bring my mind to believe that in some circumstances existing, it is said, in Nebraska, the statute might not be regarded as a reasonable or even necessary method of reaching the desired result. But if it is reasonable it is not an undue restriction of the liberty either of teacher or scholar.' [278]

I suggest you do not forget this attitude of Holmes. Put it to yourself either way you like. It is the necessary approach to the whole of our immense problem.

However, two years later, in 1925, the water went over the sill in the Gitlow case. The Court laid the proposition on the line that the due process clause protected freedom of speech. There is no particular reason why this happened at this particular time. It was long delayed. It was inevitable. The Court acted as if it were unaware of what it was doing, like a small boy opening a new knife without comment. What the Court said was, 'For present purposes we may and do assume that freedom of speech and of the press — which are protected by the First Amendment from abridgment by Congress — are among the fundamental personal rights and "liberties" protected by the due process clause of the Fourteenth Amendment from impairment by the States.' [279]

The Court turned the assumption into action in a syndicalist case from Kansas in 1927. Fiske's conviction for recruiting for the I.W.W. was reversed on the ground that it had not been shown that the I.W.W. advocated either crime, violence, or revolution, and the application of the statute to Fiske's activities was held a violation of due process.[280]

Then, in 1931, came a California case, on a law which prohibited any display of a red flag. Miss Stromberg, a young teacher in a children's camp, had devised a ceremony that we might keep in mind when we come to the Gobitis case. It was a salute to the red flag of the U.S.S.R., and the children recited, 'To the Workers' Flag, and to the cause for which it stands; one aim throughout our lives, freedom for the working class.' Her conviction could not stand, the Court said, over the dissent of McReynolds and Butler. 'The conception of liberty under the due process clause of the Fourteenth Amendment embraces the right of free speech.' [281] That, the Court said, is 'no longer open to doubt.' [282]

An Antiquarian Attitude

It was no longer open to doubt that the states were going to have to respect free speech and that the due process clause of the Fourteenth Amendment had somehow brought this about. But just how and just why were still open to discussion. The Court's difficulties with the New Deal in the next few years confined its attention so closely to property rights that this discussion was prorogued until those troubles were over and the Court had been reconstructed.

The Court had done for personal rights no more and no less than what their predecessors had done for property. What that was Holmes had told them. 'I have not yet adequately expressed the more than anxiety that I feel at the ever increasing scope given to the Fourteenth Amendment in cutting down what I believe to be the constitutional rights of the States. As the decisions now stand,[283] I see hardly any limit but the sky to the invalidating of those rights if they happen to strike a majority of this Court as for any reason undesirable.' [284]

The Court had become potentially our conscience, the spiritual guide and father confessor of all our governments, state as well as federal, a court of honor as well as a court of law, our wise old uncle, the Hays office, if you please, of political behavior, or if you prefer, our daimon of Socrates; mediator, in brief, between man as an individual and man in society. Holmes wrote, 'The feeling of mystery and awe about my work also have diminished. It ought to be done by demi gods, but I think I can hold up my end as things are.' [285] Can you state it more precisely.

If we have to put this in terms of the Constitution, we could say that these are the rights retained by the people under the Ninth Amendment, which says, 'The enumeration in the Constitution, of certain rights, shall not be construed to deny or disparage others retained by the people.' And indeed this amendment was added to make sure that the Bill of Rights should not be considered exclusive and complete. There might be others. There may be. And whether there are and what they are, is now, under the new dispensation, open for the Court to decide, to lift them up from those retained by the people and apply them to new needs.

The Court's judgments were final. They were permanent in time. They were national in scope. National, because the Court was construing a document which spoke the voice of nothing less than We the People. The Court was no less than the surrogate of all the people. Permanent, at least they pretended to be. Decisions might be overruled, and experience had put a discerning people on guard against a new permanence, yet each decision did speak as if it were for keeps, and so far as that goes, perhaps it might be. At any rate, for all practical purposes, it had to be regarded so.

The purported permanence of a decision, however, was not so important as the indubitable fact that so long as it stood it spoke for the nation. That had an ever greater influence on its character than any expectation of permanence could have. For the more people a pronouncement speaks for, the higher standard it inevitably takes. We all have a stricter conscience and a higher standard of ethics for others. Either that or a much lower, and the Court is in no position to adopt a low standard. Take a subject which we have touched on and which is only just beginning to be a matter of legal concern, racial discrimination. We are all more ready to free India than we are to give our own Negroes equality. Negroes get more equal treatment from the Federal Government than they do from the states. The ballots the Negro can cast freely in the South are cast in the A.A.A. We all profess more justice for others than we are willing to apply to ourselves. Yes, and our judgments about them may be the sounder for not being ourselves involved. There are administrative difficulties in a large country, but it has its advantages.

A prodigious task. The Court had turned the latchkey of the law into the Keys of the Kingdom, and some of the Justices were pardonably appalled. Particularly Black. The doctrine that there is a due process of law in what a state can do as well as in the manner of its doing sat very uneasily on Black's shoulders. Time and again he quoted and requoted Holmes's anxiety.[286]

What Holmes was referring to, and what Black had on his mind, is the Court's zeal in protecting property. But the roots of due process, as we have seen, now run way under the garden plot of personal liberties. How can they be dug up without destroying what bloomed in 1922? Personal liberties as well as property rights are protected by due process of law. If you restrict due process to legal procedure, will not personal liberties, for which Black has the warmest affections, be left without protection against the States?

Black extricated himself, and those other Justices who shared his feelings, from this dilemma by a very ingenious theory. He took the position that in addition to prescribing a necessary minimum of fair procedure all the due process clause does is to reflect the Federal Bill of Rights, that is, the first eight Amendments. Thus he turned the flank of both his fears very neatly, that the Court, wielding this vast power, may overprotect property — as he had seen it do — or underprotect personal liberties — as he feared it might do. As Holmes saw 'hardly any limit but the sky' to the invalidating of the constitutional rights of the States, so Black feared that 'under the same rule, another Court, with a different belief as to fundamental justice, could at least as against State action, completely or partially withdraw Constitutional protection from these basic freedoms, just as though the First Amendment had never been written.' [287]

So Black wanted to restrict due process to procedure and yet at the same time include within it the right of free speech and what he called the 'other clearly defined protections contained in the Bill of Rights.' Here, he said, 'courts proceeding within clearly marked constitutional

boundaries seek to execute policies written into the Constitution.' Beyond those 'clearly marked boundaries,' the
courts 'roam at will in the limitless area of their own beliefs as to reasonableness and actually select policies, a
responsibility which the Constitution entrusts to the legislative representatives of the people.' [288]

Grant that the provisions of the Bill of Rights are as
'clearly defined' and specific as good lawyers with a decent
regard for the difficulties of language could make them,
though surely the terms of the First Amendment are made
so only in the light that blazed from Black's convictions.
Yet was not Black confusing clarities with values?

Cardozo said that freedom of thought and of speech was
'absorbed' by the due process clause because neither liberty nor justice could exist if it were sacrificed. For it was
'the matrix, the indispensable condition, of nearly every
other form of freedom.' [289] But not all, Cardozo went on
to say. Not, for example, the provision in the Fifth
Amendment that no person shall twice be put in jeopardy
of life or limb. Freedom of thought and of speech is on 'a
different plane of social and moral values.' Take the provision of the Sixth Amendment, that 'In all criminal prosecutions, the accused shall enjoy the right to have the
assistance of counsel for his defence.' Had it been so absorbed by the due process clause as to make it applicable
to the States?

Only some nine states make that requirement of themselves. Most of them leave it to the discretion of the trial
judge to provide counsel for an accused who cannot afford
to hire a lawyer himself. And back in the eighteenth century, at the time the Constitution was adopted, no State
required the judge appoint to counsel for an indigent de-

fendant. None of them. The most you could say then was that about half the thirteen states allowed the defendant to have counsel. Even that was a great advance over the common law. For in England, until 1836, a man charged with a felony could only have counsel advise him. His lawyer could not take part in the trial, could not examine witnesses for or against him, could not argue for him. Plainly, the Sixth Amendment was something of an innovation. Equally plainly, the right to have the state provide you with counsel was not then, any more than it is now, generally regarded as an inherent fundamental right, something demanded by a common sense of justice.

So, when a case came up where a judge in Carroll County, Maryland, refused to assign counsel to a poor defendant, and he had to defend himself, which he did, and was found guilty, the Court refused to intervene, and made it quite clear why.

'The due process clause of the Fourteenth Amendment,' the Court said, 'does not incorporate as such, the specific guarantees found in the Sixth Amendment, although a denial by a State of rights or privileges specifically embodied in that and others of the first eight amendments may, in certain circumstances, or in connection with other elements, operate, in a given case, to deprive a litigant of due process of law in violation of the Fourteenth. The phrase formulates a concept less rigid and more fluid than those envisaged in other specific and particular provisions of the Bill of Rights. Its application is less a matter of rule. Assented denial is to be tested by an appraisal of the totality of facts in a given case. That which may, in one setting, constitute a denial of fundamental fairness, shocking to the universal sense of justice, may, in other circumstances, and in the light of other considerations, fall short of such denial.' [290]

Black, Douglas, and Murphy dissented. They considered, on the facts presented, that Betts ought to have been given a lawyer. That is not important to anyone but Betts. What is important to us is what Black went on to say, that the Fourteenth Amendment made the Sixth applicable to the states. If the Sixth, so also the rest and all the Bill of Rights, and only the Bill of Rights.

Where then are we, a hundred and almost fifty years since Madison arrived in Philadelphia with his proposals? Black, Douglas, and Murphy would make it just what Madison proposed and failed to persuade Congress to adopt. The Court's view is obviously something very different, something less, as we have just seen, and potentially very much more.

What is the harm in that? There is no reason why we should not encourage the Court to do better by us than Congress saw fit to propose to our forefathers. We do not want to get stuck in the eighteenth century. Why should the Court's standards of political behavior for the States be forever eighteenth century? What Black proposes is an escape into the past for fear of the future. It is a little like a taste for antique furniture. It is as if we wanted to live in the American wing of the Metropolitan Museum. We can surround ourselves with period furniture We can dress up in period costumes. But thereby we do not put on their spirit. A battle jacket really reflects more of the spirit of Valley Forge and Yorktown than a buff lapel. Again Montaigne, *il faut vivre entre les vivants*.

It is hard to avoid becoming a doctrinaire when you act like an antiquarian. Let me give you a case, really two

cases that were heard together, where Black won over to
his views a majority of the Court.[291]   Bridges, the West
Coast labor leader, and the *Los Angeles Times* had each, at
about the same time, been fined for contempt of court for
what they had said about two California judges and how
they should decide the cases before them. You will understand they took different points of view, Bridges and the
Times, but free speech does not take sides and the point of
law raised in both cases was the same.

In one case, two labor men had been convicted of as-
sault, and, when their case was set down for sentence the
Los Angeles Times at once ran an editorial calling them
gorillas and goons and urging they be sentenced to San
Quentin.   In the other case, Bridges, who was president of
the C.I.O. longshoremen's union, published a telegram he
had sent to the Secretary of Labor in which he threatened
a strike that would tie up the port of Los Angeles and involve the whole west coast, if the judge tried to enforce a
decision he had made in favor of the A.F. of L. against
Bridges' union.   In both cases, there was obvious intent to
influence the judge in question.

You do not have to be a lawyer to recognize the necessity of having a sound independent system of courts and
judges.   Nor do you have to be a lawyer to assert that
judges and courts must be allowed a certain peace and
quiet, an interlude of some degree of calm, while they are
trying and judging a case, if they are going to be as sound
and as independent as we expect them to be.   We as well
as the judges and the lawyers have insisted on the court's
having the power by contempt proceedings to fine or even
jail a man for interrupting that bit of quiet, though, of
course, it cannot and should not be a vacuum, and the air

must not and should not be stagnant. Historically judges have always had this power, and they have exercised it. Currently they have it, and need it. Of course, once they have rendered their decision, that is another matter. They are exposed, as they should be, to all the winds of scorn and vituperation. So much the better. We believe that the anticipation of criticism does a judge good, and we expect him to welcome it. Not for nothing do we require our courts to make their decisions public and to give their reasons. No other public official is required to give his reasons. He may or he may not. We expect him to know best. But there are more than three hundred volumes of the reasons why the Supreme Court of the United States decided each case as it did. Otherwise there would not be this book.

So after a case is decided, freedom of speech may run rampant, just for the good of the court and all in the best interest of the administration of justice. But until then we leave the court more or less to itself and to the lawyers. We have cut a slice out of our freedom of speech which we sacrifice to the administration of justice. Indeed, as Frankfurter said later,[292] 'In securing freedom of speech, the Constitution hardly meant to create the right to influence judges or juries. That is no more freedom of speech than stuffing a ballot box is the exercise of the right to vote.'

In these two cases, Black wrote the opinion of the Court in a five to four decision. Frankfurter wrote the dissent, in which Stone, Roberts, and Byrnes joined. The Court held that both the *Times* and Bridges had a constitutional right to say what they did, and the fines imposed by the California court were set aside.[293]

Now this was a state court and therefore it was the Fourteenth Amendment or nothing. Yet Black turned to the First Amendment. He knew perfectly well that it was the Fourteenth he was dealing with, and he said so. But he laid the basis of his opinion on the First. For the Gitlow case, he said, had recognized in the Fourteenth Amendment the application to the states of the same standards of freedom of expression as under the First are applicable to the federal government. This, he said, was the first time since 1925 that the Court had been called upon to determine the constitutionality of a state's exercise of the contempt power and the mere existence of other since then untested state decisions could not be allowed to destroy the historic constitutional meaning of freedom of speech and of the press. 'For the First Amendment does not speak equivocally. It prohibits any law "abridging the freedom of speech, or of the press." It must be taken as a command of the broadest scope that explicit language, read in the context of a liberty-loving society, will allow.'·

That was broad enough to cover Bridges and the *Los Angeles Times*. It was broad enough, Black said, to lay down a general rule, that 'neither "inherent tendency" nor "reasonable tendency" is enough to justify a restriction of free expression.' So it would seem that neither this California court, nor any court — for, as Black said, 'We are necessarily measuring a power of all American courts, both state and federal, including this one' — had any longer the power to punish publications made outside the court room even when they inherently and reasonably tended to interfere with the orderly administration of justice in a case then before a court for consideration.

If Black had confined the Court's decision to the specific

and particular facts, to what the *Times's* editorial said and
to what Bridges said in his telegram, it would be hard to
say that he was wrong. So far as the 'dignity' of the
bench is concerned, Frankfurter was quite as caustic as
Black. 'There have sometimes,' Frankfurter said, 'been
martinets upon the bench as there have also been pompous
wielders of authority who have used the paraphernalia of
power in support of what they called their dignity.' 'Particularly should this freedom be employed in comment
upon the work of the courts, who are without many influences ordinarily making for humor and humility, twin
antidotes to the corrosion of power.' But Frankfurter,
Stone, Roberts, and Byrnes balked at construing the First
Amendment to prohibit any court from punishing any
publications outside the court room — of course, a court
can keep order inside — which interfered with its orderly
administration of justice. 'It is trifling with great issues,'
said Frankfurter, 'to suggest that the question before us is
whether the eighteenth century restraints upon the freedom of the press should now be revived. The question is
rather whether nineteenth- and twentieth-century American institutions should be abrogated by judicial fiat.'

'The consequence,' he said, 'of the Court's ruling today
is a denial to the people of the forty-eight states of a right
which they have always regarded as essential for the effective exercise of the judicial process, as well as a denial to
the Congress of powers which were exercised from the very
beginning even by the framers of the Constitution themselves. To be sure, the majority do not in so many words
hold that trial by newspapers has constitutional sanctity.
But the atmosphere of their opinion and several of its
phrases mean that or they mean nothing. Certainly, the

opinion is devoid of any frank recognition of the right of courts to deal with utterances calculated to intimidate the fair course of justice — a right which hitherto all the states have from time to time seen fit to confer upon their courts and which Congress conferred upon the federal courts in the Judiciary Act of 1789.'

It was beside the point to show Black and the majority that they were historically wrong and that the courts had this power even at the time of the First Amendment. The point is, Black was destroying an established American doctrine of the twentieth century, and he was doing it by reading into the Fourteenth Amendment the literal language of the First, dogmatized for the purpose.

Black is a zealot for free speech. He is an apostle of the rights of the individual. But he is too good a lawyer not to know that courts need some power to protect themselves. He is too experienced a statesman not to know that free speech can be as destructive of the judicial process as it is essential to the democratic process. And, if these inalienable rights are to be protected and realized, it is going to be done by the courts, strong and free. What free speech is to the democratic process, the autocratic judicial process is to free speech. Black knows all this as well as any man, and three years later he joined in an opinion which brought the Court out of a pseudo-eighteenth century and put the doctrine, and the Court, back where they both belonged in the instant present.

It was another case of a newspaper attacking a court, this time in Florida. The *Miami Herald* had led a campaign for the enforcement of law in Dade County in the course of which it had said things about some of the judges, while they were considering certain rape cases, which con-

command of the broadest scope that explicit language,
read in the context of a liberty-loving society, will allow,'
whose 'unqualified prohibitions laid down by the framers
were intended to give to liberty of the press, as to other
liberties, the broadest scope that could be countenanced in
an orderly society.' [294]

As Auden says:

> We'd rather,
> Be perfect copies of our father,
> Prefer our idées fixes to be
> True of a fixed Reality. . . .
>
> But who, though, is the Prince of Lies,
> If not the Spirit-that-denies,
> The shadow just behind the shoulder,
> Claiming it's wicked to grow older,
> Though we are lost if we turn around
> Thinking salvation has been found? [295]

You see where we are.   Read a quotation from an earlier
case and see if it is not the same, perhaps not in style, but
in content.   'The destruction or abridgment of a free
press — which constitutes one of the most dependable
avenues through which information of public and governmental activities may be transmitted to the people —
would be an event so evil in its consequences that the least
approach toward that end should be halted at the thresh-
old.   Do the people of this land — in the providence of
God favored, as they sometimes boast, above all others in
the plenitude of their liberties — desire to preserve those
so carefully protected by the First Amendment; liberty of
religious worship, freedom of speech and of the press, and
the right as freemen peaceably to assemble and petition

their government for a redress of grievances? If so, let them withstand all beginnings of encroachment. For the saddest epitaph which can be carved in memory of a vanished liberty is that it was lost because its possessors failed to stretch forth a saving hand while yet there was time.'

This is not Black. It is one of his predecessors, Four of them. In the same opinion, they made the same distinction between the First Amendment and the Fourteenth which Black was making. 'The difference between the two amendments is an emphatic one and readily apparent. Deprivation of a liberty not embraced by the First Amendment, as for example the liberty of contract, is qualified by the phrase "without due process of law"; but those liberties enumerated in the First Amendment are guaranteed without qualification, the object and effect of which is to put them in a category apart and make them incapable of abridgment by any process of law.'

This is from the dissent of Sutherland, Van Devanter, McReynolds, and Butler in the case of the Associated Press against the Labor Board [296] back in April, 1937 — note the date. The Court held that the freedom of the press was not abridged by requiring the A.P. to practice collective bargaining with the Guild. The Four were dissenting.

Is not Black saying precisely the same thing? Does not he too want to give the full benefit of the literal language of the First Amendment to the *Los Angeles Times* and to Bridges just as they wanted to give it to the A.P.? Now the right of the A.P. who wanted to fire Watson, because he belonged to the Guild, is no more like Bridges' and the *Los Angeles Times*'s than Black's attitude toward contempt is like Sutherland's, Van Devanter's, McReynolds's, or Butler's. No. But it is interesting to find Black and these Four entertaining similar rigid views toward the Constitution.

A rigid construction of the Constitution, whether the Bill of Rights or the Fourteenth Amendment as reflecting the Bill, for whatever reason, in whatever cause, has one inevitable effect. It denies powers to the government. There it was the power of Congress to pass the Wagner Act and allow collective bargaining. Here it is the power of California to punish for attempted interference with the administration of justice by its courts. In either case it is government that suffers. Go back to the days of the Old Court fighting the New Deal. In the Old Court, Stone called it a lack of self-restraint. What is the difference between the Old Court's lack of self-restraint and Black's calling in the First Amendment instead of the Due Process clause? Both say, No, you cannot do that, the Constitution forbids you to do that. Neither are willing to accept the responsibility of discretion. Call it lack of self-restraint or call it a refusal, the great refusal, to exercise discretion, as you will. Is it not really the same thing? Self-restraint is the negative of discretion. They are tails and heads of the same medal.

We are dealing with mental traits and mental attitudes that are very far from being peculiar to the Justices or even to lawyers. They may manifest themselves more readily and more clearly in lawyers than in laymen, but perhaps they are best found in the clergy and in theology. There is an obvious analogy between the Constitution and the Bible in the way men have used the words explicit in each. Out of the many theological controversies which have graced our several churches, let me refer only to one.

In the seventeenth century in England there was great controversy in the Anglican Church with the Latitudinarians, who were for reason against revelation. Let me quote one of them. Samuel Butler, not the author of *Erewhon* but the author of *Hudibras*, said, 'A Latitudinarian believes the Way to Heaven is never the better for being strait.' [297]

The First Commandment and the Fourteenth Amendment

There are several ways to heaven and men can be as strait about our freedom to choose a way as the Way itself.

Jehovah's Witnesses had been pressing an issue up to the Court and the Court had been ignoring it. Three times in three succeeding years it had dismissed the question whether one of Jehovah's Witnesses could constitutionally be required, contrary to his religious convictions, to salute the flag.[298] The issue had portentous possibilities, like everything which is symbolic. Its significance suddenly struck the Court in the Gobitis case, in 1940.

Lillian Gobitis was thirteen and her brother Walter was twelve when the teacher at the public school which they attended told them that they must join with the other pupils in the salute to the flag with which school opened every morning. They were to say, 'I pledge allegiance to my flag, and to the Republic for which it stands; one nation indivisible, with liberty and justice for all.' But they were Jehovah's Witnesses, and they had been brought up to believe this was nothing less than idolatry and a breach of the first two Commandments. 'Thou shalt have no other gods before me. Thou shalt not make unto thee any graven image. . . . Thou shalt not bow down thyself to them, nor serve them.' So Lillian and Walter refused to salute the flag and their father agreed with them and told them not to do it. But he sent them back to school. It was a public school, and attendance was compulsory unless he provided them with a private education. He insisted they had a right to go without breaking the Decalogue. The school insisted they had to salute the flag if they went.

'Some think it the Achilles' heel of democracy that, by its very nature, it cannot foster general agreement on ultimates, and perhaps must foster the contrary,' said a recent committee of Harvard professors.[299] Agreeing with them or not, we count on the school as the place where we teach our children their first steps in patriotism. At the same time, we keep religion out of our schools. Now patriotism and religion are made, more or less, out of the same stuff, and they are taught in more or less the same way. There is certain to be trouble when either encroaches on the preserves of the other. Here in the Gobitis case, that is just what happened. Whether it was patriotism which was the intruder on religion, or religion on patriotism, cannot help becoming arguable, one way or the other. However, there was the preliminary question, as there always is, who shall decide the argument? Is Lillian's refusal to salute our flag a good enough reason to make her parents pay for her education? Put yourself on the school board, who consider it their duty to require the salute of all the pupils, all, not only those who volunteer or who are willing or who do not object. Put yourself into the position of the parent, who considers his child damned if he salutes the flag, or anything else but Jehovah, and who finds that he must pay for his fears and scruples with a private education. Make believe you are the child, told as she leaves home not to rise and pledge allegiance to her country and sent home by the teacher when she obeys; figure out her feelings, and the feelings of the other children.

'Render unto Caesar the things that are Caesar's and unto God the things that are God's' was not in her Testament. Her God was Jehovah, and what Christ had said did not matter. The Constitution was now called on to decide between Caesar and Jehovah. Or was it between the Gobitis children and their fellow pupils?

On June 3, 1940, Frankfurter wrote the opinion of the Court. Only Stone dissented.[300] The Court declined to hold the regulation unconstitutional.

'A grave responsibility,' said Frankfurter, 'confronts this Court whenever in course of litigation it must reconcile the conflicting claims of liberty and authority. But when the liberty invoked is liberty of conscience, and the authority is authority to safeguard the nation's fellowship, judicial conscience is put to its severest test. Of such a nature is the present controversy.' He stated the facts, and said, 'We must decide whether the requirement of participation in such a ceremony, exacted from a child who refuses upon sincere religious grounds, infringes without due process of law the liberty guaranteed by the Fourteenth Amendment.' The Fourteenth, mark you.

Frankfurter went on to ask, 'When does the constitutional guarantee compel exemption from doing what society thinks necessary for the promotion of some great common end, or from a penalty for conduct which appears dangerous to the general good? To state the problem is to recall the truth that no single principle can answer all of

life's complexities. The right to freedom of religious belief, however dissident and however obnoxious to the cherished beliefs of others — even of a majority — is itself the
denial of an absolute. But to affirm that the freedom to
follow conscience has itself no limits in the life of a society
would deny that very plurality of principles which, as a
matter of history, underlies protection of religious toleration. Our present task then, as so often the case with
courts, is to reconcile two rights in order to prevent either
from destroying the other.' [301]

But for Stone religious belief was an absolute, not the
denial of one. There were limits, yes, even to religious
freedom. There were things a man may be made to do, in
spite of his most conscientious and profound religious
scruples. He could be drafted, and made to fight. So also,
Stone agreed, there are things he could be forbidden to do.
He could be prevented from disturbing the peace or from
offending public morals, though his conscience impelled
him to do just that. But these were outward things.
Bearing arms or disturbing the peace were conduct which
the State either required or forbade for their own sake, and
their advantages could be weighted relatively to loss of
scruple. But somewhere there was an absolute, and Stone
found it in 'the higher commandments of God.' The very
terms of the Bill of Rights, he said, precluded any reconciliation there.

Frankfurter and Stone both, and later the others, all
treated the issue as if it concerned the relation of the state
to the religious freedom of one of the churches. If the
salute to the flag offends the religious conscience of the
Witnesses, the salute becomes, at least to them, a religious
act which the state has forced them to perform. It is a

ritual which we regard as political, but which they regard as religious. Now, if the salute is not religious, there is nothing in the Constitution forbidding it. If it is religious, then it constitutes the beginning — *obsta principiis* — of the establishment of a state religion. And the First Amendment, though that was not what the Court was going to apply, forbids the establishment of a state religion quite as explicitly as it protects the free exercise of religion by any church or sect.

This is the way the case struck a friend of mine, and he went on to say that in 1789 there was no danger of the temporal power itself becoming a religion. The fanatics then were men preoccupied with their own plans for eternal salvation and the danger was that one sect by gaining control of the state would try to compel the others to conform, and finally set itself up as the state church. That was the danger which the Constitution had in mind. But with the decay of interest in eternal salvation, when many or most churches became social groups, the religious nature of man turned to the deification of the state. Nationalism became a religion and the nation became a church. The salute to the flag became an obeisance, so the Witnesses thought, to a new deity, the very image of that new deity. Thus the statute was not so much an interference with religious freedom as the incipient advance of nationalism to become itself an establishment of religion.

Lincoln asked, 'Must a government of necessity be too *strong* for the liberties of its people, or too *weak* to maintain its own existence?' Here it is the second alternative. These liberties depend upon government quite as truly as they are endangered by a strong government. Without government there can be no liberties quite as truly as there are none when the government is too strong. There in the Bridges case, and here in the flag salute case, where Frankfurter quotes this from Lincoln, we have concrete examples of the dilemma. Where would religious liberty be if there was no government strong enough to calm the religious rapacity of the majority? Only an anarchist would hesitate over the answer. Where would freedom of speech rest its head, were there no courts to protect it? The Court is weighing the sanctity of the right against the efficacy of the government that protects any right at all. The Court is engaged in a nice calculus of maximum values of loyalty to the state and an opportunity for devotion to God, of unfettered liberty of speech and that necessary serenity of mind in the courts which protect it.

To return to Frankfurter's opinion. 'The precise issue, then, for us to decide is whether the legislatures of the various states and the authorities in a thousand counties and school districts of this country are barred from determining the appropriateness of various means to evoke that unifying sentiment without which there can ultimately be no liberties, civil or religious. The influences which help toward a common feeling for the common country are manifold. Some may seem harsh and others no doubt are foolish. Surely, however, the end is legitimate. And the effective means for its attainment are still so uncertain and so unauthenticated by science as to preclude us from putting the widely prevalent belief in flag-saluting beyond the pale of legislative power. It mocks reason and denies our whole history to find in the allowance of a requirement to salute our flag on fitting occasions the seeds of sanction for obeisance to a leader.

'Even were we convinced of the folly of such a measure,

such belief would be no proof of its unconstitutionality. For ourselves, we might be tempted to say that the deepest patriotism is best engendered by giving unfettered scope to the most crotchety beliefs. Perhaps it is best, even from the standpoint of those interests which ordinances like the one under review seek to promote, to give to the least popular sect leave from conformities like those here in issue. But the courtroom is not the arena for debating issues of educational policy. It is not our province to choose among competing considerations in the subtle process of securing effective loyalty to the traditional ideals of democracy, while respecting at the same time individual idiosyncrasies among a people so diversified in racial origins and religious allegiances. So to hold would in effect make us the school board for the country. That authority has not been given to this Court, nor should we assume it.

'Except where the transgression of constitutional liberty is too plain for argument, personal freedom is best maintained — so long as the remedial channels of the democratic process remain open and unobstructed — when it is ingrained in a people's habits and not enforced against popular policy by the coercion of adjudicated law.'

And he concluded, 'Judicial review, itself a limitation on popular government, is a fundamental part of our constitutional system. But to the legislature no less than to courts is committed the guardianship of deeply cherished liberties. Where all the effective means of inducing political changes are left free from interference, education in the abandonment of foolish legislation is itself a training in liberty. To fight out the wise use of legislative authority in the forum of public opinion and before legislative assemblies rather than to transfer such a contest to the judicial arena, serves to vindicate the self-confidence of a free people.'

Black, you have noticed, joined in Frankfurter's Gobitis opinion. That was about a year and a half before the Bridges decision. Six months after the Bridges case, which was in December, 1941, he recanted. In one of the series of the Jehovah's Witnesses cases, where the Court sustained a small tax on hawking books or pamphlets in the city of Opelika, Alabama, Black dissented. He and Douglas and Murphy, all three of whom had joined in the Gobitis case, filed a short dissenting opinion in which they explained their position. 'Since we joined in the opinion in the Gobitis case, we think this is an appropriate occasion to state that we now believe that it also was wrongly decided. Certainly our democratic form of government, functioning under the historic Bill of Rights, has a high responsibility to accommodate itself to the religious views of minorities, however unpopular and unorthodox those views may be. The First Amendment does not put the right freely to exercise religion in a subordinate position. We fear, however, that the opinion in these and in the Gobitis case do exactly that.' [302] Mark you, the First Amendment.

That left the law in a state of some uncertainty. These three, with Stone who had dissented, made four now who would hold a required salute of the flag unconstitutional, and only three who would continue to sustain it, Frankfurter, Roberts, and Reed. Hughes and McReynolds had retired and the two new Justices, Jackson and Rutledge, were not committed. What was a lower court to do?

Learned Hand, in another such situation, put it this way. 'It is always embarrassing,' he said, 'for a lower court to say whether the time has come to disregard decisions of a higher court, not yet explicitly overruled, because they parallel others in which the higher court has expressed a contrary view. I agree that one should not wait for formal retraction in the face of changes plainly foreshadowed; the higher court may not entertain an appeal in the case before the lower court, or the parties may not choose to appeal. In either event the actual decision will be one which the judges do not believe to be that which the higher court would make. Nor is it desirable for a lower court to embrace the exhilarating opportunity of anticipating a doctrine which may be in the womb of time, but whose birth is distant; on the contrary I conceive that the measure of its duty is to divine, as best it can, what would be the event of an appeal in the case before it.' [303] Woodbury did the same thing, dissenting, in the Girouard case,[304] believing, as he said, that the prediction could be ventured that the Schwimmer, McIntosh, and Bland cases were 'no longer expressive of the law.'

Parker and Hand and Woodbury are doing no more than a lawyer does for his client, prophesying how the court will decide, which was what Holmes said was the law itself. These Circuit Courts of Appeal are no more willing to be reversed than a lawyer wants to be wrong or a client wants to be convicted.

When the next flag salute case came up, in West Virginia, Judge Parker did just that, and quite successfully. He counted noses and said, 'Under such circumstances and believing, as we do, that the flag salute here required is violative of religious liberty when required of persons holding the religious views of plaintiffs, we feel that we would be recreant to our duty as judges, if through a blind following of a decision which the Supreme Court itself has thus impaired as an authority, we should deny protection to rights which we regard as among the most sacred of those protected by constitutional guaranties.' [305]

Judge Parker was sustained. The Court overruled the Gobitis decision when his Barnette case was appealed, for both the two new justices joined Black, Douglas, Murphy, and Stone. It was six to three. Only Frankfurter, Roberts, and Reed stuck.[306]

Jackson, who spoke for the six, said that it was important to distinguish between the due process clause of the Fourteenth Amendment as an instrument for transmitting the principles of the First Amendment and its application for its own sake. 'The test of legislation,' he said, 'which collides with the Fourteenth Amendment, because it also collides with the principles of the First, is much more definite than the test when only the Fourteenth is involved. Much of the vagueness of the due process clause disappears when the specific prohibitions of the First become its standard. The right of a State to regulate, for example, a public utility may well include, so far as the due process test is concerned, power to impose all of the restrictions which a legislature may have a "rational basis" for adopting. But freedoms of speech and of press, of assembly, and of worship may not be infringed on such slender grounds. They are susceptible only to prevent grave and immediate danger to interests which the state may lawfully protect. It is important to note that while it is the Fourteenth Amendment which bears directly upon the State it is the more specific limiting principles of the

First Amendment that finally govern this case.' Again, the First Amendment.

In one respect we have misconceived and misstated the issue. We have treated it, as the Court did and all the Justices, as a matter between Lillian, her parents, and the school board. As the Court had more and more of these Jehovah's Witnesses cases pressed upon it, the Justices learned that neither they nor the state authorities were dealing so much with individual Witnesses as they were with an organization. As more cases came up, the facts disclosed a pattern. Jackson described it in his dissent in a case which came up from Jeannette, Pennsylvania.

In 1939, a 'Watch Tower Campaign' was instituted by Jehovah's Witnesses, in Jeannette, Pennsylvania, an industrial city of some sixteen thousand inhabitants. Each home was visited, a bell was rung or the door knocked upon, and the householder advised that the Witnesses had important information. If the householder would listen, a record was played on the phonograph. 'Religion is wrong and a snare because it deceives the people, but that does not mean that all who follow religion are willingly bad. Religion is a racket because it has long been used and is still used to extract money from the people upon the theory and promise that the paying over of money to a priest will serve to relieve the party paying from punishment after death and further insure his salvation.' This line of attack was taken by the Witnesses generally upon all denominations, but especially the Roman Catholic. The householder was asked to buy a variety of literature for a price or contribution, twenty-five cents for the books and smaller sums for the pamphlets. Often, if he was unwilling to purchase, the book or pamphlet was given to him anyway.

When this campaign began, many complaints from offended householders were received, and three or four of the Witnesses were arrested. Thereafter, the Witness in charge of the campaign conferred with the Mayor. He told the Mayor it was their right to carry on the campaign and showed him a decision of the United States Supreme Court as proof of it. The Mayor told him that they were at liberty to distribute their literature in the streets of the city and that he would have no objection if they distributed the literature free of charge at the houses, but that the people objected to their attempt to force these sales, particularly on Sunday. The Mayor asked whether it would not be possible to come on some other day and to distribute the literature without selling it. The Witness replied that that was contrary to their method of doing business and refused. He also told the Mayor that he would bring enough Witnesses into the City of Jeannette to get the job done whether the Mayor liked it or not.

On Palm Sunday of 1939, the threat was made good. Over a hundred of the Witnesses appeared. They were strangers to the city and arrived in upwards of twenty-five automobiles. The automobiles were parked outside the city limits, and headquarters were set up in a gasoline station with telephone facilities through which the director of the campaign could be notified when trouble occurred. He furnished bonds for the Witnesses as they were arrested. As they began their work, around nine o'clock in the morning, telephone calls began to come in to the police headquarters, and the complaints continued all during the day. More than the police could handle, and the fire department was called out to assist. The Witnesses called at homes singly and in groups, and some of the homes complained that they were called upon several times. Twenty-one Witnesses were arrested. Only those were arrested where definite proof was obtainable that the literature had been offered for sale or a sale had been made for a price. Three were later discharged for inadequacies in this proof, and eighteen were convicted.

At the head of the Jehovah's Witness in this country is the Watch Tower Bible & Tract Society, a corporation organized under the laws of Pennsylvania, but having its principal place of business in Brooklyn, New York. It prints all pamphlets, manufactures all books, supplies all phonographs and records, and provides other materials for the Witnesses. It 'ordains' these Witnesses by furnishing each a certificate that he is a minister of the Gospel.

Some of them are full-time and some part-time ministers. The full-time Witnesses acquire their literature from the Watch Tower Bible & Tract Society at a figure which enables them to distribute it at a profit. Some of the books they acquire for five cents and dispose of for a contribution of twenty-five cents. On others, the margin is less. Part-time ministers pay twenty cents to the Watch Tower Society and ask twenty-five cents for the books. Many of the Witnesses give away a substantial quantity of the literature to people who make no contributions.[307]

You will observe that the Witnesses are pretty well organized, that they make something of a living, and that they are intent on making martyrs of themselves. Perhaps martyrdom pure and simple may justly, or generously, be regarded as a religion of itself. The Witnesses gave every indication that they would have been disappointed if they had not been required to salute the flag and if they had not been arrested. They were, in other words, an organized pressure group intent on making a series of test cases on God. Anyhow they were pushing some of the Justices farther and farther into the transcendental ditch. There is nothing strange in finding ditches on both sides of the road.

The ordinance under which the Witnesses were convicted forbade all persons from canvassing for or soliciting orders without a license, which cost $1.50 for one day or $7.00 for a week. A majority of the Court, Douglas, Black, Murphy, Rutledge, and Chief Justice Stone, held that it could not apply to the Witnesses, under, of course, the First Amendment.[308]

'The alleged justification for the exaction of this license tax,' this majority said, 'is the fact that the religious literature is distributed with a solicitation for funds. But the mere fact that the religious literature is "sold" by itinerant preachers rather than "donated" does not transform evangelism into a commercial enterprise. If it did, then the passing of the collection plate in church would make the church service a commercial project. It is plain that a religious organization needs funds to remain a going concern. But an itinerant evangelist, however misguided or intolerant he may be, does not become a mere book agent by selling the Bible or religious tracts to help defray his expenses or to sustain him. Freedom of speech, freedom of the press, freedom of religion are available to all, not merely to those who can pay their own way.' [309]

Of course. But do we have to decide whether this was evangelism or canvassing? The line may be hard to draw, but do we have to draw it when the Witnesses choose to conduct their evangelism, their proselyting, their missionary work in a manner which does in fact amount to canvassing the sale of books? If they do, should they not pay the same tax as others do? A tax that was not aimed at them, nor did it hit them any harder than anyone else. If they collected enough, would they have to pay an income tax?

Douglas answered that this way. 'We have here something quite different, for example, from a tax on the income of one who engages in religious activities or a tax on property used or employed in connection with those activities. It is one thing to impose a tax on the income or property of a preacher. It is quite another thing to exact a tax from him for the privilege of delivering a sermon.' [310]

But again, this is a general tax on all canvassing. If the Witnesses choose to preach and deliver sermons by canvassing and soliciting why should they not pay the same tax that others paid for doing the same thing? Isn't it the same thing? The First Amendment refers to freedom of speech and of the press as well as to religion. Could newspapers claim the same exemption? Could any book agent who believes that the books he is selling are good literature? Why, for that matter, does it make any odds what he thinks of them?

Transcendental abstractions have a way of getting absurd. But it is less absurd than the Court's line of thought. It had an abstraction by the tail which it was not easy to let go. Conceptual thinking is a hard master, as we have seen in the Old Court. Jackson — who was now dissenting — drew the comparison, 'So it was with liberty of contract, which was discredited by being overdone.' [311]

We are not so much interested in the case as we are in the mentality of these Justices. One more indication, then, of their conceptual thinking. They said, 'The power to tax the exercise of a privilege is the power to control or suppress its enjoyment. Those who *can* tax the exercise of this religious practice *can* make its exercise so costly as to deprive it of the resources necessary for its maintenance. Those who *can* tax the privilege of engaging in this form of missionary evangelism *can* close its doors to all those who do not have a full purse. Spreading religious beliefs in this ancient and honorable manner *would* thus be denied the needy. Those who *can* deprive religious groups of their colporteurs *can* take from them a part of the vital power of the press which has survived from the Reformation.' [312]

The italics are not theirs, but they serve to show that it is the same argument which we have seen before, Marshall's power to tax. But the Court will still be sitting on this, as on other such questions. Here too what looks like a tangent may be a curve. As Frankfurter said in his dissent, with his own italics, 'It is irrelevant that a tax *can* suppress or control if it *does not*' and to say that it *can* is not the same as saying that those who *do* tax the exercise of this religious practice *have* made its exercise so costly as to deprive it of the resources necessary for its maintenance.[313]

Jackson had been pushed too far. This was where he dissented, a little angrily, it seems to me. 'If we should strip these cases to the underlying questions, I find them too difficult as constitutional problems to be disposed of by a vague but fervent transcendentalism.' [314] We should, Jackson said, consider the facts, 'unless we are to reach judgments as did Plato's men who were chained in a cave so that they saw nothing but shadows.' [315] I have given them to you from his dissent.

The Court had not seen the last of these cases. A year later, in March, 1944, the Court had to hear the appeal of one Follett, another Witness, who had been convicted of selling books without paying the fee of $1 required by the town of McCormick, South Carolina.[316] It was the same case really, and the same majority disposed of it in the same way, joined by Reed who now concurred out of deference to the previous decision, 'now the law of the land.'

Frankfurter, Jackson, and Roberts still dissented, and in their dissent, they met the majority on their own ground, the First Amendment. 'Follett,' they said, 'is not made to pay a tax for the exercise of that which the First Amendment has relieved from taxation. He is made to pay for that for which all others similarly situated must pay — an excise for the occupation of street vending. Follett asks exemption because street vending is, for him, also part of his religion. As a result, Follett will enjoy a subsidy for his religion. He will save the contribution for the cost of government which everyone else will have to pay.' [317]

'In effect the decision grants not free exercise of religion, in the sense that such exercise shall not be hindered or limited, but, on the other hand, requires that the exercise of religion be subsidized. Trinity Church, owning great property in New York City, devotes the income to religious ends. Must it, therefore, be exempt from paying its fair share of the cost of government's protection of its property?' [318]

'We cannot ignore what this decision involves. If the First Amendment grants immunity from taxation to the exercise of religion, it must equally grant a similar exemption to those who speak and to the press. It will not do to say that the Amendment, in the clause relating to religion, is couched in the imperative and, in the clause relating to freedom of speech and of press, is couched in the comparative. The Amendment's prohibitions are equally sweeping. If exactions on the business or occupation of selling cannot be enforced against Jehovah's Witnesses they can no more be enforced against publishers or vendors of books, whether dealing with religion or other matters of information. The decision now rendered must mean that the guarantee of freedom of the press creates an immunity equal to that here upheld as to teaching or preaching religious doctrine. Thus the decision precludes nonoppressive, nondiscriminatory licensing or occupation taxes on publishers, and on news vendors as well, since, without the latter, the dissemination of views would be impossible.' [319]

It does not seem to matter what subject binds men to their seats in Plato's cave. When they emerge, they are equally blinded by the sunlight. Freedom of speech or religious liberty does not differ in that respect from liberty of contract or the rights of property, although the social and economic consequences will be different. The exemption of religious, or even of all philanthropic, organizations from taxation and regulation might cause less tension than the exemption of government agencies or of interstate commerce. Jehovah's Witnesses are less formidable subjects than states, municipalities, and business corporations. But the course some of the Justices were taking was the same. They were reacting against the complete discretion vouchsafed them by the new dispensation of Due Process, whose *carte blanche* would have turned them directly and immediately to the facts, led them back into the more comfortable security and reliability of the old conceptions of the First Amendment, and thence to its hypostasis in transcendental dogma. It was nothing but a gradual abstraction from actuality into the security of a conceptual world. Though the consequences may be less formidable, they are potentially dangerous.

Was there nowhere else to go? Had the developments of the Due Process and its extension to personal rights as well as to property, thrown the Court into a welter of pure discretion, from which there was no asylum but dogma?

Roberts, Reed, and Frankfurter stuck to their latitudinarian guns, and in the Barnette case Frankfurter spoke for them. It was a formal defense of the position which he had persuaded the Court almost unanimously to take in the Gobitis case. It was also a personal statement. More than that, it is the manifesto of the latitudinarian attitude toward the Constitution.

Frankfurter began, 'One who belongs to the most vilified and persecuted minority in history is not likely to be insensible to the freedoms guaranteed by our Constitution. Were my purely personal attitude relevant I should wholeheartedly associate myself with the general libertarian views in the Court's opinion, representing as they do the thought and action of a lifetime. But as judges we are neither Jew nor Gentile, neither Catholic nor agnostic. We owe equal attachment to the Constitution and are equally bound by our judicial obligations whether we derive our citizenship from the earliest or the latest immigrants to these shores. As a member of this Court I am not justified in writing my private notions of policy into the Constitution, no matter how deeply I may cherish them or how mischievous I may deem their disregard. The duty of a judge who must decide which of two claims

before the Court shall prevail, that of a State to enact and
enforce laws within its general competence or that of an
individual to refuse obedience because of the demands of
his conscience, is not that of the ordinary person. It can
never be emphasized too much that one's own opinion
about the wisdom or evil of a law should be excluded altogether when one is doing one's duty on the bench. The
only opinion of our own even looking in that direction that
is material is our opinion whether legislators could in reason have enacted such a law.

'Not so long ago we were admonished that "the only
check upon our own exercise of power is our own sense of
self-restraint. For the removal of unwise laws from the
statute books appeal lies not to the courts but to the ballot
and to the processes of democratic government." We
have been told that generalities do not decide concrete
cases. But the intensity with which a general principle is
held may determine a particular issue, and whether we put
first things first may decide a specific controversy.

'When Mr. Justice Holmes, speaking for this Court,
wrote "it must be remembered that legislatures are ultimate guardians of the liberties and welfare of the people in
quite as great a degree as the courts," he went to the very
essence of our constitutional system and the democratic
conception of our society. He did not mean that for only
some phases of civil government this Court was not to
supplant legislatures and sit in judgment upon the right
or wrong of a challenged measure. He was stating the
comprehensive judicial duty and rôle of this Court in our
constitutional scheme whenever legislation is sought to be
nullified on any ground, namely, that responsibility for
legislation lies with legislatures, answerable as they are

directly to the people, and this Court's only and very narrow function is to determine whether within the broad
grant of authority vested in legislatures they have exercised a judgment for which reasonable justification can be
offered.

'The reason why from the beginning even the narrow
judicial authority to nullify legislation has been viewed
with a jealous eye is that it serves to prevent the full play
of the democratic process. The fact that it may be an
undemocratic aspect of our scheme of government does
not call for its rejection or its disuse. But it is the best of
reasons, as this Court has frequently recognized, for the
greatest caution in its use.

'If the function of this Court is to be essentially no
different from that of a legislature, if the considerations
governing constitutional construction are to be substantially those that underlie legislation, then indeed judges
should not have life tenure and they should be made
directly responsible to the electorate. There have been
many but unsuccessful proposals in the last sixty years to
amend the Constitution to that end.

'Jefferson's opposition to judicial review has not been
accepted by history, but it still serves as an admonition
against confusion between judicial and political functions.
As a rule of judicial self-restraint, it is still as valid as
Lincoln's admonition. For those who pass laws not only
are under duty to pass laws. They are also under duty to
observe the Constitution. And even though legislation
relates to civil liberties, our duty of deference to those who
have the responsibility for making the laws is no less relevant or less exacting. And this is so especially when we
consider the accidental contingencies by which one man

may determine constitutionality and thereby confine the political power of the Congress of the United States and the legislatures of forty-eight states. The attitude of judicial humility which these considerations enjoin is not an abdication of the judicial function. It is a due observance of its limits. Moreover, it is to be borne in mind that in a question like this we are not passing on the proper distribution of political power as between the states and the central government. We are not discharging the basic function of this Court as the mediator of powers within the federal system. To strike down a law like this is to deny a power to all government.

'Of course, patriotism cannot be enforced by the flag salute. But neither can the liberal spirit be enforced by judicial invalidation of illiberal legislation. Our constant preoccupation with the constitutionality of legislation rather than with its wisdom tends to preoccupation of the American mind with a false value. The tendency of focusing attention on constitutionality is to make constitutionality synonymous with wisdom, to regard a law as all right if it is constitutional. Such an attitude is a great enemy of liberalism. Particularly in legislation affecting freedom of thought and freedom of speech much which should offend a free-spirited society is constitutional. Reliance for the most precious interests of civilization, therefore, must be found outside of their vindication in courts of law. Only a persistent positive translation of the faith of a free society into the convictions and habits and actions of a community is the ultimate reliance against unabated temptations to fetter the human spirit.' [320]

17

CONCLUSION

IN THE COURT'S first exercise of judicial supremacy, Marshall told Jefferson not to do just what Jefferson intended not to do. In its second, fifty years later, exercise was still scarcely the right word, for the Court tried to shout down the nation and the nation would not even listen. The fact is, the doctrine of judicial supremacy, conceived in 1803 and having survived a near abortion in 1854, was not born until sometime shortly after the Civil War. Since then we have followed some aspects of its career, more particularly after it met the New Deal in 1933.

We have been able to describe this power, but we have been wholly at a loss for any phrase or formula by which we could fix its scope and extent, though it very clearly has its limits. It is not circumscribed in the Constitution. It is not even described. The Court itself has tried, but in legal terms that are scarcely intelligible outside of the faith, and not to everyone within it. Stone showed this to be so when he said, in his dissent in the A.A.A., 'The only check upon our own exercise of power is our own sense of self-restraint.'

Sutherland, you will recall, retorted with some vehemence that Stone's suggestion was both ill-considered and mischievous, because self-restraint belonged in the domain of will and not of judgment. Without accepting Sutherland's substitutes for Stone's self-restraint, which were the Constitution, the judge's oath of office, and his conscience, we must agree that one of the ingredients of self-restraint is will power. Then is there nothing more to be said? For will power is only brute effort. Let us put ourselves in the Court's shoes and consider.

The first thing the Court remembers, or forgets, is that it is a part of our government. No more than the King of England, can it 'move in another orbit from the people, and like some superior planet attract, repel, influence, and direct their motion by his own. He and they are parts of the same system, intimately joined and co-operating together, acting and acted upon, limiting and limited, controlling and controlled by one another; and when he ceases to stand in this relation to them he ceases to stand in any.' [321] What makes it as easy for the Court to forget this as it was for the king, is the fact that the Court is an autocratic member of a democratic process. In this country an elected official has his own emoluments of prestige in the fact that he is elected. The Court must resist all temptation to make up for this in pride.

The second thing the Court remembers, and this it never forgets, is the fact that all it does must be done from inside the Legal Tradition. It is still a mystery to me why so much of the respect which we owe to the Court comes from the fact that it is a court of law, but it is so, and the Court must therefore always work from within that tradition, extending it, adapting it, never, never leaving it. The skeleton in the Court's closet is the Council of Revision which the Constitutional Convention killed. The Court dare not forget it, far less emulate or imitate it.

The third thing is simply wisdom, of which there are two kinds. The Court must be wise for itself, as well as for the rest of us. It must be prudent. It must be wary. Partly because, as I have said, it is an undemocratic, though integral, part of our democratic process. It is an adopted child, not of the blood of the conquerors. Particularly it must be wary because, oddly and yet characteristically, its power is greatest where it is least warranted by the Constitution. Witness its use of the Due Process clause. If the Court's power rested on express warrant of law, there would be precious little left of it.

Perhaps it would be more polite to call this wisdom by other names than wariness, which perhaps overemphasizes the selfish side of it, but it is a selfishness which is more self-discipline than self-seeking. It is discretion. It is fear. Why make any bones about it? It is sophrosyne, to use a Greek word. It is that quality which is indispensable to all co-operation everywhere, for it asks the question, Who of us can do this part of the job best? In any effective work with others you must first be yourself. Co-operation and individualism are not opponents but components. The best soldiers take the best care of themselves.

There is no need of expatiating on the need of the Court's being wise and acting wisely for the country. Yet, in Sutherland's conception of its duties there is no room for wisdom, which is simply nonsense. What does the Court do when it overrules a prior, perhaps long-standing decision? To overrule an important precedent is serious business, said Jackson. It calls for a sober appraisal, he said, of the disadvantages of the innovation as well as those of the questioned case, a weighing of practical effects of one against the other.[322] And once where the Court made what he called 'a switch of abstract concepts' regarding state inheritance taxes on intangible property, he said, 'I am content with existing constitutional law unless it appears more plainly that it is unsound or until it works badly in our present day and society.'[323] The Court must sail by the wind as well as by the stars.

Finally, the Justices must keep what are called their personal predilections as far from them as they can. For, unfortunately, the intensity of your convictions is no measure of how right you are. But it is not so much personal predilections, or even prejudices, that people object to. They are likely to indulge a man there. It is the suspicion that he is partisan, and that the man is not so much indulging himself as working for some special interest.

So much for that part of Stone's self-restraint which Sutherland called nothing but a crude effort of will power. There is more to it. A great part of it is not will at all, not self-restraint, not simply a mastery of the Court's desire to have its own way, but respect for the country's desire to have its own way, and that is an act of faith, not of will.

During the forty-odd years following the Civil War the Court paid less and less respect to that desire. Holmes, Brandeis, and Cardozo, and a few others as well, did what they could against the tide, but the Court lacked faith in the democratic process. We have seen how due process of law spread from procedure to substance. The Court was willing to defer to the decision of a court which had gone about its business in the same way the Court itself would have gone about it. If there had been notice, and a hearing, at which the defendant had confronted the witnesses against him, had an opportunity to present his own witnesses, had counsel, had not been browbeaten or forced to incriminate himself, well and good, the result could be accepted with confidence. There was no need of self-restraint. The Court had faith in the judicial process. And if all the other tribunals by which a man could be deprived of his life, liberty, or property, including legislatures, had acted with the same procedure, no doubt the Court would have been satisfied. Indeed the Old Court sometimes talked and acted as if that were what it expected. Of course, legislatures and commissions cannot, and should not, and did not, proceed that way, that is, according to judicial process. There is an administrative process. There is also such a thing as political process. Each tribunal proceeds in its own appropriate way, as Bradley, Gray, and Lamar recognized it must.[324]

The trouble came, and the need for self-restraint arose, from the fact that these other appropriate processes were unfamiliar to the Court, not its own way of life, not the ancient and established method by which judges and lawyers operate. The legal mind and the Legal Tradition had to take what they did on faith, unless the result matched the judges' own personal political and economic opinions. Then, of course, no faith was needed. Most of the Justices during this period, this last half century up to the New Court, just did not have the requisite faith when they did not agree.

Had the Justices had that faith, they would have had no need for self-restraint. Respect for the political, the democratic process would have taken its place and served in its stead. But there were occasions when that process was not working and the statute before them could not be said to result from it. Then there was no reason for exercising self-restraint. The non-existence of the democratic process was the precise equivalent of the Old Court's lack of any confidence or belief in it. The Court may well treat a statute that is not the result of the democratic process with no more respect and no more restraint than a Court which had no respect for that process treated all statutes.

So we may say, Where the democratic process is not working and the statute is not its result, the Court is free to make up its own mind without the exercise of any self-restraint.

There are more statutes than you might expect suffering from this congenital vice. For one example, state regulations and state taxation of interstate commerce, where the burden falls on people out of the state. Barring out-of-state lobbyists, the state legislature is then subject to no political restraints, as it is when its action adversely affects interests within the state.[325] For the same reason the Court felt free, and acted too freely, as Bradley told them and as Marshall had warned them, when it invalidated State taxes on Federal agencies and their employees.

The Okies are another example, if you remember John Steinbeck's *Grapes of Wrath*. When they were mishandled under the Indigent Persons Act of California and it was held invalid, Byrnes said, 'Moreover, the indigent non-residents who are the real victims of the statute are deprived of the opportunity to exert political pressure upon the California legislature in order to obtain a change of policy.'[326] Action against racial groups is always suspect, when prejudice excludes them from representing themselves and participating, such as the treatment of Mexicans in Texas, or of Negroes in the South, and not only in the South. But why it should apply to a group like Jehovah's Witnesses who voluntarily cut themselves off, whether or not under the compulsion of conscience? Other considerations must be invoked to protect them.

If the Court may properly cast off restraint when the democratic process is not working, license becomes a virtue when the legislature attacks the very process itself, as it does when it restricts the right to vote, prohibits peaceable assembly, interferes with political organizations, restrains the dissemination of information. All these, as Stone said, require 'more exacting judicial scrutiny' than the general prohibitions of Due Process.[327] And surely this is obvious, so much so the Court has more often acted than spoken on the principle. Some of these examples are the subject of specific prohibition in the Bill of Rights, but it is their effect upon the democratic process that justifies the more exacting scrutiny, not the fact that they have been more specifically prohibited and seem therefore easier to apply.

So our second rule is, where the democratic process is itself attacked, the Court should exercise less than no restraint.

Neither of these rules, however, reaches the solution we are seeking. What is the Court's function and what are the limits of its self-restraint when the democratic process is working, when it is not mutilating itself, and when the legislation before the Court is the result? We must look for an answer in a larger context than self-restraint or even faith in the democratic process.

No doubt Frankfurter was right when he said, in his

Gobitis opinion, that, 'Except where the transgression of constitutional liberty was too plain for argument, personal freedom is best maintained — so long as the remedial channels of the democratic process were open and unobstructed — when it is ingrained in a people's habits and not enforced against popular policy by the coercion of adjudicated law.' But Stone was equally right when he retorted, 'I am not persuaded that we should refrain from passing upon legislative judgment "as long as the remedial channels of the democratic process remain open and unobstructed." This seems to me no more than the surrender of the constitutional protection of the liberty of small minorities to the popular will.' And so too was Jackson when he said for the Court in the Barnette case, 'The very purpose of a Bill of Rights is to withdraw certain subjects from the vicissitudes of political controversy, to place them beyond the reach of majorities and officials and to establish them as legal principles to be applied by the courts. One's right to life, liberty, and property, to free speech, a free press, freedom of worship and assembly, and other fundamental rights may not be submitted to vote; they depend on the outcome of no elections.'

It would be a perverse reading of a noble perception to take it that Frankfurter meant that the Court should not play its part. He meant that the Court cannot carry the play alone, that reliance on the Court is not enough, very far from enough, and that underlying anything the Court can do is the conduct of the community of which the Court is at best only a part.

Frankfurter's eager preference for the democratic process over the judicial process differs from Stone's and Jackson's insistence only in the extent to which we must occasionally turn to the judicial process. Surely it is not our ultimate reliance. Surely too there are times when we must turn to it. If these Justices differ, it is only just such a debate as always arises in any collaboration, where it is always a question what each participant is to do in their joint effort and what process, here either the judicial or the political, should be applied to the job in hand. Congress argues out the same question on its side. Sometimes it is equally eager that the Court should take the lead or bear the responsibility. At others it is as insistent that something is a political matter as Stone and Jackson were that the right of Jehovah's Witnesses to refuse to salute the flag depended on no elections. Any joint undertaking engenders just such debates, and if it is going to be successful, out of these debates ultimately arises a common understanding of what each can do best, and what is the proper function of each. So here. What is the proper function of the Court and the judicial process?

It is all very well to say, as we often do, that these personal rights are basic and essential to the democratic process and that any abridgment of those rights is a flanking attack on democracy itself. Democracy was made for man, not man for democracy, and these rights serve some higher purpose than keeping the democratic process alive, though they do that, too. But even if that is all they do, and their only purpose is to protect the democratic process against itself, even to do that we must appeal to something outside it. When we say that these personal rights are essential and basic to the democratic process, we are implying that they rest on something other than that process. When we are saving that process from itself, we must have something other than itself to save it with.

These rights are something more, certainly, than a legacy from the eighteenth century. That was long ago. Something more too than whatever notions were prevalent when the Justices were being brought up and educated. That also was too long ago. Surely not just their personal predilections.

The Constitution, unlike the Declaration of Independence, was not a proclamation and it was shrewdly silent on these things. It expressed no major premise. Perhaps that will be reckoned as the supreme wisdom of the Convention. For now we can impute to it the best current philosophy of the time. There always is one. What Selden said of religion is true too of a country's dominant philosophy, 'We look after it as the butcher did after his knife, when he had it in his mouth.' There is no escape from some philosophy. If men make decisions and policies on anything more stable than immediate expediency or impulse, they cannot avoid having some major premise. If the decisions are legal, the premises will be legal, but the constitutional decisions which the Court makes are not just legal. So their premises are broader and deeper than what they learned in law school or forgot in practice. Holmes called them Can't-Helps and therefore he has been accused of having none. Unjustly, and not very perspicaciously, for what he meant was that they were implicit. Those who accuse him are really finding fault only with the fact that Holmes knew that he was unable to make them more explicit.

We object to the Justices importing into the Constitution their own philosophy. It is not theirs only. It is ours. Some of us may object to the kind of philosophy it was, but that is a matter of dispute. We have cause to

complain only when it is an óbsolete philosophy, one that
we have outgrown before the Justices have. Holmes objected that the Fourteenth Amendment did not enact Mr.
Herbert Spencer's Social Statics.[328] Of course it did not.
And yet it would be a great deal to expect those Justices at
that period not to act as if it had. You and I know Herbert Spencer only by hearsay, only as he has dribbled
down to us through the minds of our fathers, of whom we
are now the true elders. We think we know more than
they did, and perhaps we are right. We forget that they
were drenched in Spencer. Holmes wrote to Lady Pollock on July 2, 1895 — that was ten years before his Lochner dissent, and it was just at the time of the Income Tax
decision — 'H. Spencer you English never quite do justice
to, or at least those whom I have talked with do not. He
is dull. He writes an ugly uncharming style, his ideals are
those of a lower middle class British Philistine. And yet
after all abatements I doubt if any writer of English except
Darwin has done so much to affect our whole way of thinking about the universe.'

The Court was importing into a silent and receptive
Constitution the philosophy which they had drawn from
their own contemporary, or juvenile, sources. Inescap-
edly and not wholly consciously, and so they mistakenly
saw it in the Constitution itself. Suppose that instead of
Spencer the Justices had been brought up on Henry
George, or on Demarest Lloyd, or Edward Bellamy, or, to
come down a few years, on Thorstein Veblen. We complain only because the Justices were listening to a different
drummer.

Do not find fault with them. It is too late. Better at-
tend to what the present Justices are thinking. It is their

philosophy that counts now. Complain only when they do not tell us, and sometimes they do not tell us because we do not want them to tell us, because we expect them to be only lawyers, and we do not want to understand the law. But they must not forget that they are dealing, not with their own, but with our convictions, our major premises, our implied assumptions, our only half articulate principles, our Can't Helps. They are sailing a great-circle course and they must keep changing their course, fixing their position from the stars as well as taking bearings from the headlands. · What Jefferson, Adams, and Franklin did for us in the Declaration of Independence in our first crisis, what Abraham Lincoln in his two inaugurals did for us in our second, what Franklin Roosevelt did for us in our third, the Court must do for our daily needs, during term time.[329]

We know the Justices are lawyers. We insist upon that. Lawyers are peculiarly fitted to handle abstractions, but only their own, no one else's. We grudgingly admit they may be statesmen. But statesmen, though fit enough to deal with the abstractions of others, know best how to use them for their own purposes. We must expect the Justices to be also philosophers.

The function of the Court, then, includes philosophy as well as law and statesmanship. Not, you will understand, the practice of metaphysics — the more sparingly they do that the better — but the function which Whitehead gave philosophy. 'I hold,' he said, ' that philosophy is the critic of abstractions.' He was speaking of the sciences and scientific abstractions, but what he said can be aptly transposed to the ethical, moral, political, and economic abstractions with which the Court must deal. In White-

head's words, transposed to these subjects, the function of
philosophy is the double one, first of harmonizing these
abstractions by assigning to them their right relative
status as abstractions, and secondly of completing them
by direct comparison with more concrete intuitions of
society, and thereby promoting the formation of more complete schemes of thought. Philosophy is not one among
the many social and political theories with its own little
scheme of abstractions which it works away at perfecting
and improving. It is the survey of all of them, Whitehead
said, with the special objects of their harmony and of their
completion, and it brings to this task, not only their evidence, but also its own appeal to concrete experience, con-
fronting them with concrete fact.[330]

Having led the Court out of the conceptual woods into
the sunny fields of fact, do not think now that by appeal-
ing to philosophy we are leading it back in again. The
philosophy which Whitehead describes and which we are
demanding of the Court stands outside of conceptions and
abstractions and handles them as objectively and as sun-
nily as facts themselves. Offer such a philosopher liberty
of contract, or the freedoms of speech and religion, or the
power to tax, or state sovereignty or any of these rotundi-
ties which are pressed on the Court, and he will turn them
over in his hand, hold them up against the light, bring out
what is implicit, reconcile them with each other, and
assign each of them to its proper place and perspective.
Out of a confusion of which we may be only half aware, he
will articulate our creed for the era. This is what we expect the Court to do for us.

APPENDICES

APPENDICES

CONSTITUTION OF THE UNITED STATES

(Cut to about one third)

PREAMBLE

We, the people of the United States, in order to form a more perfect Union, establish justice, insure domestic tranquillity, provide for the common defense, promote the general welfare, and secure the blessings of liberty to ourselves and our posterity, do ordain and establish this Constitution for the United States of America.

ARTICLE I

Congress

All legislative powers herein granted shall be vested in a Congress of the United States, which shall consist of a Senate and House of Representatives.

The House of Representatives shall be composed of members chosen every second year by the people of the several States.

The Senate of the United States shall be composed of two Senators from each State elected by the people thereof for six years, and each Senator shall have one vote.

Powers of Congress (Section 8)

The Congress shall have power

To lay and collect taxes, duties, imposts, and excises, to pay the debts and provide for the common defense and general welfare of the United States; but all duties, imposts, and excises shall be uniform throughout the United States;

To borrow money on the credit of the United States;

To regulate commerce with foreign nations, and among the several States, and with the Indian tribes;

To establish a uniform rule of naturalization, and uniform laws on the subject of bankruptcies throughout the United States;

To coin money, regulate the value thereof, and of foreign coin, and fix the standard of weights and measures;

To provide for the punishment of counterfeiting the securities and current coin of the United States;

To establish post offices and post roads;

To promote the progress of science and useful arts, by securing for limited times to authors and inventors the exclusive right to their respective writings and discoveries;

To constitute tribunals inferior to the Supreme Court;

To define and punish piracies and felonies committed on the high seas, and offenses against the law of nations;

To declare war, grant letters of marque and reprisal, and make rules concerning captures on land and water;

To raise and support armies, but no appropriation of money to that use shall be for a longer term than two years;

To provide and maintain a navy;

To make rules for the government and regulation of the land and naval forces;

To provide for calling forth the militia to execute the laws of the Union, suppress insurrections and repel invasions;

To provide for organizing, arming, and disciplining the militia, and for governing such part of them as may be employed in the service of the United States, reserving to the States respectively, the appointment of the officers, and the authority of training the militia according to the discipline prescribed by Congress;

To exercise exclusive legislation in all cases whatsoever, over such district (not exceeding ten miles square) as may, by cession of particular States, and the acceptance of Congress, become the seat of the government of the United States, and to exercise like authority over all places purchased by the consent of the legislature of the State in which the same shall be, for the erection of forts, magazines, arsenals, dockyards, and other needful buildings; and

To make all laws which shall be necessary and proper for carrying into execution the foregoing powers, and all other powers vested by this Constitution in the government of the United States, or in any department or officer thereof.

Restrictions on Congress (Section 9)

The privilege of the writ of *habeas corpus* shall not be suspended, unless when in cases of rebellion or invasion the public safety may require it.

No bill of attainder or *ex post facto* law shall be passed.

No tax or duty shall be laid on articles exported from any State.

No preference shall be given by any regulation of commerce or revenue to the ports of one State over those of another, nor shall vessels bound to or from one State be obliged to enter, clear, or pay duties in another.

Restrictions on the States (Section 10)

No State shall enter into any treaty, alliance, or confederation, grant letters of marque and reprisal, coin money, emit bills of credit, make anything but gold and silver coin a tender in payment of debts, pass any bill of attainder, *ex post facto* law, or law impairing the obligation of contracts, or grant any title of nobility.

No State shall, without the consent of the Congress, lay any impost or duties on imports or exports, except what may be absolutely necessary for executing its inspection laws.

ARTICLE II

The Executive

The Executive power shall be vested in a President of the United States of America.

The President shall be Commander in Chief of the Army and Navy of the United States, and of the militia of the several States when called into the actual service of the United States; he may require the opinion, in writing, of the principal officer in each of the executive departments upon any subject relating to the duties of their respective offices, and he shall have power to grant reprieves and pardons for offenses against the United States, except in cases of impeachment.

He shall have power, by and with the advice and consent of the Senate, to make treaties, provided two thirds of the Senators present concur; and he shall nominate, and by and with the advice and consent of the Senate, shall appoint ambassadors, other public ministers and consuls, Judges of the Supreme Court and all other officers of the United States, whose appointments are not herein otherwise provided for, and which shall be established by law; but the Congress may by law vest the appointment of such inferior officers as they think proper in the President alone, in the courts of law, or in the heads of departments.

He shall from time to time give to the Congress information of the state of the Union, and recommend to their consideration such measures as he shall judge necessary and expedient; he may, on extraordinary occasions, convene both houses, or either of them; he shall take care that the laws be faithfully executed, and shall commission all the officers of the United States.

The President, Vice-President, and all civil officers of the United States shall be removed from office on impeachment for, and conviction of treason, bribery or other high crimes and misdemeanors.

ARTICLE III

The Judiciary

The judicial power of the United States shall be vested in one Supreme Court, and in such inferior courts as the Congress may from time to time ordain and establish. The Judges, both of the Supreme and inferior courts, shall hold their offices during good behavior, and shall, at stated times, receive for their services a compensation, which shall not be diminished during their continuance in office.

The judicial power shall extend to all cases, in law and equity, arising under this Constitution, the laws of the United States, and treaties made, or which shall be made, under their authority; to all cases affecting ambassadors, other public ministers and consuls; to all cases of admiralty and maritime jurisdiction; to controversies to which the United States shall be a party; to controversies between two or more States; between a State and citizens of another State, between citizens of different States; between citizens of the same State claiming lands under grants of different States, and between a State, or the citizens thereof, and foreign states, citizens or subjects.

In all cases affecting ambassadors, other public ministers and consuls, and those in which a State shall be a party, the Supreme Court shall have original jurisdiction. In all the other cases before mentioned, the Supreme Court shall have appellate jurisdiction; both as to law and fact, with some exceptions, and under such regulations as the Congress shall make.

ARTICLE IV

The citizens of each State shall be entitled to all privileges and immunities of citizens in the several States.

New States may be admitted by the Congress into this Union. The United States shall guarantee to every State in the Union a republican form of government.

ARTICLE V

Amendments

The Congress, whenever two thirds of both houses shall deem it necessary, shall propose amendments to this Constitution, or, on the application of the Legislatures of two thirds of the several States, shall call a convention for proposing amendments, which, in either case, shall be valid to all intents and purposes, as part of this Constitution, when ratified by the Legislatures of three fourths of the several States, or by conventions in three fourths thereof, as the one or the other mode of ratification may be proposed by the Congress.

ARTICLE VI

This Constitution, and the laws of the United States which shall be made in pursuance thereof; and all treaties made, or which shall be made, under the authority of the United States, shall be the supreme law of the land, and the judges in every State shall be bound thereby, anything in the Constitution or laws of any State to the contrary notwithstanding.

The Senators and Representatives before mentioned, and the members of the several State Legislatures, and all executive and judicial officers, both of the United States and of the several States, shall be bound by oath or affirmation to support this Constitution; but no religious test shall ever be required as a qualification to any office or public trust under the United States.

THE BILL OF RIGHTS

ARTICLE I

Congress shall make no law respecting an establishment of religion, or prohibiting the free exercise thereof; or abridging the freedom of speech, or of the press; or the right of the people peaceably to assemble, and to petition the Government for a redress of grievances.

ARTICLE II

A well-regulated militia, being necessary to the security of a free State, the right of the people to keep and bear arms shall not be infringed.

Article III

No soldier shall, in time of peace, be quartered in any house, without the consent of the owner, nor in time of war, but in a manner to be prescribed by law.

Article IV

The right of the people to be secure in their persons, houses, papers, and effects, against unreasonable searches and seizures, shall not be violated, and no warrants shall issue, but upon probable cause, supported by oath or affirmation, and particularly describing the place to be searched, and the persons or things to be seized.

Article V

No person shall be held to answer for a capital, or other infamous crime, unless on a presentment or indictment of a Grand Jury, except in cases arising in the land or naval forces, or in the militia, when in actual service in time of war or public danger; nor shall any person be subject for the same offense to be twice put in jeopardy of life and limb; nor shall be compelled in any criminal case to be a witness against himself, nor be deprived of life, liberty, or property, without due process of law; nor shall private property be taken for public use, without just compensation.

Article VI

In all criminal prosecutions, the accused shall enjoy the right to a speedy and public trial, by an impartial jury of the State and district wherein the crime shall have been committed, which districts shall have been previously ascertained by law, and to be informed of the nature and cause of the accusation; to be confronted with the witnesses against him; to have compulsory process for obtaining witnesses in his favor, and to have the assistance of counsel for his defense.

Article VII

In suits at common law, where the value in controversy shall exceed twenty dollars, the right of trial by jury shall be preserved, and no fact tried by a jury shall be otherwise re-examined in any court of the United States than according to the rules of the common law.

Article VIII

Excessive bail shall not be required nor excessive fines imposed, nor cruel and unusual punishments inflicted.

FIVE OTHER AMENDMENTS

Article IX

The enumeration in the Constitution of certain rights shall not be construed to deny or disparage others retained by the people.

Article X

The powers not delegated to the United States by the Constitution, nor prohibited by it to the States, are reserved to the States respectively, or to the people.

Article XIII

Neither slavery nor involuntary servitude, except as a punishment for crime whereof the party shall have been duly convicted, shall exist within the United States, or any place subject to their jurisdiction.

Article XIV

All persons born or naturalized in the United States, and subject to the jurisdiction thereof, are citizens of the United States and of the State wherein they reside. No State shall make or enforce any law which shall abridge the privileges or immunities of citizens of the United States; nor shall any State deprive any person of life, liberty or property without due process of law, nor deny to any person within its jurisdiction the equal protection of the laws.

Article XV

The right of the citizens of the United States to vote shall not be denied or abridged by the United States or by any State on account of race, color, or previous condition of servitude.

NOTES

1. *Collected Papers*, vol. III, pp. 432, 439.
2. Goethe to von Müller, November 4, 1823.
3. *Novum Organum*, I: 84.
4. O. W. Holmes, *Collected Legal Papers*, p. 209.
5. Farrand, *Records of the Federal Convention*, vol. 2, pp. 177 and 188.
6. Farrand, vol. 2, p. 454.
7. *Coyle* v. *Smith*, 221 U. S. 559; 1911.
8. *The Federalist*, no. 78 and no. 81.
9. This is Thayer without quotation marks, from his *Life of Marshall*, pp. 64–66; Houghton Mifflin Company. I have appropriated him, though not his *ipsissima verba*, nor all he said.
10. It is now Section 342 of our Judicial Code.
11. Albert J. Beveridge, *John Marshall*, vol. III, p. 142; Houghton Mifflin Company. For more, read Charles Warren, or Marshall himself in the first volume of Cranch's reports. If you don't want to read so much, there is Thayer's *Life*, which will give you the wisest and justest view in the smallest compass.
12. Article II, Section 3.
13. *Clark Distilling Co.* v. *Western Maryland Ry.*, 242 U. S. 311.
14. *Mississippi* v. *Johnson*, 4 Wallace 475 at 492; Thayer, *Life of Marshall*, pp. 98–99.
15. Beveridge gives this letter in facsimile, III: 176–177. It is dated January 4, 1804.
16. *United States* v. *Butler*, 297 U. S. 1 at 62.
17. *Euclid* v. *Ambler Realty Corp.*, 272 U. S. 365; 1926.
18. Read Warren for that, I: 108; and the Muskrat case, 219 U. S. 346, in 1911.
19. The Gobitis case, 310 U. S. 586.

20. The Carter case, 298 U. S. 238.

21. Beveridge, III: 10.

22. March 7, 1810.

23. III: 593.

24. The Carter case, 298 U. S. 238.

25. The Adkins case, 261 U. S. 525 at 544; 'delicacy' is Marshall's word, in *Fletcher* v. *Peck*, 6 Cranch at 128.

26. 198 U. S. 45 at 76; the full text is on p. 143.

27. *Eakin* v. *Raub*, 12 S. & R. at 352; 1825. Daniel Webster insisted on the same point when he argued the Charles River Bridge case before the Massachusetts Supreme Judicial Court four years later, 7 Pickering at 442.

28. July 5, 1935.

29. 298 U. S. 513.

30. *United States* v. *Bekins*, 304 U. S. at 33.

31. Of course, it was really no distinction at all. The Court later regarded the Ashton case as overruled. See Rutledge in a footnote in *Prudential Insurance Co.* v. *Benjamin*, June 3, 1946.

32. *Helvering* v. *Griffiths*, 318 U. S. 371 at 400.

33. *Collected Legal Papers*, p. 311.

34. *Desaussure's Equity Reports*, 466 at 477; quoted in Thayer's article in 7 *Harvard Law Review*, 141–142; reprinted in his *Legal Essays*.

35. 7 Wallace 506; and see Charles Fairman in his *Mr. Justice Miller and the Supreme Court*, Harvard University Press, 1938, chap. VI.

36. Warren I, 222–225.

37. *The American Commonwealth*, I, 276.

38. Warren II, 294.

39. Act of June 19, 1862.

40. Farrand, *Records of the Federal Convention*, II: 350.

41. 157 U. S. at 532 and 553.

42. Henry F. Pringle's *Life of Taft*; Farrar and Rinehart, 1939.

43. July 1, 1909; 44 Congressional Record 4002.

44. March 28, 1910.

45. Benjamin F. Wright, *The Growth of Constitutional Law*, 1942; pp. 77, 82, 86, 148, and 180.

46. See Warren II, 742; and see the table at the end of Frankfurter's *Mr. Justice Holmes and the Supreme Court*.

47. Edgerton tried to make an appraisal in his article on the Incidence of Judicial Control over Congress, 22 Cornell Law Quarterly 299, but it wasn't much use, I think.

48. *United States* v. *Butler*, 297 U. S. 1.

49. See Lilienthal's *TVA — Democracy on the March*; Harper and Brothers, 1944.

50. *Collected Legal Papers*, p. 310.

51. *The Will To Believe*, p. 195; Longmans, Green and Company, Inc., 1915.

52. *Political Science*, vol. II, pp. 330–331; 1877.

53. In a Lincoln Day address, 15 National Corporation Reporter 849.

54. *American Bar Association Journal* for May, 1937, p. 365.

55. *The Golden Bough*, by J. G. Frazer, one-volume edition, p. 171; The Macmillan Company, 1940; I abbreviate.

56. *The Business of the Supreme Court*, by Frankfurter and Landis. The figures following also come from them, pp. 302–307.

57. *The Constitution Revisited*, Columbia University Press, 1938, p. 5.

58. Holdsworth, vol. V, p. 430.

59. 37 *Harvard Law Review* 1002; 1924.

60. 2 Cranch 179.

61. This letter is quoted by Donald G. Morgan in his all too short article in 57 *Harvard Law Review* 328.

62. *Marine Insurance Co.* v. *Young*, 5 Cranch 191.

63. 261 U. S. 525.

64. *Arizona* v. *Sardell*, 269 U. S. 530.

65. 300 U. S. 379.

66. *Collected Legal Papers*, p. 173.

67. *Yale Law Journal* for February, 1937.

68. *Norton* v. *Shelby County*, 118 U. S. at 442; 1886.

69. *Chicot County District* v. *Bank*, 308 U. S. 371; it had been held unconstitutional in the Ashton case.

70. 287 U. S. 358 at 364–365.

71. See Cardozo's *The Nature of the Judicial Process;* Gray's *The*

Nature and Sources of the Law, p. 547; and Jackson's book, *The Struggle for Judicial Supremacy*, pp. 307–308; Alfred A. Knopf, Inc., 1941.

72. The Passenger Cases, 7 Howard 470.

73. *Barden* v. *Northern Pacific Ry.*, 154 U. S. 322.

74. *West Coast Hotel Co.* v. *Parrish*, 300 U. S. 379.

75. *Tigner* v. *Texas*, 310 U. S. 141.

76. Brandeis has listed them in a footnote in *Burnet* v. *Coronado Oil & Gas Co.*, 285 U. S. on 406–407.

77. *Rabelais*, Book IV, chapter 51.

78. Bertrand Russell, *Problems of Philosophy*, p. 156; Oxford University Press.

79. *Bulletin of the Boston Society of Natural History*, April, 1931.

80. *Spector Motor Service* v. *Walsh*, 139 Fed. 2d 809 at 823; 1943. Jowett said much the same thing somewhere in his notes to the *Republic*, but I can't find it again and no matter.

81. *Allen Bradley* v. *Union*, 325 U. S. 797 at 806.

82. E.g., *New York* v. *United States*, 326 U. S. 572.

83. The Gobitis case, 310 U. S. 586.

84. *Brown* v. *Maryland*, 12 Wheaton 419; 1827.

85. 4 Wheaton 316.

86. The context is on p. 206.

87. *Panhandle Oil Company* v. *Knox*, 277 U. S. 218 at 223.

88. *Hannegan* v. *Esquire*, 327 U. S. 146.

89. Henry F. Pringle's *Life of Taft*, p. 971.

90. Pringle, p. 971.

91. Pringle, p. 1044.

92. March 30, 1930.

93. 310 U. S. at vi; 1940.

94. *My Wayward Parent*, The Bobbs-Merrill Company, 1945. Elizabeth Cobb's life of her father, Irvin S. Cobb.

95. 290 U. S. 398.

96. 291 U. S. 502.

97. 293 U. S. 389.

98. 294 U. S. 240.

99. Quoted in the report of the case, 298 U. S. 330.

100. 295 U. S. 330.

101. 378.

102. 364–365.

103. 379.

104. 381.

105. 372.

106. 351.

107. 374.

108. *California* v. *Anglim*, 129 Fed. 2d 455.

109. *The Road We Are Travelling*, p. 43.

110. *Schechter* v. *United States*, 295 U. S. 495.

111. *Panama Refining Co.* v. *Ryan*, 293 U. S. 388.

112. *United States* v. *Socony-Vacuum Oil Co.*, 310 U. S. 150 at 170–171.

113. *Panama Refining Co.* v. *Ryan*, 293 U. S. 388.

114. 443.

115. The Schechter case, 295 U. S. 495. The fact is, occasionally the defendants purchased from commission men in Philadelphia. See p. 520. The Court were wise enough to ignore this bit of interstate commerce. It was a test case and they treated it as such.

116. 543.

117. 546 and 548.

118. 554. Hand's opinion is in *United States* v. *Schechter Corp.*, 76 Fed. 2d 617.

119. *Ex parte* Yarborough 110 U. S. 651; 1884.

120. 44.

121. 297 U. S. 1.

122. President Roosevelt misquoted this clause in his radio address of March 9, 1937. He quoted it as reading, 'to levy taxes . . . and provide for the common defense and general welfare of the United States.' It is a power to levy taxes to provide for the common defense and general welfare, not an independent power to provide for the general welfare. Professor Powell said, 'The President's elliptical version, which others have also urged, would render unnecessary all the other constitutional clauses conferring descriptively named powers on Congress.

Such a version would make much of the rest of the Constitution extremely silly.' (*The Nation*, March 8, 1941.)

123. 73.

124. 71.

125. 74–78.

126. 78.

127. 24, and again at 40.

128. *Mulford* v. *Smith*, 307 U. S. 38.

129. On July 5, 1935.

130. *Carter* v. *Carter Coal Co.*, 298 U. S. 238.

131. August 30, 1935.

132. 298 U. S. at 286–287.

133. 316.

134. *Sunshine Coal Co.* v. *Adkins*, 310 U. S. at 397.

135. 336.

136. 321–322.

137. Richard Hofstadter, *Social Darwinism in American Thought*, University of Pennsylvania Press, 1945.

138. Quoted by Hofstadter, p. 31.

139. The *Oxford Dictionary* gives 1566 for the first use of the word as trade or manufacture.

140. Read R. H. Tawney, *Religion and the Rise of Capitalism*.

141. 198 U. S. 45.

142. 208 U. S. 412; 1908.

143. 243 U. S. 426; 1917.

144. Pringle's *Life*, p. 1049.

145. *Morehead, Warden* v. *New York ex. rel. Tipaldo*, 298 U. S. 587.

146. *Erie Railroad* v. *Tompkins*, 304 U. S. 64.

147. See page 88.

148. *American Law School Review* for April, 1937.

149. 299 U. S. 619.

150. 299 U. S. 515.

151. 299 U. S. 515.

152. 300 U. S. 379.

153. 389–390; Hughes calls it the Morehead case after the warden from whom Tipaldo was released by writ of *habeas corpus*.

154. 300 U. S. at 402; for what Stone said, p. 130.
155. *Helvering* v. *Griffiths*, 318 U. S. 401; March 1, 1943.
156. 321 U. S. 452 and 540.
157. See *United States* v. *Darby*, 312 U. S. 100 at 123.
158. See *United States* v. *Lowden*, 308 U. S. 225 at 239.
159. The Labor Board cases, 301 U. S. 1.
160. The Carter case, 298 U. S. at 308.
161. 301 U. S. 757.
162. 97.
163. McReynolds is quoting from the act.
164. *Martino* v. *Michigan Cleaning Co.*, 327 U. S. 123.
165. *Carmichael* v. *Southern Coal & Coke Co.*, 301 U. S. 495.
166. *Associated Industries* v. *Department of Labor*, 299 U. S. 515.
167. *Steward Machine Co.* v. *Davis*, 301 U. S. 548.
168. *Florida* v. *Mellon*, 273 U. S. 12.
169. *United States* v. *Darby*, 312 U. S. at 124.
170. *Helvering* v. *Davis*, 301 U. S. 619.
171. 644–645.
172. *Gibbons* v. *Ogden*, 9 Wheaton 1.
173. *Missouri, Kansas, & Texas Ry.* v. *May*, 194 U. S. 267 at 270.
174. Quoted in Pringle's *Life of Taft*, p. 1046.
175. 'Law and the Court,' *Collected Legal Papers*, p. 295.
176. Book III.
177. *Graves* v. *O'Keefe*, 306 U. S. at 487.
178. *Erie* v. *Tompkins*, 304 U. S. 64.
179. 88.
180. *Champion* v. *Ames*, 188 U. S. 321.
181. 357–358.
182. See Warren, II: 736.
183. 247 U. S. 251.
184. *Mulford* v. *Smith*, 307 U. S. 38.
185. 51–57.
186. *United States* v. *Darby*, 312 U. S. 100.
187. *The Federalist*, no. 32.
188. *McCulloch* v. *Maryland*, 4 Wheaton at p. 431.

189. *Panhandle Oil Co.* v. *Knox*, 277 U. S. 223.

190. *Rogers* v. *Graves*, 299 U. S. 401.

191. *Graves* v. *O'Keefe*, 306 U. S. 466.

192. 12 Wheaton.

193. Learned Hand said in 1943, 'So far as I can see, the immunity of interstate commerce from such (state) taxation as such has rested upon the same considerations which still prevail as to the immunity of an activity of the United States.' *Spector Motor Service* v. *Walsh*, 139 Fed. 2d. 809 at 823.

194. *Philadelphia Steamship Co.* v. *Pennsylvania*, 122 U. S. 326 at 346.

195. 304 U. S. 307.

196. 305 U. S. 434.

197. 305 U. S. 439.

198. 304 U. S. 316–326.

199. 304 U. S. 328.

200. 305 U. S. 449–450.

201. 305 U. S. 455.

202. 309 U. S. 176.

203. 184.

204. 185.

205. 188–189.

206. 322 U. S. 292.

207. 302.

208. *Hall* v. *DeCuir*, 95 U. S. 495.

209. *Morgan* v. *Virginia*, June 3, 1946.

210. 11 Wallace 113.

211. 11 Wallace at 128.

212. *Brush* v. *Commissioner*, 300 U. S. 352; incidentally, the last act of Congress to be held unconstitutional to date.

213. *Helvering* v. *Gerhardt*, 304 U. S. 405.

214. *Graves* v. *O'Keefe*, 306 U. S. 466.

215. Quoted in Schlesinger's *Age of Jackson*, p. 29; Little, Brown, 1945; for the same gallantry, in 1936, see McReynolds's opinion for the Court in *Ashton* v. *Cameron County*, 298 U. S. 513.

216. *South Carolina* v. *United States*, 199 U. S. 437.

217. *Allen* v. *Regents*, 304 U. S. 439.

218. *New York* v. *United States*, January 14, 1946.

219. *Diaz* v. *Gonzalez y Lugo*, 261 U. S. at 106.

220. *Chase Securities Corporation* v. *Donaldson*, 325 U. S. at 309.

221. Carr, *Concerning Administrative Law*, Columbia University Press, 1941, quoting James Hart.

222. Gray quotes this three times in his *Nature and Sources of the Law*.

223. *Nash* v. *United States*, 229 U. S. 373 at 376.

224. *International Harvester Co.* v. *Kentucky*, 234 U. S. 216.

225. *United States* v. *Elgin, J. & E. Ry.*, 298 U. S. 492 at 500.

226. *Helvering* v. *Hallock*, 309 U. S. at 123.

227. 309 U. S. at 119.

228. *United States* v. *Schwimmer*, 279 U. S. 644; *United States* v. *Macintosh*, 283 U. S. 605; *United States* v. *Bland*, 283 U. S. 636.

229. *Girouard* v. *United States*, April 22, 1946.

230. E.g., Jackson in 323 U. S. at 271.

231. *An American Dilemma*, p. 281; Harper's, 1944.

232. See Myrdal, *An American Dilemma*, footnotes on pp. 1105–1107 and 1298.

233. 323 U. S. 192.

234. 200.

235. 201–202.

236. 209.

237. 208.

238. Aluminum Co. of America, 1 N.L.R.B. 530.

239. *St. Joseph Stock Yards Co.* v. *United States*, 298 U. S. 38 at 92.

240. *Wallace Corp.* v. *Labor Board*, 323 U. S. 248.

241. For the falsity and futility of the hypothesis of the isolated individual, see Chapter Two of Elton Mayo's *The Social Problems of an Industrial Civilization*, Harvard University Press, 1945; and the rest of the book for groups, their necessity and their development.

242. Warren, II, 368 ff.; Fairman, *Mr. Justice Miller*, pp. 69–74.

243. Fairman, *Mr. Justice Miller*, pp. 86–89.

244. For a harder case, before the war was completely over, see *Duncan* v. *Kahanamoku*, February 25, 1946, 327 U. S. 304.

245. 249 U. S. 47.

246. 250 U. S. 616.

247. *United States* v. *Abrams;* 1919, 250 U. S. 616 at 629–31.

248. *The Masses*, 244 Fed. 535.

249. In *Pennekamp* v. *Florida*, June 3, 1946.

250. Abrams case, 250 U. S. 616.

251. 268 U. S. 652.

252. *Prudential Insurance Co.* v. *Cheek*, 259 U. S. at 538 & 543.

253. On May 27, 1789.

254. Farrand, II, 588.

255. Warren, *Congress, The Constitution, and the Supreme Court*, 84–85.

256. From *The Bull*, vol. 20, no. 23, Root, Clark, Buckner, and Ballantine, June 10, 1939.

257. 307 U. S. 496.

258. Par. 24–14.

259. 526.

260. *Barron* v. *Baltimore*, 7 Peters 243.

261. 16 Wallace 36.

262. 122.

263. Modern Age Books, Inc., New York, 1939.

264. Connecticut General Life Insurance Co., 303 U. S. at 85–90; here you will find his reasons, and you will find too that it were hard to call him wrong, were the question new.

265. Charles Fairman, *Mr. Justice Miller and the Supreme Court*, pages 186–189.

266. 39 *Harvard Law Review*.

267. 2 Institute 46.

268. 19 Howard 393.

269. 134 U. S. 418.

270. *Lochner* v. *New York*, 198 U. S. 45; 1905.

271. *Coppage* v. *Kansas*, 236 U. S. 1; 1915.

272. *Coppage* v. *Kansas*, 236 U. S. 1 at 14.

273. *Patterson* v. *Colorado*, 205 U. S. 454 at 465.

274. *Gilbert* v. *Minnesota*, 254 U. S. 325 at 343.

275. *Prudential Insurance Co.* v. *Cheek*, 259 U. S. at 543.

276. *Meyer* v. *Nebraska*, 262 U. S. 390.

277. Drew Pearson's column, April 27, 1941.

278. 262 U. S. at 412.

279. *Gitlow* v. *New York*, 268 U. S. at 666.

280. *Fiske* v. *Kansas*, 274 U. S. 380.

281. 283 U. S. 359.

282. *Near* v. *Minnesota*, 283 U. S. 697 at 707.

283. 1930.

284. *Baldwin* v. *Missouri*, 281 U. S. at 595.

285. Letter, dated February 24, 1903, to Mrs. Charles P. Curtis, unpublished.

286. *Federal Power Commission* v. *Natural Gas Pipeline Co.*, 315 U. S. 575 at 600, and *International Shoe Co.* v. *Washington*, 326 U. S. 310.

287. In *International Shoe Co.* v. *Washington*.

288. *Federal Power Commission* v. *Natural Gas Pipeline Co.*, 315 U. S. 575 at 601, in a footnote; Douglas and Murphy joined Black in this dissent.

289. *Palko* v. *Connecticut*, 302 U. S. at 326.

290. *Betts* v. *Brady*, 316 U. S. at 461–462.

291. *Bridges* v. *California*, 314 U. S. 252.

292. *Pennekamp* v. *Florida*, June 3, 1946.

293. 314 U. S. 252.

294. 314 U. S. 252 at 263 and 265.

295. *Atlantic Monthly*, January, 1941; later published by Random House Inc. in *Collected Poetry*, 1945, p. 275.

296. 301 U. S. 103.

297. *Remains*, II: 177.

298. 302 U. S. 656; 303 U. S. 624; 306 U. S. 621.

299. *General Education in a Free Society*, Harvard University Press, 1945, p. 39.

300. 310 U. S. 586.

301. 593–594.

302. *Jones* v. *Opelicka*, 316 U. S. 584 at 623–624.

303. *Spector Motor Service* v. *Walsh*, 139 Fed. 2d., 809.

304. 149 Fed. 760.

305. 47 F. Supp. at 253.

306. 319 U. S. 624.

307. This comes from Jackson's dissent in 319 U. S. at 167–170.

308. *Murdock* v. *City of Jeannette*, 319 U. S. 105.

309. 319 U. S. 108–111.

310. 112.

311. 319 U. S. 181.

312. 319 U. S. 112.

313. 319 U. S. 137.

314. 174.

315. 166.

316. 321 U. S. 573.

317. 580–581.

318. 581.

319. 581–582. These are, of course, not the only cases which show that these Justices were thinking in the same grooves which held the Old Court so fast. See McCann's case, 317 U. S. 269, where they as much as said that under the Sixth Amendment no one could waive his right to have counsel and try his case himself. Or, on quite another subject, there is the case of Ritter's Cafe, 315 U. S. 722, where they would have treated the right to picket simply as the right of free speech and put it under the First Amendment, though picketing plainly may become something more than simply speech.

320. *West Virginia State Board of Education* v. *Barnette*, 319 U. S. 646–671. I have skipped and omitted too much.

321. Henry St. John, first Viscount Bolingbroke, 1678–1751, about the King of England, in his Dissertation upon Parties.

322. Before the American Law Institute, May 9, 1944, printed in the Journal of the American Judicature Society in June.

323. *Commission* v. *Aldrich*, 316 U. S. 174 at 202. See too his dissent in the Southeastern Underwriters Association case, 322 U. S. 533, in June, 1944.

324. *Chicago, Milwaukee & St. Paul R.R.* v. *Minnesota*, 134 U. S. 418.

325. Stone had a footnote to this effect in 303 U. S. at 185; and another in 309 U. S. at 46; and again in 325 U. S. at 767. It is something he seemed to want to repeat at every opportunity.

326. *Edwards* v. *California*, 314 U. S. at 174.

327. *United States* v. *Carolene Products Co.*, 304 U. S. at 152–153.

328. *Lochner* v. *New York*, 198 U. S. 45.

329. 'The object of the Declaration of Independence,' Jefferson wrote to Henry Lee, on May 8, 1825, was 'Not to find out new principles, or new arguments, never before thought of, not merely to say things which had never been said before; but to place before mankind the common sense of the subject, in terms so plain and firm as to command their assent, and to justify ourselves in the independent stand we are compelled to take. Neither aiming at originality of principle or sentiment, nor yet copied from any particular and previous writing, it was intended to be an expression of the American mind, and to give to that expression the proper tone and spirit called for by the occasion. All its authority rests then on the harmonizing sentiments of the day, whether expressed in conversation, in letters, printed essays, or in the elementary books of public right, as Aristotle, Cicero, Locke, Sidney, &c.'

330. A. N. Whitehead, *Science and the Modern World*, chap. V; The Macmillan Company.

BIBLIOGRAPHY

TO YOU who have just read, or are about to read, or at least have taken enough interest to decide not to read this book, I suggest first that you ask some lawyer you know to give you a few recent copies of the advance sheets of the Court's Official Reports. They are throwaways for him as soon as he gets the bound volume. Turn the pages until you come to a dissent, the longer the better, and read that first. It indicates the presence of something important or interesting, and it will tell you why better than the opinion of the Court. Ask your lawyer to loan you the bound volume containing the full report of one of the great cases that interest you. Or your library will have a set. If it hasn't, complain. A set of the United States Supreme Court Reports takes up no more shelf space and costs no more than binding old magazines.

Better, however, the current cases, and you can subscribe to the advance sheets yourself by writing to the Government Printing Office, Washington, D.C., sending $2.25 for a year's subscription. They are now coming out months behind the times, but they are beautifully printed, light to carry, and large type, good for reading on the train. Or the advance opinions published by the Lawyers Co-operative Society, Rochester, New York, which cost $5.00 a year, and come to you within a week or so.

If you want history, begin where the Court really threw in the constitutional gears and read Charles Fairman's *Mr. Justice Miller and the Supreme Court* (Harvard University Press, 1939). It is also a good biography of a vigorous American, who started as a drug-store clerk in Kentucky in the eighteen-thirties, became a doctor, then a lawyer, and from 1862, when Lincoln appointed him to the Court, till 1890, was one of the strongest and wisest Justices the Court can boast of.

That's where to start your history, but if you want to go back to the very beginning, the first volume of Charles Warren's *The Supreme Court in United States History* (Little Brown, 1926) is the best reading far and away. Charles G. Haines's big volume on *The Rôle of the Supreme Court in American Government and Politics, 1789–1835* (University of California Press, 1944), too. I hope the following volumes will come soon.

If you want Marshall, there is Beveridge's massive and also readable life (Houghton Mifflin Company, 1916), only he didn't need to keep telling you what a great man Marshall was. But don't take those four volumes instead of the hundred-and-fifty-odd pages of Thayer's short *Life* (Houghton Mifflin Company, 1901).

For Holmes, start with the *Dictionary of American Biography*, where you will find eleven nearly perfect pages. Buy Max Lerner's compilation, *The Mind and Faith of Justice Holmes* (Little Brown, 1943), and Frankfurter's *Mr. Justice Holmes and the Supreme Court* (Harvard University Press, 1938). Just before you read either, read Catherine Drinker Bowen's *Yankee from Olympus* (Atlantic Monthly Press, 1943) and Francis Biddle's *Mr. Justice Holmes* (Charles Scribner's Sons, 1942).

For the Court's recent match with the New Deal, there is Justice Jackson's *The Struggle for Judicial Supremacy* (Knopf, 1941). As Solicitor General, Jackson was in the thick of it and he had the good fortune to have Paul Freund not only in the fight with him but also to help him on this book.

For books directly describing the Court, Hughes's *The Supreme Court of the United States* (Columbia University Press, 1928). Hughes gave these lectures nearly twenty years ago, between his two terms on the bench. What he could write now!

If you want idolatry, you can have it, in James M. Beck's book, with a preface by Calvin Coolidge for the edition that someone distributed to school children. I'd rather read Maury Maverick's *In Blood and Ink* (Modern Age Books, 1939). It takes a different point of view and it's more scholarly.

For professors of constitutional doctrine off the Court, I give you these: James Bradley Thayer, Thomas Reed Powell, and

Edward S. Corwin. Thayer's essays on the subject are included
in his *Legal Essays* (Boston Book Co., 1908); many of the best
things he said are in his *Cases on Constitutional Law* (Cambridge,
1895), and I stupidly didn't buy a second-hand copy of the first
volume the other day, because I couldn't find the second. Powell is our great expert now. He comes from Vermont and he goes
about with a wrench, with which he tightens up good doctrines
and wrecks bad. You have to look in the law reviews for his
stuff. How soon will he write it all up? I hope before it becomes
someone's duty to collect it. Corwin has written sundry short
books.

INDEX

Acheson, Dean, in the minimum wage case, 149

Adams, Henry, on Darwinism, 141; on the Hartford Convention, 185

Adams, John, President, 51, 333

Adams, John Quincy, President, 22

Agricultural Adjustment Act, 2, 3, 17, 121, 134, 188

A. A. A. of 1938, 198

Alabama Unemployment Compensation Act, 176

Aldrich, Nelson W., Senator, against an income tax, 43

American Bar Association, 37, 159, 186

Aristotle, 256

Arnold, Thurman W., on the language in dissenting opinions, 55

Auden, William H., some verses, 297

Avery, Sewall, carried out, 37

Bacon, Francis, on the true antiquity, 1; on lions under the throne, 164-65

Bailey, Joseph W., Senator, for a 3% income tax, 43

Bangor, Bishop of, on the interpretation of laws, 235

Bankhead, John H., Senator, 192

Barkley, Alben W., Senator, quotes Lincoln, 154; carries on with the Court Plan, 185

Bates, Edward, Lincoln's Attorney General, 259

Bayard, Thomas F., Senator, 36

Beck, James M., his book on the Supreme Court, 360

Bellamy, Edward, instead of Spencer?, 332

Benton, Thomas Hart, Senator, on lawyers, vii

Beveridge, Albert J., his Life of John Marshall, quoted, 13, 23, 360

Biddle, Francis, Attorney General, on Butler, 98; his Mr. Justice Holmes, 360

Black, Hugo L., Justice, brief sketch, 192; on reconciliation, 89; opinions on state tax on interstate commerce, 213; dissent in Dixie Greyhound case, 217; dissent in N. W. Airlines case, 219; concurs on Jim Crow cars, 222; on due process, 286; on your right to have a lawyer, 289; on free speech and contempt of court, 291; on the flag salute, 307

Bolingbroke, quoted, 323

Borah, William E., Senator, for a 3% income tax, 43

Bowen, Catherine Drinker, her Yankee from Olympus, 360

Bracton, 62

Bradley, Joseph P., Justice, dissent in Collector v. Day, 224; in the Slaughterhouse Cases, 274, 278; on administrative boards, 277, 326

Brandeis, Louis D., Justice, brief sketch, 97; his factual brief, 145; letter to the Senate, 160; on responsibility, 249; on liberty, 280

Brewer, David J., Justice, on criticizing judges, 42, 44, 54, 66

Brougham, Lord, Disraeli on, vii

Bryan, William Jennings, 42

Bryce, Lord, on the joint in our armor, 37

Buchanan, James, President, Dred Scott case, 39, 40

Burke, Edmund, quoted by Benton, viii

Burton, Harold H., Justice, brief sketch, 204; dissent on Jim Crow cars, 222

Butler, Benjamin Franklin, no Cromwell, 36

Butler, Pierce, Justice, brief sketch, 96; opinion in N.Y. minimum wage case, 149; dissent on Social Security Act, 180; dissent on A.A.A. of 1938, 199; on the power to tax, 208

Butler, Samuel, the author of *Hudibras*, on latitudinarians, 300

Byrnes, James F., Justice, on compromise, 76; brief sketch, 203; on the Okies, 327

Cardozo, Benjamin N., Justice, brief sketch, 98; on the Platonic existence of a decision, 82; dissent in Hot Oil case, 115; concurs in N R A case, 120; dissents in Coal Control case, 139; Hughes on, 175; opinion on Social Security, 181; opinion on old age pensions, 184; on freedom of speech, 287

Carnegie, Andrew, welcomes Spencer, 141

Carriers Taxing Act of 1935, 109

Casanova, 268

Catron, John, Justice, 39

Chase, Salmon P., Chief Justice, 36, 179

Chase, Samuel, Justice, 15, 74

Chase, Stuart, the Federal Government our receiver in bankruptcy, 112

Child Labor Acts, 45, 155

Choate, Joseph H., on income taxes, 41

Clark, Grenville, in conversation with his partner, Elihu Root, 270

Clayton Act *versus* Sherman Act, 89

Cleveland, Grover, President, 41

Coal Control Act, 28, 134

Cobb, Elizabeth, quoted, 99

Coke, Lord Chief Justice, to James I, 62; on Magna Charta, 276

Conkling, Roscoe, tells a little lie, 274

Connally Act, 116

Conscientious objectors, 239

Coolidge, Calvin, President, 96

Corwin, Edward S., thinks it was Gray, 42; on new powers, 156; his books on the Court, 361

Council of Revision, 27, 59, 61, 324

Cranch, William, 22

Cummins, Albert, Senator, for a 3% income tax, 43

Curtis, B. R., Justice, 36, 39

Cushing, William, Justice, 74

Darwinism, 141

Day, William Rufus, Justice, 44

Denman, William, Judge, his sense of the ridiculous, 110

Dewey, John, 233

Disraeli, on lawyers, vii

Douglas, William O., Justice, brief sketch, 194; dissent in the Saratoga Water case, 230; on itinerant preachers, 313; on taxing religion, 315

Eastman, Joseph B., on voluntary pensions, 101; on superannuation, 104

Esquire, the privilege of the second-class mail, 91

Fair Labor Standards Act, 155, 174, 195, 196, 200

Fairman, Charles, his *Life of Miller*, 41, 359

Field, Stephen J., Justice, on unconstitutional acts, 81; on *stare decisis*, 82

Ford, Henry, 240

Frankfurter, Felix, Justice, brief sketch, 193; the business of the Court, 60; advisory opinions, 21, 27, 67; the erosion of time, 83; conflicting radiations, 92; on a seductive cliché, 209; from opinion in Saratoga Water case, 231; nonaction by Congress, 239; the clear and present danger rule, 265; contempt of court, 291, 293; opinion in the first flag salute case, 302, 305, 329; tax exemption as a subsidy, 316; dissent in the second flag salute case, 318; his *Mr. Justice Holmes and the Supreme Court*, 360

Franklin, Benjamin, to a lady at dinner, 39; Declaration of Independence, 51, 333

Frazer, James G., on kings and taboos, 57

Freud, Sigmund, on the pleasure-ego, 66

Freund, Paul, with Jackson on his *The Struggle for Judicial Supremacy*, 360

Fuller, Melville Weston, Chief Justice, 44

Garrison, Lloyd K., on precedents, 79; for a constitutional amendment, 155

George, Henry, instead of Spencer?, 332

Gerry, Elbridge, 59

Gibson, Chief Justice, on judicial supremacy, 26

Goethe, quoted, 1, 51, 85

Gray, Horace, Justice, 42, 277, 326

Gray, John C., quoted, v

Grier, Robert Cooper, Justice, 39

Haines, Charles G., his The Rôle of the Supreme Court, 360

Hamilton, Alexander versus Madison on our general welfare, 2, 126, 182; on impeachment, 10

Hand, Learned, Judge, on deduction, 88; opinion in N R A case, 120; that words are triggers, 263; when to disregard decisions, 308

Harding, Warren G., President, 96

Harlan, John Marshall, Justice, on due process, 279

Hobbes, quoted, v

Hogan, Frank J., his reliance on legislative wisdom, 186; on landmarks, 187

Holmes, O. W., continuity with the past, 1; theory, 3; rational doubts, 25, 30; his Lochner dissent, 25, 143; Can't Helps, 31; the demand for the superlative, 51; the judges not God, 53; bound by a precedent, 75, 147; law, 79, 80; the power to tax, 90, 207; on Brandeis, 97; the naiveté of judges, 189; local law, 234; his dissent on child labor, 196; prices in an imaginary world, 237; the clear and present danger rule, 261, 264; dissent in the Abrams case, 262; not being God, 281; the sky's the limit, 283; demigods, 284; Spencer, 332

Hoover, Herbert, President, on F.D.R.'s judicial appointments, 97, 98

Hughes, Charles E., Chief Justice, brief sketch, 97; on unconstitutional acts, 81; on stare decisis, 83; dissent on railroad pensions, 103; on delegation of legislative power, 115; opinion on N.R.A., 118; dissents in Coal Control case, 139; opinion in Washington minimum wage case, 161; opinion on National Labor Relations Act, 171; on Cardozo, 175; his The Supreme Court, 360

Jackson, Robert H., Justice, on interpreting the Constitution, 3; asked some questions by Swedes, 100; brief sketch, 203; quoted, 219; on union membership, 251; opinion in the second flag salute case, 309, 329; describes Jehovah's Witnesses, 310; his The Struggle for Judicial Supremacy, 100, 360; on Plato's cave, 315; on the need for wisdom, 325

James I, to Coke, 62

James, William, 'Take any demand . . . ,' 52

Jay, John, Chief Justice, 72

Jefferson, Thomas, Declaration of Independence, 51, 333, 358

Johnson, Andrew, President, 14, 27, 36

Johnson, William, Justice, on dissenting opinions, 73

Judiciary Act of 1789, 60

Kelvin, Lord, his little models, 18

Kepler, his little demons, 18

Lamar, Lucius Quintus Cincinnatus, Justice, 277, 326

Landis, James M., on the business of the Court, 60

Landon, Alfred M., on minimum wages, 154

Lawyers Co-operative Society, their advance opinions, 359

Lerner, Max, his The Mind and Faith of Justice Holmes, 360

Lewis, John L., recognized by General Motors, 166

Lincoln, Abraham, from the First Inaugural, 40, 43

Lloyd, Demarest, instead of Spencer?, 332

Lodge, Henry Cabot, Senator, against an income tax, 43

Lowell, A. Lawrence, on pooling minds, 71

McIlwain, Charles H., on where we ought to begin, 62

McKenna, Joseph, Justice, 44, 151, 227

McKinley, William, President, 42, 266

MacLeish, A., 'A poem should . . . be,' 7

McReynolds, James C., Justice, brief sketch, 95; dissent on National Labor Relations Act, 172; dissent on Social Security Act, 179; on teaching modern languages, 281; on legislative approval, 238

Madison, James, versus Hamilton on our general welfare, 2, 126; drafts the Bill of Rights, 267

Maitland, F. W., on the day before yesterday, 1

Marshall, John, Chief Justice; in Marbury v. Madison, 13, 38, 64, 94; on impeachment and the recall of decisions, 15, 155; Beveridge on Marshall, 13, 23; for unanimity, 72; on distinctions, 90; from opinion in McCulloch v. Maryland, 206; on the Bill of Rights, 272

Martin, Luther, 3

Mason, George, 4

Maverick, Maury, on prestidigitation, 274; his In Blood and Ink, 360

Merryman case, 259

Miller, Samuel F., Justice, quoted, 121

Minnesota moratorium on mortgages, 99

Monroe, James, President, 36

Montaigne, on living, 20

Moody, William H., Justice, 44

Morris, Gouverneur, 4

Municipal Bankruptcy Act, 29

Murphy, Frank, Justice, brief sketch, 202; concurs on union discrimination, 246

Myrdal, Gunnar, says Page exaggerates, 243

National Association of Manufacturers, on the real worth of things, 237

National Labor Relations Act, 46, 155, 166, 243

N. R. A., 112, 167

New York Criminal Anarchy Act, 266

New York Milk Control, 100

New York Minimum Wage Act, 140, 147, 155

New York Unemployment Compensation Act, 156

Norris, George W., Senator, 98

Page, Thomas Nelson, on the slaves' monopoly, 243

Parker, John J., Judge, rejected, 96; counts noses, 308

Paterson, William, Justice, 74

Peckham, Rufus W., Justice, 227

Pendleton, Edmund, a letter from Madison, 269

Pepper, George Wharton, Senator, arguendo, 125, 131, 133

Pierce, Franklin, President, on the indigent insane, 179

Pinckney, Charles, 12

Plato, that good judges had best be simple-minded, 189; his cave, 315

Pollock, Sir Frederick, Holmes writes him about the espionage cases, 263

Powell, Thomas Reed, on a President's ellipsis, 350; our great expert on the Court, 361

Railway Labor Act, 244

Randolph, John, of Roanoke, on sovereignty and chastity, 227

Reconstruction Acts, 14, 27

Reed, Earl F., advises his clients, 188

Reed, Stanley F., Justice, defends the A.A.A., 125; colloquy with Sutherland, 170; brief sketch, 193; opinion on Jim Crow cars, 221; on the Bridges case and contempt of court, 295

Richberg, Donald R., picks out poultry, 23, 117

Rimbaud, on the color of the vowels, 18

Roberts, Owen J., Justice, brief sketch, 96; on judicial supremacy, 17, 19; from Nebbia opinion, 100; opinion on railroad pensions, 101; opinion in A. A. A. case, 126; opinion on the A. A. A. of 1938, 199; effect of re-enacting a statute, 238

Robinson, Joseph, Senator, his sudden death, 160, 185

Rockefeller, John D., on the American Beauty rose, 142

Roosevelt, Franklin D., President, his Court Plan, 37, 68; on constitutional doubts, 28, 135; on the N. R. A., 112; on Wages and Hours Act, 155; misquotes, 350

Roosevelt, Theodore, President, his recall of decisions, 15, 155

Root, Elihu, Senator, against an income tax, 43, 56; on the word 'secure,' 270; opposes Brandeis, 97

Russell, Bertrand, on the world of universals, 84

Rutledge, Wiley B., Justice, brief sketch, 203

Sanford, Edward T., Justice, 75, 96

Selden, John, on religion, 331

Sherman Act *versus* Clayton Act, 89

Shiras, George, Justice, 42

Sixteenth Amendment, 44

Snell, Bertrand H., in shame and sorrow, 28

Social Security Act, 155, 177

Socrates, his first argument for immortality, 82; his daimon, 284

Soil Conservation Act, 134

Spencer, Herbert, as our intellectual tutor, 141; and the 14th Amendment, 143; Holmes does justice to the Philistine, 332

Stanton, Edwin M., Secretary of War, 259

Steinbeck, John, on indigent non-residents, 327

Stevens, Thaddeus, no Cromwell, 36

Stone, Harlan F., Chief Justice, brief sketch, 97; self-restraint, 46, 322; dissent in A. A. A. case, 130; dissent in N.Y. minimum wage case, 151; the Tenth Amendment, 181; opinion on the Fair Labor Standards Act, 200; from opinion in Saratoga Water case, 232; opinion on union discrimination, 245; the flag salute and religion, 303, 329

Story, Joseph, Justice, on due process, 276

Sumners, Hatton W., Senator, 29

Sutherland, George, Justice, brief sketch, 95; the presumption of validity, 25; opinion on Coal Control Act, 136; from opinion on minimum wage, 145; dissent in Washington minimum wage case, 162; colloquy with Reed on interstate commerce, 170; dissent on Social Security Act, 179; freedom of the press, 297; Stone's self-restraint, 163, 323, 325

Taft, William H., Chief Justice, about an income tax, 43; to Butler, 96; opposes Brandeis, 97; on Hughes, 97; dissents, 145

Taney, Roger B., Chief Justice, in the Dred Scott case, 39, 94; on *stare decisis*, 82; in the Merryman case, 259; on due process, 276

Thayer, James Bradley, quoted, 11; his *Life of John Marshall*, 360; his *Legal Essays* and his *Cases on Constitutional Law*, 361

de Tocqueville, Alexis, quoted, viii

Trinity Church, N.Y., its investments exempt from taxation?, 316

Tucker, Thomas Tudor, 268

Turner, Frederick J., 98

Underwood, Oscar, Senator, 192

Vallandigham, Clement L., exiled, 260

Van Buren, Martin, President, Benton writes to him, vii

Van Devanter, Willis, Justice, on meaning, 19; brief sketch, 95; retires, 185

Veblen, Thorstein, instead of Spencer?, 332

Wade, Benjamin Franklin, no Cromwell, 36

Wages and Hours Act, *see* Fair Labor Standards Act

Wagner Act, *see* National Labor Relations Act

Wallace, Henry A., Secretary of Agriculture, 123, 198

War Labor Board, on the internal affairs of a union, 249

Warren, Charles, quoted, 277; his *The Supreme Court in United States History*, 360

Washington, George, President, asks the Court its opinion, 20

Washington Minimum Wage Act, 160

Waties, Chancellor, on all men of sense and reflection, 32

Wayne, James Moore, Justice, 39

Webb-Kenyon Act, 14, 27

Webster, Daniel, argues for days, 69; on judicial supremacy, 347

Wheeler, Burton K., Senator, 159

Wheeler, William M., on naturalists and biologists, 85

White, Edward Douglass, Chief Justice, 44, 227

Whitehead, Alfred N., on abstractions, 87; on philosophy as their critic, 333

Wilkes, John, 268

Wilson, Woodrow, President, on getting over being a lawyer, vii

Woodbury, Peter, Judge, 308

Woolsey, Theodore Dwight, judges as the servants of God, 54

Youmans, Edward L., 141